Zipper

a
l
s
o

b
y

R
o
b
e
r
t

Pioneer Plastic

F
Edison's   Electric Light
r

i
e
d
e
l

Z I P P E R

An Exploration in Novelty

Robert Friedel

W W Norton & Company, Inc

New York • London

Printed in the United States of America

First Edition

"If I Only Had a Heart," E. Y. Harburg and Harold Arlen, Copyright © 1938, 1939 (renewed 1966, 1967) Metro-Goldwyn-Mayer, Inc. c/o EMI Feist Catalog Inc. Reprinted by permission of CPP/Belwin, Inc., Miami, FL. All Rights Reserved.

The text of this book is composed in Stempel Garamond with the display set in Futura extra bold condensed, and Gill Sans bold condensed.
Composition by Crane Typesetting Service, Inc.
Manufacturing by Courier Westford.
Book design by Jaye Zimet.

Library of Congress Cataloging-in-Publication Data

Friedel, Robert.
    Zipper : an exploration in novelty / Robert Friedel.
        p.   cm.
        1. Inventions—History—20th century.   2. Inventions—
    History—19th century.   3. Zippers—History.   I. Title.
    T19.F75   1994
    609—dc20   93-27997

ISBN 0-393-03599-9

W. W. Norton & Company, Inc., 500 Fifth Avenue, New York, N.Y. 10110
W. W. Norton & Company Ltd., 10 Coptic Street, London WC1A 1PU

1 2 3 4 5 6 7 8 9 0

Contents

Introduction: Why Zippers? vii

Acknowledgments xi

1 "Witty Inventions and Thinking Men" 1

2 Hustle and Bustle 26

3 Hookless 62

4 Novelty in a New World 91

5 Zip 123

6 "Growin' like the Deuce" 150

7 *Bye-bye Buttons* 173

8 "Alligators of Ecstasy" 204

9 The End of Novelty 225

Notes 255

Index 279

Introduction: Why Zippers?

Why zippers? That is a question that can be asked about both this book and its subject. On one level the simple answer is that the story of how the zipper was invented one hundred years ago and, through almost a half century of trying and pushing and slipping and edging forward, finally succeeded is a good yarn. It involves a cast of characters that includes the archetypal oddball inventor, the smooth small-town lawyer, the fast-talking door-to-door salesman, the immigrant engineer, the rube in the big city, and so forth. We all are attracted to good tales, and the zipper's story is a dandy.

But there is more to this than the drama of inventive inspiration and perspiration. The zipper has a place in our world that is worth some reflection. It can be argued that zippers are the first machines that any of us learn to master in our childhood, and they remain the most common mechanisms of our daily lives. It may in fact be just a little startling to think of zippers as machines, but surely that is what they are—carefully fitted pieces of metal or metal and plastic that must move in close coordination under our control to exert forces to accomplish a simple but nevertheless sometimes vital task. Of course, we do not normally think of them that way, but that is precisely why it is so important that we analyze carefully what these things really are and why we relate to them as we do. It is in part just because the zipper has become an invisible but inescapable part of daily life in the mid and late twentieth century that it is such an appropriate subject for an exercise in what the Swiss critic Sigfried Giedion called "anonymous history."

One of the goals of this kind of history is to understand better what the things that we make and use in our daily lives reveal about ourselves—values, ambitions, intentions, and prejudices that we may not even be conscious of. The zipper does this extraordinarily well because it is ubiquitous yet superfluous. In other words, while zippers are used everywhere, they are almost never necessary. There are many tasks that a zipper does better than alternatives do, but hardly any that can't be done more simply. Buttons will handle a trouser fly or skirt placket very nicely, snaps or clasps will fasten a purse or a pocket with no difficulty, a flap and buckle will close a suitcase, a spring will keep a tobacco pouch secure, and so forth. Yet we trust these tasks to a mechanism that requires enormous ingenuity and precision to make and that is never immune to failure. Few things combine simplicity and complexity so thoroughly as a zipper. Its working could hardly be more straightforward, but the technical requirements that must be met to ensure it are particularly demanding. Why, then, should we put ourselves at the mercy of such a device?

The answer to that question is not simple, and the reader is warned not to look for it in some quickly digested form. The interplay among such basic human impulses and concerns as the urge to invent, the desire to get rich, the ambition for fame, and the anxiety of fashionableness is a complicated one. No particular model or structure of analysis is put forth to comprehend all this. Instead it is hoped that the reader will notice that this kind of anonymous history is not anonymous at all but is peopled by individuals who shape events and outcomes by their own values, talents, and ambitions. Lest this be mistaken for a kind of "heroic history," however, it should also be noticed that the history of the zipper is testimony not simply to the capacity of individual men and women to make a difference but also to the limitations of individuals in shaping the ultimate outcomes of their actions. In other words, in technological change, as in much of life, results come neither from technical and cultural imperatives nor from individual and institutional will but from the constant interaction of these elements. Some readers will therefore note that one of the central messages of this is a negative one: that technologies are not to be explained by their own autonomous logic or by simplistic concepts such as "need," "demand," "function," or "failure." They are, instead, to be understood as human creations, produced by imagination interacting with the most fundamental values of everyday existence.

There is yet one more message in this story, and it is another one that tells us important things about the culture and values of twentieth-century America. The constant force behind the zipper, throughout the first half of its one-hundred-year history, is its novelty itself. This is not to say that the slide fastener was a spectacularly new invention, striking observers with its uniqueness. No, in fact, the examiners in the Patent Office had to be convinced, in the typical way of inventions, that the first versions of the zipper were indeed novel enough to fit the demands of the patent law. The spectacular thing about the zipper's novelty was not its initial appearance but its persistence. The zipper was novel for two generations, and it relied on its novelty for its first taste of success. For this reason, the story of the zipper tells us something interesting about the place of novelty in our lives, the extent to which we, our parents, and our ancestors back to the middle of the nineteenth century have lived with novelty as a fundamental and expected part of our condition. This is one of the most extraordinary things about modern times, setting us off from the past in a way as fundamental as any element of modernity. And what better way to appreciate the extraordinary than through the experience of one of the most ordinary things around us?

I could stay young and chipper,
And I'd lock it with a zipper,
If I only had a heart.
—Tin Woodman, in
The Wizard of Oz
(MGM, 1939)

Acknowledgments

I confess to often having felt guilty while writing this book, for it has been great fun, more than one is generally supposed to have while doing historical scholarship. Beyond that, however, it has afforded much pleasure, particularly by bringing me into contact with women and men in both Europe and America who have been generous in their encouragement, assistance, and advice. This note is a modest effort to acknowledge them, undertaken in the full knowledge that there is really no way I could fully convey my sense of debt and gratitude.

The first thanks must go to those who introduced me to this topic and prodded, encouraged, cajoled, and otherwise pointed the way: Helen Sydavar, Fred Allen, Julian Bach, and, especially, Edward Tenner. Next, my friends and colleagues at the Smithsonian Institution's National Museum of American History were patient and indulgent and usually knew just when to laugh and when to look serious. Steven Lubar and Robert Post read large portions of the manuscript and tried hard to keep me honest, Deborah Warner gave me a crucial nudge of assurance,

xii

•

A

C

K

N

O

W

L

E

D

G

M

E

N

T

S

the Division of Electricity gave me a place to hang my hat, and Joan Mentzer provided some much needed faith. On a more practical level, Francis Gadson gave me access to the museum's zipper collection, Peter Liebhold taught me some things about machinery, Claudia Kidwell and the Division of Costume taught me even more things about dresses and the clothing industry, and, as always, Jim Roan and the staff of the museum's library were gracious and helpful.

Other friends and associates indulged me in various ways, by reading portions of the manuscript, listening to my stories and problems, pointing out interesting anecdotes or sources, giving me a platform on which to try out my approaches, or even giving me old zippers. For their various kindnesses I thank Leonard Reich, Toby Appel, Bonnie Kaplan, Bernard Mergen, Joyce Bedi, Helen Samuels, Jeffrey Meikle, Susan Oetken, Ellen Miles, Alex Magoun, David Murphy, Birgit Otter, and Otto Mayr. The University of Maryland was similarly supportive. In addition to my associates in the Department of History and the Committee on History and Philosophy of Science who kept me going on this effort, even through the inevitable discouraging moments, I want to acknowledge some crucial early assistance from Helen Sydavar and the reference and interlibrary loan staff of the McKeldin Library, as well as the steady support of the secretarial staff of the History Department.

One of the real joys of working on this subject has been the new people and institutions to which it has introduced me. Both general subjects and specific topics that began as complete mysteries to me were illuminated only through the kindness and expertise of a far-flung group of individuals. It was obvious to me at an early point that the entire subject of clothing history was a large and complex area of study with which I would need much assistance. Besides those at the Smithsonian, among others who were particularly generous in this area were Robert Kaufmann of the Costume Institute of New York's Metropolitan Museum of Art, Madelyn Shaw and her colleagues in the Textile Department and the library of the Fashion Institute of Technology, and Elizabeth Ann Coleman of the Museum of Fine Arts, Houston. Jan Harold Brunvand kindly shared his knowledge of urban folklore, and Jerry Gould answered my questions about the zipper business in New York.

The location of the archival records documenting the history of the zipper was sometimes a formidable challenge, and I could never have overcome it without a bit of luck and a lot of help. At an early and particularly frustrating stage the staffs of the National Archives demonstrated to me once again why they represent a special treasure for anyone attempting to piece together a part of American history. In particular the staffs of the Washington National Records Center and the branches at Philadelphia, Bayonne, New Jersey, and Los Angeles provided me with legal and patent materials that filled in otherwise baffling gaps in the record. The records of the Slide Fastener Association were made available to me through the kindness of Mary Ann Eubanks and her staff in Columbia, South Carolina.

While this work does not in fact do full justice to the non-American side of the zipper story, some effort was made to suggest at least the outlines of the European and Japanese experience with the novelty. This was made possible by the generous assistance of a number of individuals and institutions. The Archives Department of the Birmingham (England) Central Library gave me access to the valuable records deposited there by the Metals Division of ICI. Paul Willer of the Lightning Fastener Company shared his extensive knowledge of that firm's history to supply additional information. In Prague Shannon McKeen and the staff of Koh-i-Noor were extraordinarily gracious in their hospitality and efforts to glean information about the pioneering efforts of Jindrich Waldes. Additional information in this connection was supplied by Otto Smrček of the Czech Academy of Sciences and Milo Waldes. In Stockholm Inger Björklund of the Archiv/Bibliotek in the Tekniska Museet very generously made available to me information gathered by the museum documenting Swedish and Swedish-American interest in the zipper.

In Germany I had much good fortune in many directions. In Munich the staff of the library and research institutes of the Deutsches Museum helped me continue a number of research pursuits. In addition, others at the museum, especially Hans-Liudger Dienel and Hartmut Petzold, pointed out unexpected directions of inquiry. A special delight was meeting Helmuth Hartmann in northern Germany, whose enthusiasm for the zipper and the stories surrounding it was a joy to behold. Dieter A. Laule of Opti-Werk GmbH generously opened the doors of his factory in Rhauderfehn to give me a look at modern zipper production. My knowledge of the important work of the Japanese zipper industry, and particularly of Tadao Yoshida, has come through the kind efforts of E. Alex Gregory and Nick Tsubokawa of YKK (U.S.A.).

Of all the assistance I received on this book, none has been more central to my efforts or more personally rewarding than that from individuals in Meadville, Pennsylvania, the former home of Talon, Inc. This book really began with a visit many years ago to Meadville and the Crawford County Historical Society. Over the years individuals associated with Talon and the historical society have been a source of encouragement, advice, and information that have sustained this study through thick and thin. At Talon Barbara Horner and her front-office staff were wonderfully tolerant of the unpredictable intrusions of a nosy historian and gave me constant proof that the vicissitudes of their company had not diminished the good and optimistic spirit that had supported it from the beginning. One of the first individuals to whom Barb introduced me was a former Talon executive, David Conner, whose steady belief in the importance of his company and the technology it pioneered was matched by an appreciation for its history. Dave helped me in more ways than I can recount here. Another individual I was soon introduced to in Meadville was Ruth Klingener, the daughter of zipper inventor Gideon Sundback. It was Ruth who gave me precious glimpses into the mind and work of her very private father. She and Dave also, unwittingly, I suppose, gave me a glimpse at the fine spirit of pride and gentility that had characterized not only Gideon Sundback but also his indispensable (but very different) colleague in the zipper enterprise Lewis Walker. Ruth alerted other members of the Sundback and Klingener families to my interests, and they were always gracious in responding to my queries. I want to give a special thanks to Alice Klingener for assisting me with translations of Swedish-language materials.

Zipper

"Witty Inventions and Thinking Men"

1

The September 9, 1893, edition of *Scientific Ameri-can* ("The Most Popular Scientific Paper in the World") featured, as it had for weeks, articles about the spectacular world's fair then taking place on Chicago's Lake Michigan shore. Pictures showed the triumphal arch that graced the fair's Court of Honor and the canals and bridges that wove the Lake Michigan lagoon and the city into an intricate display of the City Beautiful think-ing that was to inspire American urban planners for decades. The Woman's Building got its own article, and a spectacular view was offered of the fair's popular Midway Plaisance, from the top of the famous Ferris wheel. The more thorough reader would find, however, a downbeat note or two in the journal, such as the report of the depression then gripping much of the country. Almost half a million jobs had been lost in the manufacturing sector that had been the star of the great industrial boom of the previous decade. The companies that were of greatest interest to the *Scientific American* reader, the technological pioneers of the day, were not so affected, and their prosperity was hinted at by the advertisements on the back page: Kodaks could be bought from six to one hundred dollars, Otto gas engines—state of the art in internal combustion—were available with from one-third to one hundred horsepower, the General Electric Company advertised its own motors, and the American Bell Company reminded everyone that it owned the most valuable patent of the day, Alexander Graham Bell's number 186,787.

This last advertisement might add motivation for a reader to turn to the inside pages, where *Scientific American* always listed the Patent Office's latest issuances. This week could be found the 378 patents granted on August 29, running in alphabetical order from an air brake to a zither stand. Easily lost among these offerings were two in the name of Whitcomb L. Judson, of Chicago, for shoe fasteners. There was very little remarkable about these two newly announced inventions. Indeed, they were of the most typical kinds of things that were certified from the large, handsome classical building that the Patent Office occupied on Washington's F Street; their novelty seemed modest, their application was extremely limited, and, perhaps most typical of all, they didn't work very well. Some study of the patents suggests, in fact, that the inventions therein described didn't work at all, if they were actually ever constructed. The Patent Office having abolished just a few years before the requirement that working models accompany inventions (except for perpetual motion and flying machines, for which the skeptical commissioner of patents continued to require models), there was no need for Whitcomb Judson to make the devices he described.

It had taken a bit of effort on the part of Judson and of his lawyer to convince the Patent Office that his devices were sufficiently novel. They only claimed to be shoe fastenings, so Thomas Hart Anderson, the assistant examiner who took on Judson's applications, was surely reasonable when he suggested that there were a host of patents that covered this sort of thing. Perhaps Anderson was also a little put out by the fact that the first invention of the pair he was reviewing had been submitted for patenting in early November 1891, and the second sent in a full nine months later, as "an improvement" on the earlier one. While it was not an unusual practice for an inventor to continue to work away at perfecting his creation before the Patent Office got around to giving its blessing, an examiner might be justified in thinking that the would-be inventor was fishing for valid claims when he wasn't too sure whether his ideas were novel or not. The customary give-and-take between examiner and lawyer went on for months, but once the last amendment requested by Anderson had been filed, in May 1893, it took only ten days for the examiner to inform Judson's Washington attorney that the patents would be allowed. When they were finally issued on August 29, they were assigned numbers 504,037 and 504,038 (for some reason, the earlier number was given to the second— 1892—application).[1]

Among the half million-plus patents that had been issued in the fifty-seven years since the Patent Act of 1836, there had been some very important inventions, a few of which had already transformed life by the last decade of the nineteenth century. Some of these—such as Charles Goodyear's 1839 patent for the vulcanization of rubber, Elias Howe's sewing machine patent of 1846, Alexander Graham Bell's 1876 patent for the telephone, or the crucial carbon filament patent issued to Thomas Edison in 1880 as the cornerstone of his electric lighting system—were quite famous. They constituted, however, only a tiny fraction of the country's inventive output. Far more common were those patents that were simply modifications, often of no importance, of a well-known technology, or minor little gadgets and designs that might get brief tryouts but then fade into deserved obscurity, or, perhaps most common of all, impractical, irrelevant, unwanted devices that were hardly much more than gleams in an inventor's or promoter's eye. To the practiced student of such things, the two patents Whitcomb Judson received that August would certainly promise to be of this last sort. Why and how they turned out to be much more are questions that go to the heart of understanding how people make new things a part of their world.

Whitcomb Judson had received fourteen patents before those for his shoe fastener, and he was to receive fourteen more before his death. Of all these, only the fasteners (including the improvements he made after 1893) were to have lasting significance. The others, however, were eloquent testimony of the kind of world that Judson inhabited and what he wanted to make of it. He was in his early forties before he began in seriousness his life of invention, but by that time—the 1880s—the prestige and possi-

4

•

Z

I

P

P

E

R

ble gratification awaiting the successful inventor were an irresistible lure to a man who had spent much of his life working with and selling other men's machinery.

Perhaps he was moved by the notoriety of his contemporaries who were reshaping the nineteenth century by their technical legerdemain. Thomas Edison, already a very famous man, was about a year younger than he and, like him, had come out of the Middle West equipped with little more than technical aptitude as he sought his fortune in the East. Unlike Edison, however, Judson had been just old enough to join the regiments in the Civil War (the Forty-second Illinois Cavalry) and had had at least passing acquaintance with a college education (Knox College, in his hometown of Galesburg, Illinois). His exposures to technology were not in the fast-moving and exciting world of telegraphers and electricians, like Edison, but rather in the older, more established, yet pivotal department of agricultural machinery. This was a realm that might not be so thoroughly brushed with the breath of the future as electricity, but it was one in which a young man could look forward to a life of steady, progressive work, contributing in one way or another to the agricultural enterprise that was still at the heart of a rapidly industrializing civilization.

Whereas Thomas Edison had his first biography in 1878, when he was thirty-one years old, and subsequently led a life as thoroughly chronicled and documented as a celebrity's could be, Whitcomb Judson's life has to be pieced together from the meagerest bits of evidence. We can only speculate, therefore, on what moved him, as he approached middle age, to leave the business of selling such machines as the self-binding harvester, made by the Osborne Machinery Company of Auburn, New York. We cannot even say which came first, the spiritual move to an inventor's uncertain life or the physical move that found him in Minneapolis, Minnesota, in 1886. We do know, however, that at about the time he moved to Minnesota, so did another Osborne salesman—one Harry Earle. The paths of Judson and Earle were to be tightly interwoven for the next decade and a half, and their relationship shows neatly the respective roles of technical ingenuity and entrepreneurial savvy in fostering novelty to a society alternately intoxicated and repelled by it.[2]

The Minneapolis city directories identify Whitcomb Judson

Whitcomb Judson, the original inventor of the slide fastener (1846–1909), was a machine salesman turned inventor whose penchant for complication led to dozens of patents but no solid success.

TALON, INC.

as a "traveling agent" in its listings for 1886–87, but they do not reveal just for whom he was a salesman. They tell us that Harry Earle was employed as the manager of the Pitts Agricultural Works, and it is reasonable to speculate that Judson may have been working for this firm, in his customary line of business. A couple of years later we can be a bit more certain about what was going on, for Earle was listed as the head of his own outfit, the Earle Manufacturing Company, makers of "Band Cutters, Grain Scales, Etc.," and Judson was one of his salesmen. It is precisely at this time, 1888–89, that he began his inventive efforts in earnest, receiving his first patent, for a "mechanical movement." Indeed, in 1889 Whitcomb Judson was granted six patents, all dedicated to the creation of a new technology that was to be the primary focus of his energies for several years—a "pneumatic street railway."

All fourteen of the patents that Judson received before his shoe fasteners were concerned in one way or another with this

6

•

Z

I

P

P

E

R

dream of a streetcar system that could be propelled by compressed air. Such a concept, in its most general form, had been around for most of the nineteenth century, but Judson took it in a novel, one might even say bizarre, direction. A brief look in this direction suggests just what sort of inventor he was trying to be. The most straightforward notion of a pneumatic streetcar system is one in which cars are pushed by air pressure by means of pistons running in underground tubes. Such a streetcar would resemble, at least superficially, a cable car, with the pistons suspended beneath the car, just like a cable car's grips, and the air pressure cylinder lying underneath the tracks, somewhat like the cable conduits. Such systems were tried from time to time in the nineteenth century, but they invariably ran into the problem of sealing. There was simply no way to provide the streetcar piston with access to the compressed air tube without permitting extensive leakage of pressure. Most typically, leather flaps would cover an open slit in the top of the air cylinder running just beneath the ground. It was hoped that the flaps would permit the passage of the streetcar piston, while still keeping the cylinder more or less airtight when the piston was not passing through. One does not have to be a mechanical engineer to realize that the seal provided by such flaps would not be very airtight under the best of conditions and that matters would quickly deteriorate in tubes running for many miles in all kinds of weather, with dirt and street filth constantly being pushed into them and with, most important, the constant wear from the pistons themselves tending to destroy the flaps. By the mid-1880s these difficulties were well known and posed seemingly insurmountable obstacles to using air pressure for urban transport.

From the vantage point of the twentieth century it may be a little hard to imagine why such obstacles should still be seen as inviting challenges to the would-be inventor, but the decade of the 1880s represented one of those occasional moments in technological history, visible only in hindsight, where there was a clear gap between a widely perceived need of the day—improving transportation in cities and towns undergoing astonishingly rapid growth, much of it concentrated in already congested centers—and the solutions of the future—transport systems dependent upon electricity and the internal-combustion engine. It is also easy to forget from the modern vantage point that compressed air, which could be readily generated at central stations by means of water turbines or steam engines and distributed at relatively great distances, was a very attractive form of power to nineteenth-century engineers. In the 1880s numerous systems were built to transmit or distribute power, usually for industrial uses, by piping air under pressure. So alluring were the simplicity and reliability of this technology that the promoters who were planning the gigantic undertaking of harnessing the power of Niagara Falls for transmission twenty miles or so to the city of Buffalo were on the verge of choosing a compressed air system when, almost at the last minute, they were persuaded that electricity, with all its unknowns and apparent dangers, was the unstoppable way of the future.[3]

If the great European and American engineers consulted by Niagara's Cataract Construction Company could not quickly decide between electricity and compressed air, small wonder, then, that Whitcomb Judson should believe that solving the problems of a pneumatic transport system would be a path to fame and fortune. The rewards for the person who could devise a workable urban streetcar technology were widely apparent. The steam locomotive, king of all land transport, seemed less and less likely to provide acceptable solutions to the increasing congestion and distribution problems plaguing the rapidly growing cities of the industrialized (and industrializing) world. Horsecars were seen more and more as inadequate to the challenge. While electric systems, such as that built by Frank Sprague in the city of Richmond, Virginia, in 1887, were presenting a widely acknowledged alternative for progressive engineers, the hazards and difficulties of such systems were substantial enough to raise questions in many sober minds. Besides, Judson did not know electricity, but he did know mechanisms, and he clearly believed that he had devised a clever solution to the apparently insurmountable difficulties of compressed air.

It should be said right away that the Judson system did not work very well. It certainly had little or no effect on the development of urban transportation, although it was tried out at least once. Judson's pneumatic streetcar is of interest not because of its importance for technology but because of what it tells us about Whitcomb Judson. In brief, the Judson system consisted of a metal tube, about six inches in diameter, placed in

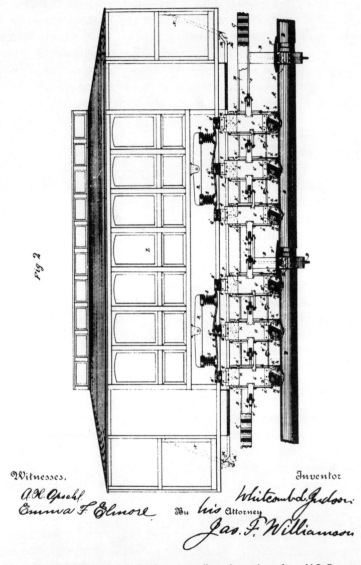

This example of Whitcomb Judson's street railway inventions, from U.S. Patent 402,934 (1889), illustrates the inventor's penchant for complex mechanisms. The car is driven by friction wheels pressing against the long shaft at the bottom, which is kept rotating by compressed air. *U.S. PATENT & TRADEMARK OFFICE*

a conduit running beneath streetcar tracks. This tube was kept turning, at a constant speed, by small engines, run off compressed air and placed several hundred feet apart. Cars were moved by friction wheels suspended beneath them and in constant contact with the rotating tube under the tracks. If the wheels were perpendicular to the tube, no motion was imparted to the cars. If, however, they were turned to other angles, then the friction between them and the rotating tube would cause the latter to propel the cars, in the manner of a screw. At a slight angle, the velocity imparted to the car would be small, but the traction relatively great; as the angle of the friction wheel was increased, so, too, was the velocity imparted, with likewise decrease in traction. In principle, Judson's system functioned like well-known power transmission systems, but applied on a scale hitherto unimagined. In construction, his pneumatic streetcar relied on costly combinations of air engines, bearings, conduits, tubes, and mechanical linkages that would have made it one of the most expensive transport systems ever built or operated.[4]

Judson's invention tells us of a man taken by mechanical cleverness—indeed, perhaps a bit too taken by cleverness itself. It suggests a mind quite ready to apply complicated solutions to problems (even, perhaps, to simple ones). The invention was certainly seen by his contemporaries as testimony to Judson's originality, if not his practicality. He himself had no qualms about practicality, however. With the assistance of Harry Earle, who turned out to be as avid a business promoter as Judson was an inventor, he organized the Judson Pneumatic Street Railway Company, and only months after the first patents were issued work was under way on a demonstration line in Washington, D.C. The readiness of Washington promoters to invest in the strange new technology deserves a comment, for it is a fine illustration of how specific political, social, and economic conditions can shape technological opportunities. By 1889 it had already become apparent to many observers that electric streetcars, using the kind of overhead trolleys seen in the Sprague system at Richmond, offered the greatest promise for solving urban transport problems. In the city of Washington, however, the guardian of public aesthetics and safety—the Congress of the United States—forbade overhead electrical lines in the city center (south of today's Florida Avenue). At almost the same time, however, Congress expressed its displeasure at the filth from horsecar lines and threatened to suspend franchises for companies failing to convert to other forms of traction. Entrepreneurs thus scrambled for alternatives that would keep the capital from earning the reputation of a technological backwater. Already cable car lines ran from the city's core, and it was at the end of one of these, along what is today Georgia Avenue, that about a mile of single track of the Judson system was built in the first part of 1890. It was a minor miracle that the system was completed and operated at all, but it was not more than a few weeks before the technical problems of Judson's scheme became overwhelming. The cable car company purchased the line and shortly thereafter electrified it.[5] Although Judson's company continued to exist for a while longer, backing for further trials was not forthcoming.

When Whitcomb Judson died in 1909, in Muskegon, Michigan, he was not a famous man, but his obscurity was not so great that the *News Chronicle* of that town didn't take some detailed notice of his life. Therein the most prominent notice is given to the fact that he "INTRODUCED PNEUMATIC STREET CARS," including reference to the construction of "a suburban line out of Washington, D.C." The obituary goes on to admit that his system was quickly made obsolete by electric lines. To get a fuller picture of the kind of man he was, we must turn to the few personal observations left by those who knew him. These do little more than confirm the image that emerges from contemplating the complexities and eccentricities of his inventions. Colonel Lewis Walker, who entered Judson's life as an investor in the streetcars and was to remain as the champion of his fasteners, remarked, "In overcoming the difficulties to be met in the development of mechanical inventions, Mr. Judson invariably tried to meet these difficulties by adding invention to invention. . . . His inventive capacity was great; his practical utility of that capacity was almost nil." Whatever his weaknesses, however, he struck a man like Walker as "of sterling character, of limited educational advantages, and striking personality; a genius of unusual mechanical resourcefulness."[6] The surviving photograph of Whitcomb Judson shows a large man, balding, with a dark, bushy beard and prominent ears. None of these details, however, tells us much about why Judson, his passion for his streetcar system

largely spent, should be inspired to invent the shoe fasteners that
are so interesting to us.

We can dismiss as fantasy the story sometimes told that
Judson's fasteners were devised because he found it tiresome to
bend his sizable body to lace his boots. Such explanations are
the creation of minds for whom invention is invariably the response to need. Such "necessity is the mother of invention"
thinking not only is historically inaccurate but shortchanges the
remarkable capacity of human beings to apply their imagination
and creativity to every aspect of the world around them. Even if
the big man grunted a bit in fastening his shoes, so had large
people done ever since they started enclosing their feet. The fact
is that Whitcomb Judson left no clue to why he invented his
fasteners, and we should not be too surprised at that. By this
point in his life he had tasted the intoxication of invention,
the thrill of holding in his hands the official-looking document,
adorned with a picture of the Patent Office Building and the
ornamented words UNITED STATES OF AMERICA at the top, certified with a red ribbon and red wax seal, declaring his "exclusive
right to make, use, and vend" his discovery. The testimony of
people like Lewis Walker and the thirty patents Judson earned
in the last twenty years of his life suggest that he saw himself
first and foremost as an inventor, a candidate for joining that
league of notable men who had made names and fortunes for
themselves by turning their innate mechanical talents into creative and profitable enterprises, aided by the patent system and
the willingness of other men to put their time and money to the
cause of technological progress and personal profit.

In the last stages of his streetcar efforts Whitcomb Judson
lived in New York City, where he and Harry Earle tended the
fortunes of his Pneumatic Streetcar Company out of an office on
Broadway. By the time he applied for his first fastener patent in
1891, however, he had moved to Chicago. There is nothing to
tell us why he moved west again or how he spent most of his
time there. He continued to use his Minneapolis patent attorney,
James Williamson, and the fact that he signed the required oath
for his second fastener application, in August 1892, while in
Kansas City, Missouri, might suggest that he had resumed his
earlier work as an agricultural machinery salesman, traveling

about the country's midsection. We also don't know exactly where Earle was at this point, although he seems never to have been far from Judson. When the patents were issued in 1893, Earle became the chief champion of his friend's new invention and even acquired one-half interest in the patents.[7] And in 1894 Earle took the lead in organizing a company in Chicago to promote the fastener. With the organization of the Universal Fastener Company, the story of the zipper turns away from the airy world of Whitcomb Judson's imagination toward the real world of investors, promoters, sellers, and, eventually, users.

The invention that inspired promoters and investors was, in fact, a very unpromising one. The creations of 1891 and 1892 were clever but complicated solutions to the simple problem of securing the flaps of a shoe. The patents themselves are revealing both for what they claim and for what they do not say. While they incorporate the obligatory language referring to the inventions as "new and useful" devices for fastening shoes, they do not, as many other patents did, detail precisely why these devices were superior to their traditional predecessors. They are also striking for their lack of reference to any prior inventions, devices, or patents. While examiner Anderson had made some reference to at least a half dozen prior patents in his early reaction to the 1892 application, the replies of Judson's lawyers were sufficiently persuasive to eliminate the ordinary discussion of the "prior art" in the body of the patent itself. In other words, the essential originality of Judson's invention was largely apparent.

What is not apparent today in looking at these patents is the workability of the devices they describe. There were essentially two parts to these inventions: a fastening "guide," as Judson called it, and the "clasps," which is what he called the fastening elements themselves. The guide was the first form of the slider of the modern zipper and was unquestionably the most original (and permanent) of Judson's creations. In both patents the guide functioned for the most part like a zipper slider. It was a flattened device, roughly triangular in form, with two openings at the wider end and one at the opposite. Within, two channels from the wide end converged into a single one at the apex. With these characteristics, Judson may be said to have invented this portion of the modern zipper. It is impossible to find, as the Patent Office examiner admitted, any real precedent for this invention.

W. L. JUDSON.
CLASP LOCKER OR UNLOCKER FOR SHOES.

No. 504,038.   Patented Aug. 29, 1893.

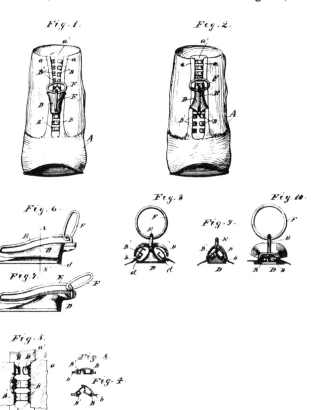

Fig. 1. *Fig. 2.* *Fig. 6.* *Fig. 8.* *Fig. 10.* *Fig. 7.* *Fig. 9.* *Fig. 5.* *Fig. 3.* *Fig. 4.*

Witnesses.   Inventor.
U. U. Opsahl.   Whitcomb Judson
E. F. Elmore   By his Attorney.
                                          Jas. F. Williamson,

Patent illustration for Whitcomb Judson's first slide fastener, applied for in 1891 (U.S.P. 504,038). Note particularly the complex form of the clasps and the interior of the slide. Note also the reversed orientation of the slide on the two shoes; the slide was pulled in the same direction either to open or to close and was removed when not in use. *U.S. PATENT & TRADEMARK OFFICE*

The other portion of the inventions—the fastenings—were another matter. What Judson describes in his patents were simply unworkable devices. Indeed, so awkward and unlikely do these elements appear that both drawings and artifacts produced over the years to depict "the first zipper" of 1891 never show what Judson actually described. Since none of these actually dates from the early 1890s, they are certainly figments of the imagination, confusing later models of the fastener with Judson's awkward first creations. In the patent application of 1891 the guide was designed to pull together "clasps," which, in the words of the patent, "have underreaching and overlapping projections or lips at their forward ends, which prevent the engagement or disengagement of the hook-portions of the clasps, except when thrown upward, so that the parts stand at an angle to each other of about ninety degrees." In other words, the clasps, attached to each side of a shoe's flaps, would, when unfastened, stick out from the shoe. The guide had the job of bringing each pair of opposing clasps together and then attaching them to each other by pushing them down on each other. The guide's design, therefore, was actually a bit more complex than that of a zipper slider since it needed to be shaped carefully to carry out two motions: bringing the opposing clasps toward each other and, at the same time, forcing them down on top of each other. One other aspect of the guide distinguished it from its modern counterpart. Once it had done its job of bringing the rows of clasps together in sequence, the guide continued to be pulled until it came off the shoe. If the guide had been pulled up to fasten the shoe, it would then be removed from the top of the fastener. To unfasten, Judson specified that the guide should be turned around and pulled in the same direction as for fastening, so that in this case it would again be pulled from bottom to top, but with the narrow end facing topward, the separated clasps issuing from the bottom end. When Judson entitled his 1891 application "Clasp Locker or Unlocker for Shoes," he was referring to his guide alone. As a later observer remarked, he had invented only half the zipper at this point.[8]

The "improvement" that led to the other patent of 1893 (no. 504,037) indirectly acknowledged some of the problems of the earlier invention but resulted in no more serviceable a product. The guide was shaped and used largely as before. The somewhat

W. L. JUDSON.
SHOE FASTENING.

No. 504,037.   Patented Aug. 29, 1893.

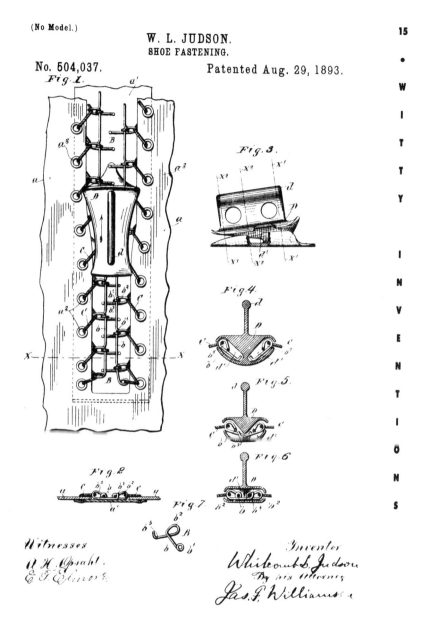

Witnesses
A. H. Opsahl.
E. F. Elmore

Inventor
Whitcomb L. Judson
By his Attorney
Jas. F. Williams

Patent illustration for Whitcomb Judson's second slide fastener, applied for in
1892 (U.S.P. 504,037). The complex form of the fastening elements has been
considerably simplified, but performance still seems dubious.

U.S. PATENT & TRADEMARK OFFICE

bulky clasps of the early form were replaced by lighter wire hooks. More important, as a conceptual advance these hooks were linked together on each side of the shoe flap into chains. The chains could then be laced into a boot or shoe, using the preexisting lace holes and lacing. In the earlier design each pair of clasps functioned completely independently (the patent even specified that each pair could be fastened successively by hand, dispensing with the guide altogether). In the new fastener the opposing chains of hooks were clearly meant to function as coordinated units, and in that modest way at least, they presaged the modern zipper. The means by which these hooks were to fasten to each other, however, was particularly unpromising. Each piece of steel wire in the chain consisted at one end of an eyelet (to which would be attached the adjacent wire hook in the chain), a short straight length, a loop in the middle (used for lacing the chain to the shoe) and, at the other end, a ninety-degree bend, which was to act as the hook, engaging the straight length of its opposing number on the other side of the shoe opening. Judson as much as admitted the fragility of this hook by stating the hooks were "held in their engaged position by the upward pressure of the foot against the tongue of the shoe." It takes little imagination to see that such attachments would be fickle indeed.

A little more than a year after Judson received his fastener patents, he and Harry Earle, joined by others, including Lewis Walker, formed the Universal Fastener Company in Chicago. The company's name provides a slight clue to what might have motivated investment in such unlikely-looking devices. Judson's patents claimed that his inventions, while described as shoe fastenings, were "equally applicable for fastening gloves, mail-bags and generally, wherever it is desired to detachably connect a pair of adjacent flexible parts." While the potential of a complex and relatively costly device as a shoe fastener would seem to be inherently limited, if not downright unpromising, that of an invention with possible application to many different fastenings, some of them with special and demanding requirements, could more plausibly have been viewed brightly. Even more persuasive to investors, perhaps, was the fact that Judson was continuing to modify and improve his designs. About a month before the company's founding, he applied for two more fastener patents, both ultimately assigned to the Universal Fastener Company. These patents, eventually granted in 1896, still described shoe fastenings, but they covered inventions that advanced Judson's original ideas considerably. They also provided the real foundations for a serious manufacturing effort that in twenty years' time, was to produce the modern zipper.

U.S. Patents 557,207 and 557,208 incorporated changes that were important, even if their utility was not fully appreciated at the time. For example, the "guide" in the first of these is described as "a cam-action slider which is somewhat similar to the locker and unlocker shown in my prior patents, but which in this combination operates with a somewhat different action involving an automatic movement of the slider backward in the uncoupling action of the chains, and which slider is in this case designed to remain permanently on the shoe." Even more striking, perhaps, is the design of the fastening elements themselves. The two patents actually describe a variety of designs, but one of them involves fasteners in which the opposing elements on each side of the fastener are identical to each other and fit together by the engaging of "pintles" and "sockets." The principle is described in 557,207 in this fashion: ". . . each link of each chain is provided both with a male and female coupling part, and when the chains are coupled together the female part of each link on one chain is engaged by the male part of a link on the other chain." This is as clear a description as one could wish of the principal fastening mechanism of the modern zipper. Judson did not, in fact, commit himself to this principle in most of the devices he subsequently made, but he seemed to understand at least the theoretical superiority of a design in which, as he put it, "every link has a double coupling with the opposite chain."

While the appeal of a "universal" fastener is evident in the patent claims—this time corsets are mentioned as an alternative application—Judson kept his focus on shoes. Now he felt moved to assure the examiner "that all statements of fact herein made as to the action of this device are based upon actual usage of a working device on a wearable shoe." Even more striking was the introduction of a clear argument for the utility of the invention:

From the foregoing statements it must be obvious that
a shoe equipped with my device has all the advantages

peculiar to a lace-shoe, while at the same time it is free from the annoyances hitherto incidental to lace-shoes on account of the lacing and unlacing required every time the shoes were put on or taken off the feet and on account of the lacing-strings coming untied. With my device the lacing-strings may be adjusted from time to time to take up the slack in the shoes, and the shoes may be fastened or loosened more quickly than any other form of shoe hitherto devised, so far as I am aware. (U.S.P. 557,207)

On the basis of such claims, in a period of severe business contraction, the Universal Fastener Company set out to join the ranks of American industry.

The impetus to enterprise that led to the founding of companies like Universal Fastener is one of the enduring mysteries of American economic life. The limited applicability, the technical uncertainty, and the dismal business climate that surrounded Judson's invention and the effort to make it go would suggest that investment in such schemes was hardly the product of rational economic decisions. To gain some understanding of what could move otherwise sober American businessmen to devote their wealth and, as it turned out, their lives and reputations to this kind of gamble, we must look a bit more closely at the men themselves. This is not always easy, for, as is often the case in such histories, the individuals who make their mark in these dramas are typically not literate, effusive sorts, leaving behind clues to their lives or their personalities in the form of memoirs or reflective letters. They are, instead, "practical" men and women, the sort for whom self-reflection is, if it ever takes place at all, a private and short-lived act, leaving behind no record for the inquisitors who may follow.

Such a person was Harry L. Earle. Whereas, upon his death, Whitcomb Judson left a legacy of thirty patents, a son who was already a successful manufacturer in his own right, and a reputation for mechanical cleverness, if not technological astuteness, Earle left little legacy at all. Yet it could be argued that without Harry Earle, Whitcomb Judson and his clever mechanisms would have been nothing—possibly with no patents, not even clearly articulated inventions, and certainly no chance for making a real mark on the material world. The Universal Fastener

Harry Earle was the salesman and promoter whose persistent hustle kept Whitcomb Judson's inventions alive. For several years his entrepreneurship sustained the slide fastener, until he was displaced by Lewis Walker.

TALON, INC.

Company was formed two days after Earle's fortieth birthday, and it represented the latest in a series of flirtations with technology and enterprise that went back to his youth in the same Midwest that had nurtured Whitcomb Judson. At age seventeen Earle became a station agent for the Lake Shore & Michigan Southern Railway, probably in his native Ohio. After six years at this, he took a turn for a year and a half as a telegraph operator for Western Union. By 1880 this was perhaps not the sort of training ground for aspiring inventors and mechanics that it had been fifteen years earlier, when Thomas Edison had spent his youthful years in such service. Nonetheless, such experience marked, at least very generally, the directions in which Earle's ambitions seemed to lie. The year 1883 saw Earle a salesman for the agricultural machinery outfit that employed Judson at the time, and there began a relationship that lasted for more than twenty years.[9]

Because of the role that Earle played as a promoter of Judson's pneumatic streetcar and then of his fastener, it would be easy to characterize him as simply the hustler for Judson's inventive schemes. For a time, however, we know that Judson worked as a salesman for Earle, soon after both men moved to Minneapolis. The fuller description of Earle's business suggests that not all the technical ideas flowed in one direction. The Minnesota incorporation papers for the Earle Manufacturing Company, filed in October 1887, specify that the firm's business was to be "the manufacturing, selling and dealing in the Earle Automatic Bagger & Tallyer, the Earle Automatic Band-cutter & Self-feeder," and other devices it might add later.[10] The same year his company was formed, Earle received two patents, one for an automatic grain scale (U.S. Patent 369,698). By the 1889–90 city directory, however, Earle was no longer listed as the president of his own company, and the next year's directory informs us that he had "removed to New York City," and the company was nowhere to be found. We know at this point that Earle was deeply involved in promoting Judson's pneumatic railway, but it is not clear whether his devotion to this cause was in spite of his other commitments or, as seems more likely, due to the collapse of these enterprises. When, late in his life, Earle was asked to list his occupations, he characterized his activities in the twenty years after 1886 as "In business for myself, promoting various things, one of them is now known as the 'Zipper.' " At this point, in the depths of the Great Depression, Earle could not claim to be a success. He was applying for admission to a charity home "for Aged and Respectable Bachelors and Widowers," and was forced to admit not only his own poverty but that of his offspring as well. But forty years before he had been the crucial man in giving a new technology a push toward the future.[11]

It was Harry Earle who took it upon himself to find the kind of backing for Judson's fasteners that would allow manufacturing to begin. The inventor could (and did) continue to experiment, concentrating on ways of making his devices as well as on improved designs. But if this effort were not to die aborning, sufficient capital would have to be located to provide the tangible elements essential to any industrial enterprise—machines, tools, buildings, raw materials. While it is not clear quite how he did it—perhaps by drawing on friendships and trust that went back to his days as an agricultural machine salesman farther east— Harry Earle managed to locate investors in the small town of Catasauqua, Pennsylvania. There, in late 1895, the Universal Fastener Company was invited to begin manufacturing in the Bryden Horse Shoe Company's shop.[12]

The first slide fastener to be manufactured was this design of 1896. It is often depicted as the original 1891 design, but a glance at the earlier patents shows the radical difference. While far easier to manufacture than the earlier designs, it still did not function well. The item shown here is almost certainly a later replica.

TALON, INC.

Eastern Pennsylvania's Lehigh Valley must have seemed almost ideal as a location for the new company; it was a region in which metalworking was certainly no novelty, and thus both materials and skilled workers could be expected to be in plentiful supply. One other feature of the Bryden shop may have had an additional appeal to the Universal Fastener organizers. Just a couple of years before their arrival this company became perhaps the first firm to begin producing horseshoes by "presswork." In other words, while the old blacksmith forging of horseshoes had long been displaced by machinery, the Bryden works went one step farther, using large machines to punch the nail holes in the formed shoes (and perhaps even to make blanks of the shoes themselves). In June 1893 the Catasauqua shop took delivery of a thirty-eight-ton punching press from the Ferracute Company of Bridgeton, New Jersey. A few months later it received two even larger presses, of fifty-two tons. Thus the initial manufacture of Judson's invention was undertaken in a shop that was pioneering the use of large powered machines for the careful forming of metal. That such machines, appropriately designed for precisely stamping out parts of the fastener, would be crucial to the success of their endeavors may have become quickly evident to Earle, Judson, and company. They had placed themselves in just the right spot to take advantage of machinery and expertise.[13]

Only the sketchiest of information about this inaugural manufacture survives, but apparently by early 1896 a real product—largely handmade—emerged from the old Bryden shops. Surprisingly, perhaps, it wasn't a shoe fastening, but one of the Judson designs applied to mailbags. The logic of this is not difficult to see and, in fact, represents a form of thinking to be found in almost every inventor and entrepreneur in American history, from Eli Whitney and his claims for interchangeable parts to the Wright brothers and their airplane to the biotechnology pioneers of the 1990s: If a technology appears to have uncertain markets at the outset and also has large capital requirements or poses considerable technical challenges, then all efforts must be made at the outset to sell it to the government. Even the most vocal champions of laissez-faire cannot effectively deny that such thinking has so frequently moved American invention. In April 1896 representatives of the Post Office Department were able to inspect the Judson fastener on a mailbag, and pronounced it satisfactory. The second assistant postmaster general gave an order for twenty sacks equipped with the fastener, and Earle and his colleagues must have thought, at least for a moment, that they had success at hand. The Post Office's order was never repeated, however, and the Catasauqua effort was quickly in trouble.[14]

By late 1896 the Universal Fastener Company's minutes begin to reflect the unstable nature of the enterprise. Meetings were no longer held in Catasauqua but at Harry Earle's offices in New York City, and the company's activities ground to a temporary halt. The source of the difficulty was not solely the lack of orders but stubborn technical problems that clearly surprised the company's backers by their intractability. In December 1895 the Connecticut machine builders of Blake & Johnson were given the order to produce fastener-making machinery from Judson's designs. It was early apparent that the fastener would have to be made by machinery to be economically viable. Six months later Judson reported to his partners that the equipment was due to be finished in about sixty days. After three more months he reported that it was "practically completed, and should be ac-

cepted" by the company. Soon after this, however, the optimistic
reports ceased, the work in Catasauqua stopped, and the local
backers of the effort apparently lost heart. The well-connected
Earle had little difficulty picking up the slack, however, for he
was able to persuade a banker from Elyria, Ohio, the eponymous
George H. Ely, to bankroll the Elyria Fastener Company to take
a license from Universal Fastener and even to take Whitcomb
Judson himself as an employee, in order to find successful applications of the invention. It is important to note here that the
challenges facing Judson and his backers were perceived largely
in terms not of developing further their fastener's design but of
coming up with—both technically and economically—successful
applications for it. Ely was particularly attracted to the idea of
the fastener's use in leggings and "overgaiters," applications of
a novel device to uses that seem peculiarly anachronistic to a
modern eye. The move to Elyria in early 1898 coincided with
the first trials of the machinery, finally shipped from Connecticut. When the intricate mechanisms were put to the test, however, nothing but trouble was encountered.[15]

When he was faced with the difficulties of his machine designs, it would seem that Whitcomb Judson was out of his league.
The machine builders from Manville Brothers, Waterbury, Connecticut (who inherited the Blake & Johnson contract), were
called to Elyria to try to modify their handiwork, but the result
was little more than enormous bills. In spite of these problems,
the optimistic Harry Earle went ahead with plans to promote a
European Universal Fastener Company and even went to England in an attempt to sell interest in it. The combination of bad
economic times and little concrete progress to report from home
doomed these efforts quickly. George Ely, for his part, began to
lose patience. He complained as early as May 1899 that he had
"spent more money than he had planned in the development and
operations of the company," and a few months later he apparently told Harry Earle that he had had enough. In February
1901 the Elyria Fastener Company sold its assets, including its
Universal Fastener license, to Harry Earle. At this point the
fortunes of Judson's invention were really little further advanced
than they had been when Earle's promotional efforts had begun
six and a half years before. Only hard-earned lessons and some
faulty machinery had been won to the cause.[16]

•

z

I

P

P

E

R

As the new century opened and as Whitcomb Judson's fastener idea approached its tenth anniversary, there was still nothing to distinguish visibly this invention from the host of similar misbegotten schemes and inspirations that moved in and out of the Patent Office year after year. To be sure, companies had been organized, investors recruited, and a few products had seen the light of day. This was farther than many an inventor's efforts got, but it was certainly a long way from profitability. There is little evidence of flagging faith on the part of the original promoters, however. The lure of the golden invention was a hard one to deny. Perhaps inventors and promoters alike were moved by the same faith enunciated by the commissioner of patents in 1901, when he declared that "the century just closed stands out preëminently as the century of invention," in which the prosperity of the country could be traced to "the combination of witty inventions and thinking men."[17]

More likely, these champions of invention and enterprise were more motivated by a different kind of faith, given voice by Washington patent attorney Fred G. Dieterich in his 1899 guide to the prospective patentee. Although not all patents were remunerative, the prospects of success were generally bright, Dieterich promised, and the possibility of true enrichment was enough enticement to the efforts required:

> To be sure, thousands of patents have been granted whose merits have never been tested, and no doubt many patents have caused their owners' disaster, as it will be found to be the case in any business: but as a general thing, a large proportion of patents granted are productive of handsome profits upon a very trifling financial outlay. Compare the costs of all the patents issued up to date with the known worth of a prominent invention. Reckoning the average cost of a patent to be $60, the amount invested would be but $36,000,000; whereas, among the earliest of patents issued by this government, the Sewing Machine has yielded the owners and inventors more than $100,000,000. These are facts which cannot be disputed.[18]

No doubt many inventors could have been found with more skeptical views about the value of patents. Even the most enthusiastic patenter of them all, Thomas Edison (in his report for 1900 the commissioner of patents noted that Edison had been issued 742 patents; he was to receive more than 350 more before his death), had declared that a patent was "simply an invitation to a lawsuit" and that he had "lost all faith in patents, judges & everything else relating to patents."[19] The average of 40,000-plus applications received by the Patent Office each year during the 1890s testified to a deeper faith both in the patent system and in the prospective rewards of invention. While the patent attorney's claim that "a large proportion of patents granted are productive of handsome profits upon a very trifling financial outlay" can be dismissed as professional hucksterism, many wanted to believe exactly that. Whitcomb Judson clearly shared that belief, and men around him, while quickly disabused of any notions that they might be dealing with "a trifling financial outlay," were moved by their own faith in the eventual returns from the combination of "witty inventions and thinking men."

Hustle and Bustle

2

In 1901, when Harry Earle took possession of the assets of the Universal Fastener Company, Lewis Walker was forty-five years old. He had established himself well in his adopted town of Meadville, Pennsylvania, in which he had lived for almost three decades, ever since he came as a student to Allegheny College. To be sure, he owed some of his success to his marriage the year he was graduated, 1877, to Susan Adelaide Delamater, offspring of one of Meadville's richest and most prominent families. Lewis Walker was able to establish quickly that he knew how to take the best advantage of his new social standing. He parlayed his study of law into a position of considerable responsibility for overseeing various business and real estate dealings of his wife's family and, in fact, never set up an independent law practice of his own. By his early thirties Walker had made himself into a corporate attorney of some influence and authority, dealing with as many as sixteen different enterprises at one time. He did not neglect the other things that were important in establishing a respectable name in late-nineteenth-century

Lewis Walker (1855–1938)—the Colonel—was the single most dominant figure throughout most of the zipper's first forty-five years. In both appearance and manners he was the model of the small-town lawyer and businessman, and in his youth, as this picture suggests, he could even be a bit the dandy. *TALON, INC.*

small-town America. Civic responsibilities were met through service in the Pennsylvania National Guard, which resulted in his acquiring the rank and lifelong title of Colonel when he was thirty-five. A reputation for courtesy and sobriety was enhanced by his slender, upright bearing, and his elegantly groomed mustache punctuated a suavity that impressed acquaintances and strangers alike.[1]

This was the man who, more than any other, stood at the center of the zipper story. Lewis Walker claimed no great technical capacities, although he certainly thought himself capable of judging those of others. He invented nothing, yet the transformation of Whitcomb Judson's peculiar ideas into a ubiquitous and indispensable technology owed as much to Walker's perseverance and leadership as to the technical ingenuity of tinkerers and engineers. It can even be argued that Lewis Walker was no great salesman himself and that the marketing trials and eventual triumphs that marked this story owed little to him. Yet no participant or observer could effectively deny the Colonel's central role. This is why understanding that role is such a help in comprehending the real place of individuals in the shaping of modern technology. If the creation of a new thing is but a matter of solving technical and economic problems, then we can easily (although we do not have to) believe that technological paths were determined largely by physical laws, economic and social conditions, and all the other anonymous forces that we customarily conjure up to explain the dimensions of our world. If, on the other hand, more is involved, if men and women are seen as active agents in creating our material culture, then we must sit up and take notice of a story like that of Colonel Walker and the zipper. We can then hope to measure better what difference a personality can make, what changes are wrought by an individual's faith or prejudice, and how much of our world is truly contingent on the people who inhabit it.

Reminiscing about his relationship with Whitcomb Judson, Lewis Walker sometimes spoke of first encountering Judson and his fastener on an 1893 stop in Chicago en route to the West Coast. Perhaps he simply wanted to forget that his ties to the inventor extended back to the ill-fated days of the pneumatic railway. While Walker's friendship with James Williamson, Judson's Minneapolis patent attorney, was the likely source of his introduction to Judson and his schemes, the Colonel's involvement went beyond casual interest and investment. In 1890 the Delamater interests, under Walker's direction, purchased several hundred thousand dollars' worth of stock in Judson companies, and Walker did not hesitate to put some of his own money into the ventures as well. In fact, he went so far as to work out a contract for the exclusive rights to market the Judson system in the state of Pennsylvania, Even after financial disaster struck the Delamaters at the end of 1890, Walker kept up with the activities of Judson's companies, closely watching the arrangements surrounding the Washington experiments in early 1891.[2] There can be no question that Lewis Walker was high on the little list that Harry Earle seemed to have of prospective investors for the enterprises on which he wished to build the future.

The small group that got together in Chicago in November 1894 to form the Universal Fastener Company certainly constituted a peculiar mixture of men, yet each of the principal figures (there were others, but they were of little consequence to the story) can be seen as particularly apt representatives of the forces at work in shaping their century. Whitcomb Judson's bounty of schemes, so often rife with complexity and overcleverness, almost appear as broad strokes in a caricature of the ingenious but impractical Yankee inventor. His self-schooled background, peripatetic career, and reliance on others for promotion all contribute to the impression that he makes on the modern observer of a man very much the product of his time and circumstance, the sort of figure that would have been unimaginable in an earlier age and out of place in the next century. Harry Earle, too, possesses some of the same dated aura—that of the hustler who seeks to expand the theater of his pitch but who seems somehow never to escape from the small platforms that would have been so comfortable to the seller of threshers and automatic grain scales but that were so inadequate in a world being made over by Rockefellers, Morgans, and their ilk.

Only Lewis Walker, college graduate, lawyer, maker of companies and contracts, seems to belong to the future. Sure enough, he alone of the three survived the first struggles of the new technology that captivated them all, and he alone was to build a sound personal prosperity upon it. But even in his success and the modern air that he projects, he poses for the modern viewer perhaps the greatest puzzle of all. Why? Why did he cast his lot in with this effort? What moved a man, so well along in his career, so much a creature of home, family, and community, so self-possessed and marked by personal courtesy and grace, to seek his fortune with devices and desires so bizarre, untried, and uninspiring? While the Colonel, as we shall see, was a prolific letter writer, he was not, as far as his surviving correspondence reveals, a reflective one. Indeed, one could not expect a man of his background and businesslike approach to life to speak much of motives or special ambitions. Later in his life he seemed to regard himself as somehow above the kind of ambition that normally drove men to put their hopes and money in uncertain enterprises. Reflecting on his beginnings with Judson's fastener, he spoke of "time unlimited, money almost unlimited" as the primary requirements for a new invention:

> ... and in the early stages this money is obtainable generally from the class we might designate as "gullible investor"—the individual expecting big returns from small investment, quickly realized, accepting the enthusiasm of the inventor or promoter as evidence of the immediate value of the invention, and that practical utility is ready and waiting for the use of the invention—with the investor's experience and avarice leading him on to part with his savings, and with no realization of the fact that practically every invention is the acorn only that produces the oak tree after Nature's law has nurtured the nut through years of slow growth, resulting in the many acorns.[3]

Clearly Lewis Walker did not see himself as ever belonging to this class of men.

The Walker involvement in the Universal Fastener Company waxed and waned in those struggling early years. Walker, Earle, and Judson were among the seven company directors chosen in June 1895, although it quickly became evident that it was largely a Judson and Earle effort at this point. In 1898, with the company's fortunes particularly low, the colonel was a vocal advocate for George Ely's participation, and shortly after the move to Elyria, Walker took Whitcomb Judson's place as company presi-

Peter Aronson was a mechanic who had emigrated from Sweden to Connecticut, where he worked for the machine foundry of Manville Brothers. In 1903 he moved to Hoboken, New Jersey, to work on the machinery for making Judson's fasteners. His daughter Elvira worked in the Hoboken shop, where she attracted the attention of Gideon Sundback. *TALON, INC.*

32

•

Z

I

P

P

E

R

dent. When Harry Earle took charge of things again in 1901, the colonel apparently was happy to make way for him.[4]

Earle organized the Fastener Manufacturing and Machine Company in New Jersey and sought out additional investors in the area to support renewed manufacturing efforts. He still had not lost his touch, and seems to have had little trouble infecting a wealthy New Yorker, J. F. O'Shaughnessy, with the fastener's fever. With this backing, Earle located his new company's works in a small brick building in Hoboken, undoubtedly encouraged by northern New Jersey's already impressive record as an incubator for new technologies. Almost precisely a century before Hoboken's own John Stevens had demonstrated convincingly the power of steam to do work on both land and water. More recently such full-time inventors as John Wesley Hyatt, creator of everything from roller bearings to plastics, and Thomas Alva Edison had shown how congenial rapidly urbanizing Hudson and Essex counties could be to the technological pioneer. Even more important than his new shop, however, were Earle's new men. The substantial investment in machinery from Connecticut's Manville Brothers was now supplemented by substantial technical skill, in the form of two Manville employees, John G. Lepper and Peter Aronson. Lepper became the chief manager and technical adviser at the Hoboken shop, but in an indirect way it was Peter Aronson who was to have the greatest long-term effect on the fastener story. Not only was he to contribute his own inventions to the effort, but the Swedish-born mechanic was to be directly responsible for bringing one of his countrymen to the task of finishing what Whitcomb Judson had only started.[5]

With a new shop and the influx of new funds, Harry Earle was able, for the first time, to begin plotting a sales strategy. The relocation to the New York City area opened up avenues that simply had not been available before. In particular, a real range of applications for the fastener could be promoted, going beyond the very casual speculations that Judson had included in his patents. It was necessary, as well, to confront the more subtle problem that every new technology must face: how to claim and identify its place in the general scheme of things. Every new product must develop an identity that will allow onlookers to understand how they are to judge its novelty, its utility, and just why they are to be attracted to it. Rarely does an invention

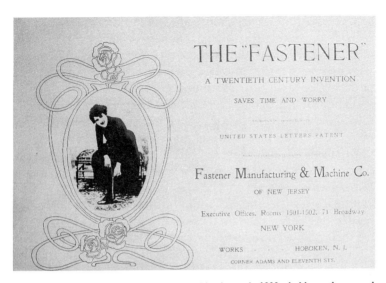

This promotion for "The Fastener," issued in the early 1900s, held out the appeal of a "Twentieth Century Device" and attempted to give the Hoboken company the appearance of an established New York City firm. *TALON COLLECTION, CCHS*

The promotion for "The Fastener" illustrated a variety of applications, in gloves, gaiters, skirts, boots, and the like. *TALON COLLECTION, CCHS*

appear with such a character ready-made; just as in the case of individuals making their debuts on new stages of life, so, too, must things stake out the basis for their reputations. And just as with individuals, this effort is generally a combination of actual performance and calculated appearance.

The Fastener Manufacturing and Machine Company set out to make a reputation in a thoroughly modern manner: It promoted itself in print. At some expense Earle had an elaborate illustrated brochure produced, introducing his product, its applications, and even the setting of its manufacture. Nothing better portrays than this publication the way in which Earle and his colleagues saw Judson's invention as fitting into the scheme of modernity. Oddly enough, they could not think of a better name for their product than "The Fastener." The makers of this device (and its more successful successors) always were surprisingly awkward about devising good monikers; the term "zipper," as we shall see, was in the end foisted upon them. In these opening years of the new century it was incumbent upon the promoters to announce their product as "a Twentieth Century Device," one appropriate for "this busy and progressive age." The primary purpose of their literature was to explain just what "The Fastener" was and how it worked, and since it was "so radically new," it was only through photographs that they could "make it clear, that it is a most remarkable invention; remarkable in its . . . simplicity, rapidity, security, utility." The pages of photographs and explanations that followed showed a fastener that was different from any in Judson's U.S. patents, although it was described in a British patent (B.P. 6998 of 1896). The two chains of the fastener consisted of links with hooks curving out to face the opposing chain and eyelets between them to receive the opposite hook. This somewhat fierce-looking device was shown applied to skirt plackets, gloves, corsets, boots, shoes, leggings, and government mailbags. The women's uses depicted happy, satisfied, respectable users, clearly pleased with the convenience of the new device. Perhaps most encouraging of all, and suggesting that the real target of the promotion was potential stock purchasers, each application was accompanied by an estimate of the numbers produced each year: "We are reliably informed that there are more than 175,000,000 dress-skirts made and sold annually in the United States . . . 300,000,000 pairs of

gloves, . . . there are more than 200,000,000 pairs of corsets and
corset waists made and sold annually in the United States, . . .
50,000,000 pairs of leggins [sic] and overgaiters, . . . 250,000,000
pairs of boots and shoes, . . . more than 300,000 new sacks are
purchased annually. . . ." Photographs of the Hoboken factory
attested to the substantial nature of the manufacturing establishment, and a final photograph purported to show the "Executive
Offices" in a Manhattan skyscraper—71 Broadway, in which
Harry Earle had a small office.[6]

At least one newpaper picked up the material in this booklet,
publishing a description under the heading A TWENTIETH CEN-
TURY DEVICE. Here was an appreciation of "the 'little things' of
which the patent office record hundreds every week" that added
as much to human happiness as the great inventions of the age:

> One of the most ingenious and useful of these to come
> under our notice recently is what is known as "The Fas-
> tener," made exclusively by the Fastener Manufacturing
> and Machine Co., of New Jersey. This ingenious device is
> really sui generis, stands in a class all by itself. Yet it is very
> simple, and equally strong and effective. As a saver of time
> and worry, it is unequalled. [Here follows a description of
> its appearance and operation.] It is simply and easily oper-
> ated, beating buttons, hooks and eyes and all such things
> hollow. As a placket fastener for ladies' dresses, as a glove
> fastener, a corset fastener, a legging fastener, and a shoe
> fastener it is unequalled, and experts have declared it the
> most perfect and satisfactory device for the fastening of gov-
> ernment mail sacks.

A reproduction of the photograph sequence of a smiling woman
fastening a boot completed the publicity. While this puffery
probably made Earle's shareholders feel good, it is not clear that
it translated at all into sales. It is, in fact, the only evidence
remaining that the Fastener Manufacturing and Machine Company produced anything.[7]

Not long after the Hoboken shop had received its machinery and the frustrating task of trying to make it work had resumed, Lewis Walker reentered the picture, this time with an
increasing level of involvement that was never to slacken. On

36

February 8, 1904, he became a director of Fastener Manufacturing and Machine. Ten days later the company became the Automatic Hook and Eye Company, the name under which it was to market its products for nine years. On May 11 Walker was elected the company's vice-president, and, just as significantly, his brother-in-law, Victor Delamater, became company secretary and treasurer. These events marked the beginning of a permanent shift in the active cast of characters in this tale, a shift that culminated a couple of years later in the final exit of Harry Earle and Whitcomb Judson.[8]

It was about this time that the inventor made his last substantial contribution to the development of his brainchild. Although Judson had been working off and on with the fastener's promoters, investors, and machine builders, his inventive heart had really been elsewhere for almost ten years. Since receiving his 1896 patents, he had taken out eleven more, but only one was directed toward helping the fastener, that being for his ill-fated chain-making machine. The others had largely been devoted to a much more alluring technology, that of the automobile. This was, after all, the technology that was to make his son, Ross Judson, a multimillionaire well before any of the fastener's developers were to see riches. Whitcomb Judson's last patent, however, issued in 1905, was for a "separable fastener" (U.S. Patent 788,317), which was one step forward and one backward in the progress toward a practical device. The step forward was the move away from the chain links that had been such a constant element of the device. In this latest design Judson specified that the fastening elements were to be attached on either side of the closure by being clamped to cloth tape, which could then be sewn into their final application. This simplified both the fabrication of the fastener itself and its installation. The backward move was to reshape the fastening elements themselves so that they resembled more than ever traditional hooks and eyes. Instead of the innovative designs of the 1896 patents, with their identical, staggered, interlocking pieces, this last patent described a fastener with a row of hooks on one side and one of eyelets on the other. The renaming of the company Automatic Hook and Eye was an attempt at a literal description of the new product, as well as an attempt to identify with a widely recognized American penchant

Whitcomb Judson's final fastener design consisted of hooks on one side, opposed by eyes on the other, clamped to beaded cloth tape. It was the first slide fastener to be sold widely.

TALON COLLECTION, CCHS

C-CURITY
FASTENER
1902

for things that promised to save labor through machinery, things "automatic."⁹

The most important virtue of Judson's new design was that it could be made. In 1905 Automatic Hook and Eye brought the C-curity fastener to market. After more than ten years there was a fastener that could be manufactured and sold. Making the C-curity was relatively simple, although laborious, since it was finally decided that there was no machinery adequate to the task. Punch presses were used to cut and bend small pieces out of thin sheets of steel and form the hooks and eyes. These tiny pieces were then finished off by smoothing rough edges and applying a protective coating. "Girls" then put them into steel racks and fed these into an assembling machine, which brought cloth tape to the hooks and eyes and allowed the workers to clamp them together with the right spacing. Other women then inspected the so-called stringers coming out of the assembling machine, replacing bent, misplaced, or absent hooks or eyes or rejecting stringers that could not be fixed. The final step was to bring together a stringer of hooks with one of eyes and adding the slider. The fastener was not finished, however, until the slider was run up and down the finished article enough times to assure smooth operation. This sort of hand fabrication fell far short of the mechanical ideals of the Automatic Hook and Eye men, but it at least worked and was to sustain the company for almost a decade.[10]

With the introduction of the C-curity, the fastener makers deepened their commitment to a market that Whitcomb Judson hardly even imagined when he began: women's skirts and dresses. In announcements of the device it was described as a "placket fastener," which would generally be interpreted as referring to women's garments. The Hoboken manufacturers were sure of their target, and confident that they had chosen well. One advertisement depicted three famous singers, past and present:

> *In 1782 Mrs. Siddons was laced into her costume at the Drury Lane Theater.*
> *In 1850 Jennie Lind depended on hooks and eyes at Castle Garden.*

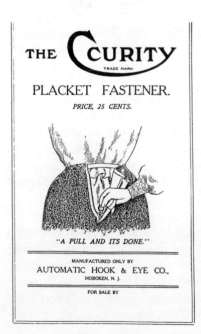

THE C CURITY
TRADE MARK
PLACKET FASTENER.
PRICE, 25 CENTS.

"A PULL AND ITS DONE."

MANUFACTURED ONLY BY
AUTOMATIC HOOK & EYE CO.,
HOBOKEN, N. J.

FOR SALE BY

The appeal to modernity was the key to selling the C-curity, but this was accompanied by an off-putting complexity in instructions for its installation and use.
TALON COLLECTION, CCHS

In 1901 Lillian Russell used Snaps at the Weber and Field's Music Hall.

And then:

A Pull and it's Done! No More Open Skirts. No old fashioned Hooks and Eyes or Fasteners. Your Skirt is Always Securely and Neatly Fastened. The C-curity Placket Fastener.[11]

Could the fastener's champions have possibly imagined how their pitch was foreshadowing images and feelings that were to make their product (in its later, refined form) so much a part of how men and women in the twentieth century thought about the glamour of dress and undress? To refer openly to the laces, hooks and eyes, and snaps that had secured famous women was probably as provocative as a 1907 publicist was willing to be, but there was no going back now. Whitcomb Judson had not thought about his invention as invading the more intimate realms of daily life, but that was exactly where Lewis Walker and his associates were taking it.

The sales strategy that accompanied this approach was straightforward and initially successful, although it created problems later. The C-curity was unabashedly promoted as a novelty item, sold largely door to door by fast-talking salesmen who persuaded their largely female customers that this was the device that would guarantee their reputation for being modern and efficient women. The promise of "A Pull and it's Done!" was to be part of a "drummer's" spiel, and the manner in which the Hoboken operators readily handed over their new technology to such salesmen spoke volumes about how they saw their creation in the general scheme of things. The most vigorous sales efforts began to pour from the tidy brick building on the corner of Hoboken's Adam and Eleventh streets. The key women's magazines were plied with touts for the novelty. *Vogue* could be quoted as saying that the patent fastener belonged "in a class quite above the usual thing in this line." The *Woman's Magazine* called it "one of the most ingenious little devices ever constructed, and a perfect boon to woman in this day of skirts with snugly fitted hips." *Woman's Home Companion* and the *Ladies'*

Z
I
P
P
E
R

World illustrated the C-curity, along with brief instructions on how it might be fitted. The sentiment of the *Companion*'s author, expressing astonishment at "how many women will wear a gown with a gaping placket hole," seems to have been an easy one to plant in the journals whether or not it was true. It was actually an idea that zipper makers harped on for the next thirty years.[12]

All this, however, was simply ammunition for the real sales effort, which was the force of commission agents that the company began to recruit vigorously. In June 1907 newspapers throughout New England ran this little come-on: "MALE AND FEMALE: The new C-curity Fastener for skirts and trousers. Best agency offered anywhere. Establish repeat orders. Big orders. Not sold in stores. Write for particulars. AUTOMATIC HOOK AND EYE COMPANY. Hoboken, N.J."[13] Farther west, one Burt A. Martin in Verdi, Nevada, sponsored an "Agents Wanted" notice directed at Long Beach, California. *Collier's Weekly* that fall ran another advertisement promising "$3000 a year up . . . for reliable men capable of hiring and managing" a sales force. "Sales repeat themselves automatically . . . new necessity for both men and women," the piece assured readers.[14] Some of the notices offered to send samples of the fastener for thirty-five cents, which was its retail price. The materials prepared by the company in support of this campaign were just what one might have imagined. One polished little leaflet led on with its cover: "THE OPPORTUNITY—MAKE YOUR SPARE TIME PAY. WHY LET IT PASS?" On the inside:

> AN OPPORTUNITY.
> For one active man and woman for every town and city in this country.
> To please every other man and woman in that town.
> To solve for others the most difficult problem in the art of dressmaking and tailoring.
> AND
> To make more money in SPARE HOURS than it is possible to make in most lines of business in a whole day.
> In other words to sell our C-CURITY PLACKET and TROUSERS FASTENER.

This pitch is followed by assurances that this opportunity was limited to men and women "of good social standing." After descriptions of the great virtues of the fastener, the company's sales approach is explained by noting that this is a product that requires a personal approach to customers rather than "by selling through stores where clerks are oftentimes indifferent even to the point of discourtesy when the sale of an article needs personal instruction for its application and use."[15]

The fact is that the C-curity did indeed require "personal instruction," and this was no great virtue of the device. Automatic Hook and Eye tried to meet the problem with an instruction booklet that was to be distributed with each fastener sold. This attempted to make installation seem an easy matter for any ordinary dressmaker or tailor, although a note of anxiety emerges with the reminder of "the importance of following these directions with care." The likelihood of initial frustration is hinted at in the assurance that "After having sewn on one you will find it easier to put the second one on. . . ." The instructions for using were only slightly less formidable than those for applying, but they betrayed how strange the new fastener must have been to most people:

> *To open, unhook and pull on waist band with both hands, as you would tear in two a piece of paper or cloth.*
> *To close, take hold of the ring and pull up slide, holding garment below opening with other hand. Pull steady, don't jerk.*
> Important*!!! If, in moving the slide, it tightens, push it back just a little; this will ease it. Don't pull hard if it stops; push it back.*
> Smooth out the folds of underskirt, so they will not get caught in the slide.
> *If skirt is to be washed remove fastener.*

Remove fastener? Yes. The steel hooks and eyes of the C-curity were given a finish to protect them, but this would not have prevented their rusting under the stress of laundering, not to mention damage to the exposed parts of the device. Modern readers will recognize (and sympathize with) the danger of catching underwear in the slider, but the additional complications will not seem so familiar. Unlike Judson's original designs, the opening of this fastener was not done with the slide but by

42 ripping apart the sides of the fastening. A little reflection will suggest that this meant that opening was perhaps just a bit *too* easy. It is also not hard to detect a sense that the motion of the slider often was not smooth at all but rather could require a bit of a struggle. "A Pull and it's Done!" seems to have been a mite too sanguine a characterization of the fastener's performance. The instruction booklet apparently went through several editions, as the makers struggled with the obvious distress of users. After the involved installation directions in one edition, this almost plaintive note was appended: "CUSTOMERS WILL CONFER A FAVOR UPON US BY REPORTING ANY DIFFICULTY IN APPLYING FASTENER, IN WHICH CASE WE WILL BE PLEASED TO SEND MORE DETAILED INSTRUCTIONS." Perhaps "ominous" would be a better description of this plea, surely no source of confidence for the first-time user.[16]

The C-curity was simply not very good. While the Judson hook and eye design had real advantages over his first models, both in fabrication and in use, when put to the test of the real world—of people standing up and sitting down, bending over and twisting around—it simply would not do. This fact must have been apparent to the Hoboken manufacturers pretty early, but it did little to deter them. The sales approach that had been adopted worked well enough at the outset that they could get at least a few years' mileage out of the C-curity. "It was a new and novel article and appealed to the individual minds," explained one observer years later. But, he went on to admit, "The sales were usually made, what we would call a first sale; a repeat sale to an ultimate consumer was never made."[17] The contract that Automatic Hook and Eye offered to its agents required that the salesman "agree to thoroughly prepare for the work by mastering the art of applying Fastener on the various skirts before entering the field" and "to call upon and show the merits of Fastener to every dressmaker, tailor and to the lady of every home in [the] territory. . . ." He had to promise not to sell to "jobbers, merchants, nor directly or indirectly to retail stores." If this wasn't demanding enough, the agent was also admonished in his contract to sell the C-curity for no less than 35 cents, although discounts to dressmakers were allowed if they bought in quantity. Likewise, if the agent purchased his items by the dozen, they cost him 20 cents apiece, but if his orders were three dozen or more, this was cut to 17½ cents. The diligent agent might, it was promised, expect to make as much as 4 to 6 dollars a day on this basis. This was, however, if he or she (there was an explicit invitation to women to become agents) indeed succeeded in making the promised "average of one sale in every house"—an accomplishment that could hardly have been typical.[18]

Even if the putative virtues of the fastener were as readily apparent as the sales recruiters promised (as is highly unlikely), the agent would run into another problem that would make life difficult: Thirty-five cents was a sum well beyond anything a dressmaker would normally think of expending on such an article, far beyond the cost of buttons or hooks and eyes. While the Hoboken shop was clearly organized to keep manufacturing costs as low as possible, the inescapable costs of production, as well as the need to make the effort worth the while of door-to-door salesmen, put the price into a realm that made the purchase a costly one for most prospective customers. The spring 1907 catalog of Sears, Roebuck & Company, for example, advertised skirts as cheap as 77 cents, and even more costly ones were less than $2.50. Men's trousers were to be found at under one dollar, good-quality corsets for between 60 and 90 cents, and buttons started at less than 5 cents a gross. The problem of high relative costs, relative not only to the technology it displaced but also to the "context" in which it was used—the skirt, glove, boot, or bag—was to be a serious one for zipper makers for more than three decades. Even when the device became a genuinely attractive convenience (rather than a problematical novelty), its high cost would be a source of concern for producers and prospective consumers alike. At the outset, it can be imagined, the Hoboken company may have felt compelled to adopt its pushy-gadget-salesman strategy. Here was the sort of approach already associated with the sellers of apple corers and cherry pitters, and before them with peddlers and tinkers, and afterward with the purveyors of vacuum cleaners and stain removers. This had the unfortunate result, however, of tainting the fastener with the air of fly-by-night entrepreneurialism, which was possibly acceptable to the likes of Harry Earle but was probably not the kind of thing that Colonel Lewis Walker wished to be attached to.

From the outset the men at Automatic Hook and Eye saw that other approaches were desirable, at least from a theoretical point of view. Their Hoboken location, after all, had the ostensible virtue of being almost within sight of the greatest concentration of garment manufacturing in America—Manhattan. It is difficult to judge from the surviving evidence exactly how hard they tried at this point to go after the garment trade, but to judge from later attempts, it may have been a vigorous effort for a time. At one point, at least, in these early days the approaches to the dressmakers caught the eye of an outside observer, whose brief newspaper report of what he saw was a wonderful parody of technological hustle:

JOY! BLISS! BEATITUDE!
SELF-HOOKING WAIST FOUND

*One More of Man's Ills Removed by
Genius from Hoboken, New Jersey*

That long drawn sigh is not the dying gasp of summer, but the exclamation of relief from all parts of the United States following the announcement that the death knell of hooks and eyes and large buttons for small buttonholes has been rung; and to-day an inventor from much-maligned Hoboken, N.J., is a candidate for the Hall of Fame. The announcement of the hookless-buttonless waist was made at the meeting of the Dressmakers' Protective Association now in session at Masonic Hall.

Inside fourteen models were donning and "undonning" the latest French creations, but in the hall outside a number of men were listening with awe to the Hoboken inventor who told of his epoch making discovery. Men with gnarled fingers from buttoning waists wept with joy as the man unfolded his device which makes it possible for a woman's waist to be buttoned in one second simply by turning a ring which is sewed either at the bottom or top of the garment. The dressmakers, however, have not given official indorsement to the invention as yet.[19]

The dressmakers kept their distance from the invention for almost another three decades.

The C-curity had not been on the market for very long before it became clear to Lewis Walker and his associates that their enterprise had some major problems. Sometime early in 1906 Harry Earle resigned his position with the company, and both he and Whitcomb Judson began to exit the drama they had so hopefully begun a dozen years before. From this point on Lewis Walker's central role became more and more obvious, although he chose to remain in Meadville and thus recruited a family friend, Frank Russell, for the post of president, while his brother-in-law, Victor Delamater, remained as secretary and treasurer. Peter Aronson assumed the technical leadership of the company in mid-1905 and proceeded to work on solving the obvious problems with Judson's last design. While he made some minor progress in this connection, the work convinced Aronson that the small changes he was competent to make were simply not adequate to the challenge. Aronson was a fine machinist, with experience in the Swedish mining industry before he emigrated to America in 1893, but he recognized that the mechanical difficulties of the C-curity required an analytical approach that was simply beyond his competence. What the work in Hoboken required was an engineer.[20]

"Much-maligned Hoboken" lies on the Hudson River, sandwiched between Weehawken, where Alexander Hamilton and Aaron Burr squared off for their famous duel, and Jersey City, where most of the great eastern railroads deposited passengers for the trains that ran under the Hudson on their way to lower Manhattan or Pennsylvania Station. In Hoboken itself, lying opposite about Fourteenth Street in New York, the Delaware, Lackawanna & Western Railroad terminated, and the gigantic tubes of the Pennsylvania Railroad began their way under the river. At the water's edge were the piers at which the steamships of the North German Lloyd, the Hamburg American, and the Scandinavian lines deposited their stream of immigrants. Many of these moved no farther than a few blocks from their disembarkation, giving the city an ethnic, particularly northern European character. The census of 1900 reported that of the Hoboken population of 59,364, more than 80 percent (48,439) were either immigrants or had one or both parents who were foreign-born, with a large proportion of them having a German heritage. A smaller community, located in adjacent Weehawken, was made up of those of Scandinavian, particularly Swedish, extraction.

Little wonder, then, that Peter Aronson had felt right at home
there after his move from Connecticut (indeed, throughout his
life Aronson sought the cultural comfort of fellow Swedes in
America). It is, also, no surprise that as part of this community
he should hear about and meet other migrants from his native
country as they made their way as a small part of the great flood
that was to total almost 9 million total immigrants in the first ten
years of the twentieth century.

It is possible that twenty-four-year-old Otto Frederick Gideon Sundback took his first step in the New World on one of
Hoboken's piers, but if so, he didn't linger. He made his way
straight to East Pittsburgh, Pennsylvania, where a job waited for
him at George Westinghouse's thriving electrical works. It may
not have been much of a job—he started as a tracer of engineering
drawings—but a young electrical engineer could hardly have
asked for a more exciting place to be in that winter of 1905. The
generator department of the Westinghouse Electric and Manufacturing Company had been responsible for building the gigantic
dynamos installed in the electric power project at Niagara Falls.
The attendant publicity from this and other spectacular systems
made the Westinghouse product attractive to many who wanted
to be on the cutting edge of the most important new technology
of the day. Sundback came well equipped to take advantage of
such a situation. Product of a prosperous family of Jönköping
Province, in southern Sweden, he had completed a thorough
technical education in Germany, receiving his certification in
electrical engineering at the polytechnic in Bingen in 1903. He
had been able to afford to pay the extra fees at the polytechnic
that allowed him to shorten considerably his years of training,
so the trip to America was not that of a penniless immigrant
seeking a fresh start. It was most likely the calculated move of a
young man wishing to make the best of an excellent technical
education, who had been inspired by stories sent back from the
United States by friends in very similar circumstances.[21]

While nothing could be clearer or more reasonable than his
move to the United States, the same cannot be said for Gideon
Sundback's move to Hoboken and the frustrations of the Automatic Hook and Eye Company. After about six months on
the job at Westinghouse, he was promoted to the position of
draftsman, and he worked away at this for a year longer. Always

Gideon Sundback (1880–1954) was the German-trained engineer who emigrated to the United States from Sweden to work on electric power systems, only to find himself in a few years immersed in the problem of making the slide fastener practical. He invented the modern zipper in 1913. *RUTH KLINGENER*

a sociable man, the young Sundback enjoyed visiting within the Swedish communities in the United States and cultivated his acquaintances among his compatriots. From such social contacts, he came to the attention of Peter Aronson, who suggested to Automatic's president, Frank Russell, that he invite the engineer to Hoboken to discuss work. At first Sundback resisted, but eventually, deciding that a trip to the sizable Swedish contingent in New Jersey would be pleasant, if not necessarily productive, he made his way east. Stories differ about Sundback's reaction to what he found in the Hoboken factory and to the invitation offered to him. His decision to leave Westinghouse in the summer of 1906 and to stake his career on the fortunes of a struggling little company engaged in making a balky mechanical device with a very uncertain future has to be seen as an emotional choice, rather than an economic one. It has been speculated that the technical challenges facing the fastener makers was the primary allure, and certainly Sundback must have found something attractive and potentially satisfying in the prospect of tackling and overcoming a challenge that had been more than a match for other inventive minds. There was also undoubtedly some appeal

Elvira Aronson and Gideon Sundback, at the time of their marriage, 1909.
RUTH KLINGENER

in escaping from the highly organized corporate environment of East Pittsburgh, where he was simply one of dozens or hundreds of draftsmen and engineers. Yet the idea that a young man trained in the best available schools of his day in the most advanced technology of the century would abandon the obvious potential that this held for his future, beckoned by a technical realm that might—just might—reward cleverness and careful analytical thinking but that otherwise made little use of his advanced knowledge poses a puzzle that seems to beg for another piece.[22]

That additional piece was Elvira Aronson. It is evident from the surviving pictures and letters that Peter Aronson's daughter was a lovely and intelligent young woman, the sort that many men no doubt found attractive. Sundback spoke of being smitten by Elvira, whom he probably met during that initial trip to visit Automatic Hook and Eye. This explanation for the entry of the zipper's second inventor onto the scene may strike some as simply too romantic, too distant from the material concerns that we generally think must be at the center of our technological universe. Some will resist any persuasion that such a cause as this has much of a place in describing how and why an important new thing came to be. We would be wrong to dismiss such skepticism as the inevitable product of a cynical or disaffected age or as merely the cavil of the loveless. It is, to a point, a proper insistence that historical explanation not stop at the sentimental tale or the clever connection but be part of a consistent fabric of cause and effect. There is nothing inconsistent with Gideon Sundback's own declaration that his love for Elvira Aronson was the main force that pulled him to Hoboken, for he was a man who was able to combine a Nordic self-discipline with a hearty and affectionate spirit. Besides, the historian must eventually confess that no other explanation readily surfaces.

Whatever the case, G. Sundback, as he invariably signed himself, in the middle of 1906 came into a company that was struggling to get its feet on the ground. The C-curity had been on the market only a year or so, but signs of difficulty and frustration were already showing. Harry Earle had stepped down from any leadership role in the company, and gave up his financial interest as well, though Sundback remembered years later that he hung around for a while. The Swede bought the nearly penniless promoter bottles of beer, listening to him still hustling the possibilities of the struggling enterprise, even though his own stake had disappeared. When, shortly, Earle finally departed Hoboken, he left "his trunk, his couch, and his table" to Sundback, who remembered only that some bottles of beef extract were found in the trunk. These were Whitcomb Judson's last days, too; later that year he moved off to live with his son in Michigan. Sundback saw enough of him, however, to recall his impression that the man "invented something every night." His final image of Judson was that of him standing on the pier holding "a great big blue print and . . . all a-flutter" with the excitement of some new scheme. The company's chief salesman, F. A. Wildman, left at the end of the summer, and Sundback must have wondered if he had not just come on board a sinking ship.[23]

The engineer took some time in identifying and tackling C-curity's problems. By about the middle of 1907 he believed he had made enough progress to begin recasting the fastener in an image more to his liking. The central functional problem was not that hard to identify. Sundback described the flaw succinctly: "When the fastener was being bent, the hook was snapped out of interlocking engagement with the eye, and the fastener opened up. When one hook is out of engagement, the rest of them, by a simple tear operation, will get out of engagement, and the fastener is in most cases made entirely useless."[24] The true significance of this he once put even more pithily: "When the fastener was put in the placket of a ladies' [sic] skirt, and the lady bent over, the fastener would pop open."[25] That a device named C-curity should be so fundamentally insecure was probably no irony; its makers were at the same time aware both of the most crucial function of a dress fastener (that it stay closed) and of the most problematic quality of what they were selling (that it didn't). That its sellers should wish to promise security at the very time that they were aware they couldn't quite deliver it does not necessarily betray any particular corruption or hypocrisy but was simply the norm of hopeful hustling.

Nonetheless, such a situation was clearly intolerable to Gideon Sundback. It was also, of course, very bad for business. His solution was not a complicated one, although it constituted enough of a change in the last Judson design to merit a patent, the first of many Sundback was to earn for his fasteners (1,060,378, granted 1913). He described the essential feature of his improvement: "The major problem I tackled first, that is, to make the fastener more flexible, and I devised a new eye in the Plako fastener, which at the time was thought to give us a perfect solution. The solution of the problem was successful to the extent that the hook would not snap out of the eye when the fastener was being flexed. . . ."[26] The term "Plako" had been quickly devised for the new device, which worked on the same principle as the C-curity and looked much the same but for the eyes. In the earlier fastener the eyes were short metal protrusions from one side of the fastener, with enough space for the short hook to fit between the protrusion and the cloth tape. The Plako's eyes, on the other hand, were substantial units themselves, sticking out from the tape on which they were attached and providing oval openings to receive more snugly the corresponding hooks. The carefully analyzed fashion in which the Plako attempted to correct the primary deficiencies of its predecessor marks it as the product of an engineer's mind, and Gideon Sundback never let it be forgotten that an engineer was what he was.

The Plako was introduced sometime in 1908, and Automatic Hook and Eye went forward again with renewed confidence that markets would follow. "Everybody was enthusiastic," Sundback recalled, "until we had the fastener in production." New problems were not long in showing themselves, sometimes with the same obstinate perversity that had made the C-curity so infuriating. Sundback told the tale of Lewis Walker's brother-in-law leaving for a party one evening, a Plako installed in the fly of his trousers; upon his return, pins were seen keeping the pants decent. If a bit of fabric got caught in the fastener, it not only was inoperable but might be ruined. It still could be washed only with great care, and assembly was unchanged from the labor-intensive methods of the C-curity. Indeed, the tighter fit of the Plako's hooks and eyes added problems. Once the hooks and eyes were installed, and the slider put on, it was necessary to secure the slider with little hammerblows and to run it up and down many times by hand to wear the hooks and eyes smooth enough to allow it to run properly. Even at six-dollars-per-week wages for the women in the shop, this made for an expensive device.[27]

The selling of such an article presented enormous problems. Some of these were inherent in the technical problems of the

The Plako fastener was Gideon Sundback's first substantial contribution to the slide fastener's design. It was a more secure form of Judson's C-curity and sustained the fastener company for several years, but it was still a hook and eye device and thus suffered from most of the basic flaws of the earlier designs. *TALON, INC.*

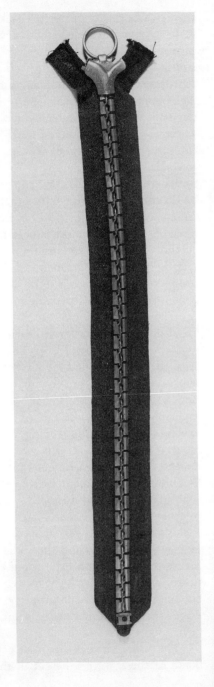

device; repeat sales were rare. Some problems were the legacy of past activity; in Sundback's recollection, "the old C-curity had been so thoroughly canvassed by our sales force that it left a trail of smoke." Instead of devising a significantly new strategy, however, Automatic Hook and Eye intensified the familiar hustling methods. In January 1908 the company contracted with Howard Clarke to organize sales, and an experienced agent, Thomas J. Cooper, was recruited to operate the Clarke Sales Company out of a Park Avenue office in New York. Here Cooper put together a sales pitch that managed to make even the C-curity's campaign seem tame by comparison. An excerpt from one of his general solicitations to agents shows how completely the makers of the Plako had put themselves into the hands of what nineteenth-century Americans had called drummers:

> *Dear Friend:—*
>
> *This is to inform you that I am now connected with this Company* [Clarke Sales]. *You have sold books for me from my Chicago Office in the past and as I already feel acquainted with you I prefer to have you act as our agent in your territory than to secure someone whom I know nothing about.*
>
> *The enclosed circular will give you some idea as to what the* PLAKO *garment fastener is. We consider it the greatest invention of the age, and so does every one else who has examined it or tested it's [sic] merit by actual use. One agent in Texas sold 1200 dozen during the month of January, many others have done nearly as well. This should give you some idea as to what can be done in your field. We will undoubtedly sell several million fasteners this year and I want you to share in the profits that will result from this great sale.*

There was much more in this vein, with Cooper assuring his reader, "You will sell PLAKO ten times as fast as you ever sold books."[28]

The last three decades of the nineteenth century have been called the heyday of the commercial traveler, the period when they not only flourished but became a cultural artifact. Whereas the 1870 census enumerated a mere seven thousand "commercials," the number had reached ninety-three thousand by 1890 and continued to grow into the new century. The book salesman established himself as the "prototype of the species," in the words of one observer. When Christopher Morley endeavored in his 1917 novel *Parnassus on Wheels* to provide a picture of the traveling salesman's life and character, his Roger Mifflin advertised "Good Books for Sale—Shakespeare, Charles Lamb,

The promotion of the Plako differed little from that of earlier designs, emphasizing security and ease of working, while clearly betraying the complexity of application and hinting at its fragility (especially in laundering). *ROBERT FRIEDEL*

R.L.S., Hazlitt, and all others." Such salesmen were not regular
peddlers or seasonal visitors; they came only once, hawking
Bibles and Shakespeare, spreading literature to the countryside,
and then moved on to other territory. This pattern of selling had
its antecedents, but it came to its flower in the age of the railroad.
Now it was possible for the commercial to cover a considerable
territory in a relatively brief time and to replenish his stock
through freight agents. A close cousin to the book salesman, also
an irregular traveler, was the seller of gadgets, novelties, and
inventions, the purveyor of material advancement in its most
titillating and meretricious form. Such salesmen not only had to
be sharp and glib but needed to possess a preacher's capacity for
converting the simpler soul to the paths of modernity. Such
paths would be marked by everything from patent eggbeaters to
internal-combustion engines, and the salesman was characterized
by an infectious conviction that only the ignorant or the lazy
passed up the opportunity to march to the drumbeat of mechanical progress.[29]

The selling of the Plako called forth the highest art of salesmanship. From the Clarke Sales Company poured letters and
solicitations, repeating the message that the fastener was a sure
route to riches. One letter addressed to a James M. Joyce, of
Lewiston, Maine, probably much duplicated all over the country, admonished the recipient to "Go out in the street and look
at the back of every skirt worn and then count and see if nine
out of every ten doesn't need an invisible and secure fastener to
close the skirt opening. Ask every woman you know and see if
she won't agree with you that all her neighbors' skirts are not
fastened neatly." The selling points of the new device were not
subtle: "How easy to sell a fastener for the waist which eliminates
gaping or opening when on, and wonder of wonders, THE
WEARER CAN FASTEN THE BACK OF HER OWN WAIST!" Even amid
the exhortations, however, may be detected signs of the continuing difficulties of selling the Plako. A general letter sent to agents
at the end of 1908 spoke of the progress made to date and the
promise of the coming year, but along with the usual salesman's
boosterism can be found a more plaintive note: "Let's all forget
the past hard year and concentrate our every energy on the new."
Another "Important Notice" to salesmen sent out over Thomas
Cooper's signature began: "As a few of our representatives and

56

their customers have reported difficulties in applying the Plako Garment Fastener, we hereby advise you, that if you will send us any garment with which you have had trouble, WE will attach Plako to it and return it AT ONCE AND WITHOUT DELAY, paying the express charges BOTH WAYS OURSELVES. If you can show us a skirt that we cannot apply a Fastener to we will make you a present of FIVE DOLLARS IN CASH." Sales agents were reminded of the importance of wearing the Plako themselves, and this was directed toward women as well as men. Yet another form letter from Cooper, directed to new agents, while promising that "you will find this work entirely different from selling books or any other article that the people *do not want*," emphasized the importance of learning how to install and operate the fastener correctly. All this adds up to a curious mixture of bravado and caution, as if the exigencies of the hard sell were in constant battle with the inescapable limitations of the technology itself. This is probably not an uncommon circumstance as an invention makes its first, tentative steps in the real world, but rarely is it so well documented as in the case of the Plako.[30]

These efforts met with some modest success at first. The novelty value of the fastener had not been completely spent by the C-curity, and Plako salesmen constantly sought out new territory for their efforts. More important than new territory, however, was the recruitment of good agents, and Automatic Hook and Eye acquired the services of one who was described as "the type of salesman who could sell bridges in the Sahara Desert [*sic*]." Wilson Wear may have started with the company selling C-curity, but it was the Plako that brought out his talents. Stories were told of his energy and perseverance; while traveling from town to town, he would canvass the railroad cars, selling men on the virtue of the fastener for their wives' skirts, and ladies on its desirability for their husbands' trousers. In this Wear seems to have hit upon an effective bit of psychology, selling the fastener not to the end user but to the person most likely to observe the user's clothing critically. He concentrated on making his sales to country and small-town storekeepers, whom he could convince to take a gross or two at a time. Later zipper salesmen spoke admiringly of Wear's technique: "He was smooth; he was spectacular; he was convincing. When he canvassed a community he did it thoroughly, and never made the blunder of returning too soon." Wear's success had its down side, however, as illus-trated in the story told of Wear and Sundback, many years later, visiting a country store in Harmonsburg, Pennsylvania. When Wear happened to mention that he had been a fastener salesman, the storekeeper at the counter looked at him for a second, recognized him as the man who years before had sold him a lot of Plakos, and promptly took after him with a meat cleaver. In hasty retreat Wear offered to buy back the fasteners but was spurned. The man then explained that annoyed as he was with the salesman, he wouldn't part with the Plakos since they served as an important means of resisting further such purchases. A mere glance at the fasteners gathering dust on a top shelf was sufficient to stiffen his resolve and spur him to toss any aspiring salesman out on his ear. This may have been the Plako's most successful service.[31]

Willie Wear kept up the Plako's fortunes as best as he could for as long as he could. Indeed, even after Gideon Sundback had finally devised solutions to the problem of a successful slide fastener, Lewis Walker kept Wear at work hustling the Plako. Wear's prodigious salesmanship may, in fact, have been the primary thing keeping Automatic Hook and Eye afloat in the years from 1908 to 1913, at least as far as its fastener business was concerned. Sundback continued to struggle with the Plako's clear deficiencies, but progress was so meager and the company's fortunes were so shaky that he was compelled to improvise to keep the wolf from the door. At one point, when he was the only one left in the Hoboken plant with any authority, he was approached by the salesman for Roebling and Sons, the Trenton wire makers who provided the metal for the Plako. Automatic was finding it difficult to pay its bills, and Sundback had to plead for more credit from Roebling. Seeing that the alternative was to drive the little firm out of business, the salesman agreed to keep supplies coming, as long as some payments could be made. Sundback had to seek outside metalwork to keep money flowing in. He designed machinery for a local printer, manufactured paper fasteners and other trinkets, made models for other inventors, and otherwise kept the shop active. Alternative products were introduced: The Plako Hose and Sleeve Supporter was billed as "the hole that holds"; this was a metal clip meant to replace garters to hold up socks, shorten sleeves, or keep men's drawers from

Peter Aronson with Gideon
Sundback, about the time of
Sundback's marriage to Elvira
Aronson, 1909. *RUTH KLINGENER*

slipping down. These devices were made of more exotic metals than the steel used in the Plako—German silver (a copper alloy with nickel and zinc) and aluminum were experimented with— and this may have given Sundback useful experience with these materials. The Plako was, in the hands of a Willie Wear, a salable product, but to a Gideon Sundback it was a technical embarrassment, and to a Lewis Walker it was an unsatisfactory foundation for commercial prosperity.[32]

Discouraging as much of the experience with the Plako was, its promoters had high hopes for its future for several years. One of the most typical expressions of such commercial dreams was the pursuit of overseas opportunities, and the Plako quickly became the subject of foreign ambitions. By the middle of 1908 the financial state of Automatic Hook and Eye was sufficiently straitened that the company yielded all non-U.S. rights to his fastener patents to Gideon Sundback, to use as he saw fit. This arrangement, apparently in lieu of more appropriate payment for his work, continued in subsequent years and was put to good use by Sundback. At this stage, however, it became the basis for an ill-fated venture in France. Peter Aronson, who had left the

LE FERME-TOUT

—— AMÉRICAIN ——

PERFECTIONNÉ

BREVETÉ S.G.D G.

LE FERME-TOUT se compose de deux rubans portant l'un des crochets, l'autre des œillets qui s'ouvrent et se ferment instantanément par une glissière centrale.

Hier
Inconvénients des vieux systèmes qui s'ouvrent inopinément

Remplaçant les boutonnières et agrafes dont la pose est longue, LE FERME-TOUT procure par sa souplesse, **sécurité et rapidité.**

Toute femme élégante et pratique l'adoptera.

Elle évitera ainsi l'ouverture fréquente et si disgracieuse de ses jupes et corsages. Elle trouvera en outre, toute commodité pour s'habiller rapidement et sans le concours de personne.

Aujourd'hui
Corsages et Jupes sont hermétiquement. fermés avec le FERME-TOUT américain

r. 4.50 M

LE FERME-TOUT est *INVISIBLE et INUSABLE*

Se fait en 5 nuances

Noir, Blanc, Bleu, Gris et Brun

POUR PANTALONS

Tailles : 21-23-26 cent.   **Prix : 1 25**

POUR JUPES 2 tailles :

26 centimètres. . . .   **Prix : 1 25**

32   — ' . . . .   — 1.45

POUR CORSAGES 4 tailles :

33 centimètres. . . .
36   —   . . . .
38   —   . . . .   } Prix : 1 75
40   —   ' . . . .

Peter Aronson traveled to Europe to promote the C-curity and Plako fasteners, with modest success. The French promotion emphasized the identification of the fastener's potential market with women's clothing. *TEKNISKA MUSEET, STOCKHOLM*

Hoboken factory and become Sundback's father-in-law in 1909, went to Paris with the intention of selling rights to both his own fastener invention (that for a "separable fastener") and Sundback's to French investors. He attracted enough interest to begin manufacture and promotion of le Ferme-tout Américain (the American close-all). Every effort was made to associate the novelty with the image of elegance and convenience, and promises made for it were similar to those made for the Plako. A departure in the sales approach, however, was noted in the announcement that *le ferme-tout* could be found "in all the best fabrics stores and notions counters." The hustle of the American door-to-door salesman would have to give way to the calmer precincts of the French *maisons de mercerie et magasins de nouveautés*. Bravado was not missing from the French sales approach, nonetheless, as customers were warned *refuser toutes imitations*. For all of Aronson's success in getting this enterprise started, however, he could not overcome the fact that the fastener, whatever it was called and wherever it was sold, was not a reliable or attractive device. The accounts of Automatic Hook and Eye showed shipments of machinery, hardware, and fabric to the "Societe Francaise" [*sic*] until the summer of 1912. Aronson also arranged much smaller shipments to the Lightning Fastener Company in England, but this appears to have been an even less successful venture (its name, however, was to be perpetuated with great success in coming years).[33]

By the time the twentieth century entered its second decade, the slide fastener that had started as Whitcomb Judson's brainchild was, in one guise or another, almost twenty years old. This is, in fact, not a young age for many technologies or for enterprises formed to promote inventions. Within three years of Thomas Edison's invention of his electric light bulb, for example, entire light and power systems could be found in a number of cities, and in only a couple of more years the technology was flourishing in many corners of Europe and America. Hardly more than a decade after the Wright Brothers made their first flight in 1903, armed forces throughout the world began to organize air forces. Other notable inventions of the nineteenth and twentieth centuries—telegraphs, telephones, motion pictures, plastics, radio, and the like—could be used as examples of the fact that technological development can be quite rapid under a variety of circumstances. The slide fastener, however, did not benefit from such speedy perfection. It could be argued that this was due to its triviality; such a small, simple, unimportant thing could hardly inspire the kind of inventive effort that moves great innovations along quickly. While there is some truth to this, it does not take away from the fact that extraordinary persistence was required to make this particular technology a reality. In the years between 1891 and 1913 a range of individuals, from eccentric inventor to sober businessman to clever engineer to hustling salesmen, were sufficiently motivated to maintain an effort to force this novel thing into being. Their motivations were not necessarily noble, if we recognize the desire for comfortable wealth, intellectual satisfaction, community respectability, and simply the means for an honest living as so ordinary as to hardly evoke any sense of nobility. But it is important that we recognize the force of such motivations, harnessed to clever invention and competent enterprise, to change the world. The first two decades of the zipper's story were not glorious ones; they were as frustrating and bedeviling as any invention's beginning could be. But these decades emphasize, perhaps more than anything else, the extent to which dogged individual faith is often at the heart of technological change.

Hookless

3

The origin of an idea is the happy period of creative mental work; when everything seems possible because so far it has had nothing to do with reality.

The carrying out is the time for preparing all the means that will assist in the realization of the idea; still creative, still happy, the time when nature's obstacles are overcome; from which one emerges steeled and exalted even when beaten.

The introduction is a time of struggle against stupidity and envy, apathy and evil, secret opposition and open conflict of interests, the horrible period of struggle with man, a martyrdom even if success ensues.[1]

Rudolf Diesel's 1913 description of the stages of technological innovation has not been improved upon. To be sure, economists and other students of technology have applied a sometimes useful jargon of "invention," "development," and "innovation" to the sequence and have provided more precise (though no less controversial) definitions of each phase. But none of them could speak from the heart like the Bavarian engineer, whose twenty-year struggle to develop his ideal internal-combustion engine was precisely contemporaneous with the first years of the slide fastener. In the same year that Whitcomb Judson received his first patents, 1893, Diesel published his *Theory and Construction of a Rational Heat Engine*, in which he outlined his ideas for an internal-combustion engine that would generate the maximum amount of work out of the heat produced by its fuel. More experimental work followed, but by 1899 Diesel had a factory in Augsburg that was producing models of his design, and by 1913, when he was drowned at sea (apparently a suicide), his motor was becoming an important new addition to the world's prime movers. Despite the air of frustration and tragedy that Diesel conveyed in his memoirs, he made enormous progress in those years from 1893 to 1913.[2]

Indeed, those two decades, between the closing of the Columbian Exposition in Chicago and the eve of the First World War, were as fruitful a period of technological change as there ever was. The great fair had shown off the electrical power system of George Westinghouse in wonderful splendor, and in the next twenty years such electrical systems spread to every corner of the Western world. By 1913 the internal-combustion engines that had been rather minor curiosities at Chicago had already begun their wholesale reshaping of personal transportation. Henry Ford, who had introduced his Model T five years earlier, opened his first assembly line that year, and Charles Kettering was promoting his electric self-starter as a means to make automobiling available to everyone. The electromagnetic radiation that had been no more than a laboratory curiosity in 1893 was, by 1913, an accepted means of worldwide communication. Only the year before, wireless had demonstrated its indispensability as the key tool in bringing rescuers to the hapless *Titanic* as it foundered in the icy North Atlantic. Even more rapid and wonderful to many was the appearance of airplanes in the skies throughout the world, a sight that would have sounded preposterous indeed to even the most optimistic of Chicago's fairgoers. Just ten years after the Wright brothers' flight at Kitty Hawk, the airplane might still be a technology in search of a use, but the coming of war soon demonstrated its power to everyone.

•

Z

I

P

P

E

R

Decades like these make us realize that the rapid transformation of the world by invention was a phenomenon with which our grandparents and their parents before them were well familiar.

In Diesel's case, the sequence from "origin" to "carrying out" to "introduction" was unambiguous, for he saw himself as a crusader determined to realize the theoretical ideals that seemed to emerge naturally from an understanding of the laws of thermodynamics. His engine was an instrument for approaching an ideal, which he defined in terms of achieving the highest fuel efficiency possible in a heat engine. An invention, in his words, was "the result of a struggle between thought and the material world," and the final product "always appears quite different from the original imagined ideal which will never be attained." But how well does Diesel's picture correspond to most inventions? While an inventor must, at some point, be driven by an idealized picture of what he wishes to create, this ideal may be a very fluid thing indeed. Time and again we find inventors seeking one thing and coming up with another, and the successful ones are able to transfer their preconceptions and even their goals to correspond to their observations of what nature seems to have to offer. The products of accidental discovery, from the phonograph to Teflon, constitute no small part of our technological inventory.

Between the invention born of an intellectual ideal and that stemming from a chance observation there lies a large, difficult-to-define realm to which the zipper belongs. The idea that came to Whitcomb Judson in 1891—that of pulling a series of clasps together through the action of a camlike slider—was a clever way of dealing with a small problem. It was not born of the knowledge of science or of new phenomena in nature. It came not from an effort to exploit novel substances or powers. It was, rather, like most human innovations: a modest attempt to apply ingenuity and common experience to make something that would be appreciated for some distinctive quality or combination of qualities, such as efficiency, quickness, convenience, economy, beauty, or even simply novelty itself.

The central problem (though not the only one) with which Judson and his backers had to deal over the next twenty years was that his means of dealing with a small problem was not a good one. This was a judgment widely shared, at least in the testimony of later years, and reflected by the sales approaches adopted by the Automatic Hook and Eye Company. The reliance on hustling traveling salesmen, the failure to create or sustain a stable retail business, the lack of any serious progress in developing novel applications all testified to the functional deficiencies of the company's product. Finally, the modern eye can see with little trouble what a problematic technical advance the Plako represented. As one tugs on the awkward pull ring attached to the slider, there is a slow, grudging dividing of the two halves of the fastener, each of them emerging from the top of the slider, forced apart in almost opposite directions. Because the slider must bring together (and separate) the opposing hooks and eyes at an angle that facilitates their engagement (and disengagement), it must bend these two sides of the fasteners apart from each other with a force that is awkward to deal with. This creates above the slider a large opening, which promises to be closed again only by an almost violent pull on the slider that will be sufficient to rejoin the opposing rows of hooks and eyes. When the fastener is closed, it looks and feels very unbending; it does not at all invite or even allow the ready flexing that one would ordinarily seek in a skirt placket or trouser fly. The individual hooks and eyes (especially the hooks) possess a fragile appearance that should worry the most careful user, not to mention the conscientious launderer. Users were no longer admonished to remove the fastener when washing the garment but were still put on notice that it "should not be put through a wringer and should be thoroughly dried" (the fastener's blued steel could easily rust). The Plako was indeed an "automatic hook and eye" device, but it accomplished its mechanical task through carefully applied labor.

It is, of course, impossible for a modern person to look at or try the Plako without comparison to a zipper. By such a test, the Plako was a miserable failure, and it is useful to understand this, if only to appreciate better just what challenges Gideon Sundback overcame. But it is important not to allow such a comparison to blind one to the much more important comparison for our story, that with the Plako's contemporary competition. Since the perceived application of the Plako was pretty much confined to skirts, dresses, "waists" (waistcoats or blouses), and trousers, the list of competitors was not long. In the 1920s British author Christopher Morley remarked that "there are three ages of human beings in this matter: (1) Safety-pins, (2) Buttons, (3) Studs, or (for females) Hooks and Eyes."[3] The comparison usually made in advertising was to hooks and eyes. This was in part to make the Plako's function—as an "automatic hook and eye"—more transparent to the audience, but it also reflected the importance of hooks and eyes, especially for women's garments. Less explicit, but no less obvious in application, was the comparison with buttons, which carried the burden of tradition for most clothing. In better gentlemen's clothing, the button might give way to a metal stud, a more exclusively masculine closure. If one recognizes that the safety pin with which Morley so identified the fastening of infants was but a modern, industrialized version of the fibula that the Romans used to close their togas, then it is evident that the universe of fasteners was not only a small one but an ancient one as well. Only buckles and lacing need be added to provide a comprehensive list of traditional fastenings.[4]

Even the nineteenth century saw only modest changes in the appliances or customs of fastening garments. The most original (and permanent) innovation was the invention in the latter part of the century of the metal device that Americans know as snaps. This and one or two similar metal closures were first introduced in France, primarily for use in fastening the small, tight gloves that had replaced the looser gauntlet. By about 1890 the snap fastener had been sufficiently well developed that it began to find application in a wide range of garments. The construction of this device, while considerably simpler than that of the zipper, possessed its own subtleties, and its success owed much to the development of metal punch presses and associated techniques that were not too distant from those used in Automatic Hook and Eye's Hoboken factory. The true extent of the snap's application to everyday clothing, however, remained limited. It always filled some specialized role, like that of dainty glove fastenings, or in theatrical clothes, or, in its heaviest version, for upholstery. It was not an item that challenged traditional fastenings in their most important uses.[5]

From at least the late thirteenth century buttons had been a key feature in Western dress. The button itself in some form can be traced back to ancient Egypt, but the medieval clothiers are

given credit for inventing the buttonhole, thus integrating the
device into the garment to make it a fastening in the modern
sense. Having begun, however, as a largely decorative device,
the button never lost this function in clothing. The simplicity of
buttons allows them to be manufactured from an astonishing
range of materials, which have been used throughout history to
announce the wearer's wealth, status, and taste. Pearl buttons
might be used to convey a sense of daintiness, while bejeweled
buttons would proclaim loudly a secure prosperity. Metal buttons could be particularly sensitive gauges of status, for utilitarian
brass and pewter would clearly mark a man beneath one who
flaunted silver or gold. Most button materials could be carved
or molded into fancy shapes without affecting function; thus
buttons became wearable evidence of an artist's skill. By the late
nineteenth century expensive or ornate buttons had a very limited
place in most wardrobes, but the norms concerning button materials, shape, and size still were widely accepted elements in defining the status and taste of clothing, from the haute couture of
Paris salons to the machine-made garments of the mail-order
catalogs.[6]

Perhaps most significant for the would-be inventors, hustlers, and businessmen, buttons worked. So did, for the most
part, all the other traditional fasteners. There was no general
sense that this was an area begging for improvement, much less
replacement. To be sure, buttons came off, hooks and eyes might
pop open, and lacing could be slow and laborious. This was not
a realm characterized by perfection, but neither was it one in
which the shortcomings of available techniques and devices beckoned obviously to a century "mad for improvement." Changing
fashions would make some changes in the requirements and expectations for fasteners. In the 1890s, for example, the bodice
that required a long row of hooks and eyes was a common feature
of many women's wardrobes, and this might be perceived as
somewhat laborious. A decade or so later there was some experimentation, as in a 1911 dress style that used rows of alternating
hooks and snaps to close up. Nonetheless, fastenings were an
area that received little attention from either the designers or the
reporters of fashion.[7]

This is not to say, however, that would-be inventors had
ignored the possibilities entirely. None other than Elias Howe,

whose lockstitch machine made the modern sewing machine a reality in the mid-nineteenth century, took out perhaps the earliest patent for an "improvement in fastenings for garments" in 1851. A glance at the illustration for Howe's patent specification (U.S.P. 8,540) can be a bit startling, for it seems to be nothing less than a zipper (of a sort). Closer scrutiny reveals that Howe's invention was no such thing, for it actually consisted of, in the exceptionally clear words of the patent, "a series of clasps united by a connecting cord, the said clasps running or sliding upon ribs formed of any suitable material." In other words, an opening could be closed by pulling on one end of a cord that was connected to a series of small, evenly spaced clasps. When the cord was pulled, the clasps would be brought up and distributed at intervals of perhaps an inch over the length of the fastening. This was actually a simple and clever invention, a variation on the drawstring, that was resurrected in the twentieth century, but in Howe's day there is no evidence that it was ever manufactured. Variations on the Howe principle reappeared in later patents, applied both to clothing and to such articles as mailbags. Indeed, so lucrative did mailbag closures apparently seem to would-be inventors that this was a popular context for fastening inventions in the nineteenth century.[8] All these efforts enjoyed the same fate of most patents: They disappeared into well-deserved obscurity.

The originality of Whitcomb Judson's patents of 1893 was judged against this background. Although it took the examiners awhile to appreciate fully the creativity of Judson's invention, especially its most novel element, the slider, once the patents were issued, they defined a distinctive territory into which no others entered for many years. Through the entire period that Judson was experimenting with his fastener, until he received his patent for the C-curity in 1905, no other inventor tried his hand at improving on Judson's work. The Universal Fastener Company and the Automatic Hook and Eye Company had the field to themselves those years and could comfortably pursue improvements without giving consideration to competition. Of course, the experiences of these companies would hardly encourage would-be competitors in any case; there was little enough business, and the technical problems of the Judson products did not present themselves as ripe targets for the clever innovator.

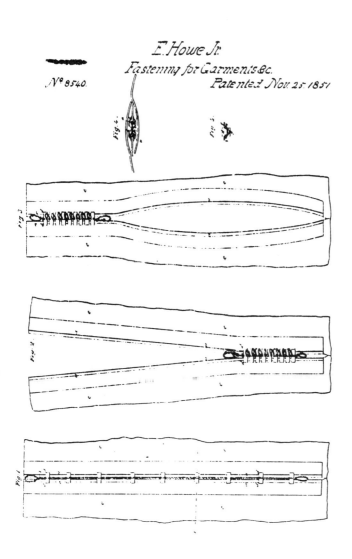

Elias Howe's 1851 patent for a garment fastener (U.S.P. 8,540) superficially resembles a zipper at first glance, but it is actually little more than a kind of drawstring. *U.S. PATENT & TRADEMARK OFFICE*

After Judson's departure from the scene, however, others, seeing new possibilities for invention and profit, entered the arena.

The patent record of these new inventors is not extensive. The first to make inroads in Judson's formerly exclusive territory was Peter Aronson, Automatic Hook and Eye's chief mechanic. He applied for a patent on an improvement in the C-curity design in late 1906. Because of the patent examiner's broad reading of Judson's patents, however, Aronson's claims were rejected at first. The examiner even requested that Aronson submit a working model, a demand rarely made of inventors at that time. Perhaps as the result of Aronson's preoccupation with other work (especially his overseas ventures) and possibly as the result of Sundback's contributions, which Automatic Hook and Eye clearly judged to be of greater value, it was not until 1913 that Aronson's patent was issued. In fact, it was issued the same date as Sundback's patent on the Plako design, which had been filed in the spring of 1908. The five years required for Sundback to receive his first fastener patent was due, again, to the difficulty of distinguishing his invention from Judson's earlier claims, although it has to be wondered if the attorney handling both the Aronson and Sundback applications wasn't a bit slow himself, since the Patent Office was generally quick in its responses. The lack of competition and the fact that it controlled the Judson patents gave Automatic Hook and Eye little incentive to speed up the patenting process.[9]

Competition, however, was on the horizon, and other inventors began to seek out openings. Even before Sundback had made his first contribution, a clever and original patent application was made by one Frank Canfield, of Denver, whose patent for a "skirt-placket" was applied for in April 1907 and issued in August 1908 (U.S.P. 896,689). Canfield adapted Judson's slider mechanism to guide opposing rows of balls and sockets into a fastening. The slider was used just as in earlier devices, feeding the opposing elements toward each other and bending them at just the right angle as they joined, leading the ball-like elements on one side between the socketlike elements opposite and then straightening and feeding the joined elements out the other end. Just as in the C-curity and the Plako, the Canfield design called for relatively large individual fastening elements, and the slider bent them at a large angle in mating them. It was nonetheless a clever adaptation—an escape from the hook and eye principle that bedeviled Sundback's experiments.

In his remarks for 1900 the commissioner of patents estimated "that out of every one thousand patents one is granted to a woman" and observed that most of these were for garments and household items.[10] The patent of Ida Josephine Calhoun (U.S.P. 887,586, issued May 12, 1908), neatly illustrated with a woman modeling her fastener on a long closure in the back of a dress, fitted this pattern nicely. The application, prepared by those ever-eager patent solicitors Munn & Company (publishers of *Scientific American*), was acted upon with remarkable speed by the Patent Office. Once the claims had been amended to take into account the full range of Judson's patents, the patent was allowed barely three months after the application was first filed. The resulting invention, labeled simply a "garment-closing device," was original primarily for its two-part slider. While the fastening elements themselves were so much like those of Judson's patents that they could not be included in the patent's claims, the slider was designed to snap apart. This would allow the hooks and eyes to be separated with great ease (according to the patent) when desired. The device itself, it seems pretty clear, could never have been constructed without infringing upon the Judson patents. It is a bit hard to imagine what would have motivated such an invention. Perhaps Calhoun was simply one of the many who responded to the blandishments of Munn & Company, which used *Scientific American* to cajole would-be inventors into pursuing fame and fortune by patenting whatever clever ideas came into their heads (for a small fee, of course). For their part, it should be pointed out, the interests of the lawyers at Munn & Company were best served by making the patent application as narrow as possible and shepherding it as quickly as possible through the Patent Office. This reduced the effort put out for their fee, although it also reduced the chances of the patent holder's reaping much reward other than a fancy certificate from Washington. One suspects, in fact, that such Munn & Company clients as Ida Calhoun were often satisfied with just that.

The growing general interest in the slide fastener idea was not confined to the United States. Whitcomb Judson had received a British patent for one of his designs in 1896 (B.P. 6,998 of that year), and Peter Aronson took out French and German patents (F.P. 396,261 in 1909; D.R.P. 210,763 in 1907) to cover the basic C-curity and Plako form of fastener and added at least one French patent in later years. It should not be surprising, therefore, that alerted by these filings and perhaps by Aronson's marketing efforts, Europeans began to add their own contributions.[11] These were not, it seems, of much importance, with one spectacular exception. In June 1911 the Swiss Federal Patent Office issued its patent number 55,740 to Katharina Kuhn-Moos and Henri Forster, both of Zurich, for a *Verschluss, insbesondere für Bekleidungsgegenstände* (fastener, especially for garments). Subsequently British, French, and German patents were taken out for the same invention. In spite of the broad patenting effort (which did not reach the United States), the invention was never manufactured, and because of the patent maintenance fees levied in countries like Switzerland and Germany (where inventors or their assignees were charged an escalating scale of fees to keep a patent valid during its lifetime), the patent was allowed to lapse long before expiration. None of this detracts, however, from the fact that Kuhn-Moos and Forster patented a design that incorporated most of the key principles of the modern zipper. In particular, their fastener abandoned the hook and eye principle and substituted for it a design based on alternating identical scoops. A first glance at the original Kuhn-Moos specification reveals to the modern eye little less than a zipper. There are the two rows of identical "teeth" (technically, and more appropriately, called scoops), characterized by little nibs on their upper side and dimples or cups on the lower. The slider clearly functions as in the modern zipper, bringing the two rows together at just the right angle (a smaller angle than required by the Plako or any of the other hook and eye designs) to mesh alternating scoops so that nibs enter opposing cups and exit the slider securely attached to each other. While a few inventions prior to this one (including one of Judson's 1896 patents) incorporated the principle of meshing identical teeth, none came so close to the modern zipper's design.

Close—but it was not the same. The history of technology is replete with near misses, and the Kuhn-Moos patent is one of them. Just why it was a near miss and not the real thing will be addressed shortly, but a moment should be taken to ask what

difference it really makes. More broadly, what difference do all
the stories of unappreciated firsts, mistaken credits, and close
calls make in our understanding of who has shaped our world
and how they did it? In law they make a difference because our
concept of intellectual property is exclusionary: Only one person
or group can be given credit (with all the benefits that flow
from it) for an invention or discovery, and the claimant who
demonstrates the earliest accomplishment of the feat is the sole
recipient of the credit. These stories of firsts and near firsts are
more important, however, for their cultural meaning. Invention
is fascinating to us not simply because it has been one of the
primary ways in which our world has changed over the last two
centuries but because it is an example—sometimes a spectacular
example—of human creativity at work. The inventor can claim
to have produced, from his or her mind, something truly new in
the world. The capacity for doing that is a source of awe and
wonder, to those who possess it as well as to those who behold
it. It thus means something to us to know just *how* new, *how*
original an inventor's creation was. We judge the greatness of art
or music or any other creative act both by its effect on us—
measured often in terms of beauty or aptness or harmony—and
by its creative force. If the work of an artist or an inventor is
clearly derivative, manifestly built upon some other work, then
we are less impressed by it. But even if there is no derivation or
borrowing, the judgments of history are less generous to the
creations that are foreshadowed by what has gone before. This
is true for a symphony or a building just as for an invention, for
we seek, above all, the message of human creativity, of the capacity of men and women to reach deep into their souls for something that never before was.

Thus the invention of Katharina Kuhn-Moos and Henri Forster does in some way diminish the achievement of Gideon Sundback simply because it reduces the full extent of the originality
with which we can credit him. We do not know, in fact, whether
Sundback borrowed from or even knew of the Swiss invention;
the skimpy records of his work do not say. We do know, however, that the patent examiners knew of it (through the British
patent) and that Sundback quickly was compelled to explain and
defend the novelty of his work. This he had to do repeatedly in
subsequent years, as the value of his patents grew and made the

challenging of them worthwhile for a multitude of would-be competitors. The priority of Kuhn-Moos was inevitably at the heart of these challenges, though for the purposes of the Patent Office and the courts, it was never sufficient to undermine Sundback's essential claims of invention.[12]

Upon his arrival in Hoboken in 1906, Gideon Sundback lost little time before he was actively wooing Elvira Aronson. This was undoubtedly made easier by the fact that Elvira spent her time in Automatic's factory, along with a dozen or so other young women, who assembled the C-curity hooks and eyes or sewed garment sections for demonstrating the fastener's application. As the manager's daughter, of course, Elvira had her privileges. She modeled skirts, gloves, and boots with the fastener, and it is her smiling face that adorns a number of the early advertisements. She was also able to take extended vacations, retreating in the summers of 1907 and 1908 from the hot city either to the seaside retreat (and Methodist camp meeting town) of Ocean Grove, New Jersey, or to Mountainhome, in the Poconos of eastern Pennsylvania. From here she wrote her "dear Gidde," describing her leisure through the pursuits of a well-bred young woman of her class: taking photographs, walking on the boardwalk, playing the piano, writing letters to all her friends. In his replies, at least in the beginning, Sundback asked his "Vira" for help with his English, although his letters show that it was really only his spelling that called for occasional correction. He also reported on conditions in the factory, which on those summer days could get uncomfortably hot. Work was very uneven. If orders were coming in, he suggested that perhaps her vacation should not be extended, but it was just as likely that he might suggest otherwise: "I guess that you can figure on staying out of the factory here for a couple of weeks anyway, as the orders are not coming very fast."[13] Before another summer came around, Otto Frederick Gideon Sundback and Naomi Elvira Aronson (they shared an aversion to their first names) were married, in Hoboken, on June 5, 1909.

By that time Sundback was pretty much in sole charge of Automatic Hook and Eye, and his Plako design was the company's primary product. The Clarke Sales Company in New York, along with Wilson Wear and his brethren of the road, were struggling to distribute the Plako as widely as they could.

The company was losing money (it had turned a profit in only one semiannual period since it began sales in 1904), but the new design still held much promise of pulling the enterprise into the black. Besides, the chief engineer (the *only* engineer) was making continuing improvements. By the end of 1909 he had devised a new, tougher slider, had improved the coating put on the fastener to retard rust, had designed a long, separating fastener that could be adapted to "waists," and had, in general, made himself master of the novel technology to which he had attached his ambitions.[14]

The end of 1909 probably marked the nadir of Automatic's fortunes. In December, the same month that Whitcomb Judson died in Muskegon, Michigan, the company books showed that it had lost $3,870 over the course of the year. The company's chief officers and representatives of the Meadville interests, Victor Delamater (the Colonel's brother-in-law) and Frank Russell, left before the end of the year, the latter going to work for Wilbur and Orville Wright's aircraft company. When they left, the company owed Delamater almost $3,000 and Russell more than $8,000 in unpaid salary. Russell, who had been president, tried to convince Sundback that the company was headed for certain bankruptcy and that he, too, would be well advised to seek other work. He also probably tried to persuade his younger brother, Alger, to leave, despite the fact that he now held Delamater's position as company secretary. It isn't clear why the two didn't leave at this point; instead Sundback began to devise the small alternative products and to take in the outside work that kept money coming in. Since this was just the time that his father-in-law, Peter Aronson, was making plans for taking the fastener abroad, it was perhaps a sense of family commitment that kept Sundback plugging away in Hoboken. He also probably shared Aronson's faith that a little more tinkering and a little more hustling would allow the business to turn the corner. For his part, Alger Russell may have been reluctant to attempt to find other work since his profound deafness would have put him at a considerable disadvantage.[15]

Over the next several months things did begin to improve. The Swedish engineer managed to get production costs under better control and negotiated a new contract that gave him 25 percent of the savings for reducing the cost per fastener under six cents. He and the younger Russell were able to manage company

76 affairs with little help, so that the absence of Delamater and
Frank Russell made little difference in operations. By the middle
of 1910 losses averaged only about one hundred dollars per
month, and by the end of the year profits were averaging better
than five hundred dollars per month. This rate of return was not
to last, but for the next couple of years Automatic Hook and
Eye ran in the black.[16]

Also contributing to the improved state of things was the
fact that Willie Wear was hitting his stride. He was selling,
through much of this period, as much as fifty gross (7,200) of
fasteners per month, and occasionally even more. He traveled all
over the United States, recruiting other agents (who rarely lasted
any time at all) as he went. One of Alger Russell's jobs came to
be keeping tabs on Wear and occasionally bringing him into line
when he seemed to be stretching his credit a bit too tightly or
slacking off in his orders. Russell tried to impress upon Wear the
need to keep the business as steady as possible: "We have to
break in new operators when the business is beginning to boom
and to lay them off again while our agents are taking a vacation."
Such an arrangement, he emphasized, "would be very much of
a losing proposition to us." As stern as Russell might be with
Wear, he must have been well aware that the mercurial salesman
carried the company on his back. For Automatic's last two years
(mid-1911 to mid-1913), Wear's orders were typically 60 to 70
percent of the company's total sales each month, and for the last
six months they were the only shipments on the company's
books.[17]

Whatever prosperity Automatic Hook and Eye experienced
in this period was always precarious, and Gideon Sundback, for
one, was never happy with the state of affairs. His contract, for
one thing, gave him an incentive to continue improvements in
the manufacture of the Plako, and he constantly adjusted proce-
dures and machinery with the aim of reducing labor, saving
materials, or making the finished product less likely to be returned as unsatisfactory. Every month the company's books
included modest "Experimental Expenses," as Sundback continued to try out not only new manufacturing methods but also
new applications that might spur sales in an important new direction. This work certainly had its frustrations, especially since no
one except Alger Russell seemed to care much about what was

going on. Visits from the Colonel were few and far between, and even letters from that tireless correspondent in Meadville seem to have been reduced to a trickle. Nonetheless, as a good engineer Sundback must have derived some satisfaction from being able to maintain a steady output of Plakos and from the fact that for a while at least, Willie Wear, by keeping on the move, was able to make the business a profitable concern. In the summer of 1910 Sundback was prosperous enough that upon learning of his father's death, he could travel back to Sweden, where he undoubtedly not only visited his own relatives but became acquainted with the Aronson side of his soon-to-be expanding family.[18]

Then tragedy of a most personal kind struck, and Sundback lost one of the things that kept his life in balance. In March 1911, shortly after giving birth to a daughter, Elvira Sundback died. Her husband was devastated. Just as his love for Elvira had been open and visible, so, too, was his grief. Elvira's parents were still settling down to their French ventures, so Sundback felt particularly alone and burdened. He quickly decided to send the newborn, Ruth Margit, to Sweden to be raised by his mother (she did not return to America until she was almost a young woman). And then, so he told her years later, he threw himself into his work. Once again, perhaps, the story of Gideon and Elvira begins to sound like a novelist's romance rather than the substance of explanation for historical events. But Gideon Sundback did have a passionate side, one that he revealed on occasion to friends and family and that was enough to give his otherwise well-controlled life turns and bends that set him on new directions that had never been part of his calculations.[19]

With his attention now focused as never before on the technical problems before him, Sundback began to see the situation in a new light. His later recollection evoked the feelings of 1911–12: ". . . I was fed up with hooks and eyes, rusting metal and everything pertaining to the fastener. The complaints as far as our salesmen were concerned were 'here is a scratchy fastener, these hooks are awfully rough and rusted.' I decided to turn in an entirely different direction and away from hooks and eyes, and get away from the metallic appearance—make something attractive to the wearer." Sundback does not seem to have been a careful recorder of his experiments. Indeed, in later years he was chastised by the company's patent attorney for not keeping good notes of his ideas. It is thus not possible to follow his experimental efforts directly or even to date clearly the work he was doing. The accounts of the Automatic Hook and Eye Company show, however, that experimental expenses increased markedly in mid-1912. Whereas such charges were often made on the monthly accounts, they typically were less than $50. The $257.02 charge for July 1912 therefore was exceptional. That was followed, moreover, by a charge of $388.86 for August and one of $310.29 for September. Other evidence supports the conclusion that Gideon Sundback was up to something that summer, and in October he applied for a patent to demonstrate what he had to show for himself.[20]

Being "fed up with hooks and eyes," he sought to rethink the problem of the fastener at a very basic level, and what emerged was a considerable departure from anything that Whitcomb Judson had thought of. It was a clever invention that steered away from the key deficiencies of the Plako and its predecessors: It was flexible; it avoided the "metallic appearance" that made the earlier fasteners bulky mechanisms attached to a garment; it worked with a smoothness and simplicity that put its predecessors to shame. Sundback's description of how his new fastener worked is as good as any: "One side of the fastener has spring jaw members which clamp around the corded edge of the tape on the opposite side. The slider opens up the jaw members and carries the corded edge in under the jaws. [One can see] how the cord is inside of the jaw members and held against the crosswise strain which is put on the fastener when it is in active use."[21] Sundback had retained Judson's slider but changed everything else. To attach one side of the fastener to the other, he constructed one edge out of a series of closely spaced steel clamps that could be hidden in the folds of cloth tape. On the opposite side he had cloth tape with a corded edge, just as had been used to attach the elements of the Plako. Now, however, the corded edge was forced by the slider between the jaws of the steel clamps. These held the other side of the tape tightly, providing a secure, continuous fastening. Sundback spent several months refining his invention before applying for a patent in October (issued August 14, 1917, as U.S.P. 1,236,784).

To Sundback, the most striking thing about his new inven-

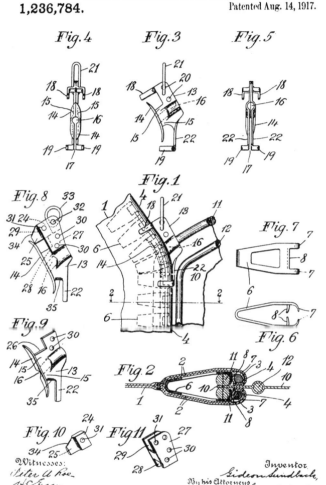

G. SUNDBACK.
SEPARABLE FASTENER.
APPLICATION FILED OCT. 22, 1912. RENEWED APR. 5, 1917.

1,236,784.

Patented Aug. 14, 1917.

Fig.4   Fig.3   Fig.5

Fig.1

Fig.8   Fig.7

Fig.9

Fig.6

Fig.2

Fig.10   Fig.11

Witnesses:
Peter U. Roe
H.C. Egan

Inventor
Gideon Sundback,
By his Attorneys
Edwards, Sager & Wooster

Gideon Sundback's first hookless fastener was a radical departure from the designs he had been working with. Its initial promise was so great that it spurred Lewis Walker to move manufacture to Meadville, although Sundback soon reported that the fastener wore out too quickly.   *TALON, INC.*

tion was that it allowed him to get rid of the hooks and eyes that so bedeviled him. He initially referred to it as the "hidden hook," although he quickly devised the more apt appellation of "hookless fastener." Already, by 1912 the term "horseless carriage" was an antiquated way of referring to automobiles. What we know as radio was still frequently called wireless, although that term, too, was on its way out, at least in the United States. There was, nonetheless, still something eminently suitable about calling a new technology or device by what it most conspicuously lacked.

Sundback's experiments coincided with a new downturn in the company's fortunes. In August he informed Colonel Walker that Automatic's poor finances, as well as, presumably, a lack of orders, had led him to shut down the factory for a while. "There is hardly any doubt in my mind that the new hidden hook will replace Plako, but before we get ready to fill orders we will want some stock and facilities to manufacture the hidden hook and that is a few months off." Meanwhile, experiments continued, and the results were not all encouraging. Again, Sundback wrote the Colonel: "It doesn't seem to me that the hidden hook is right for the trade as yet even if the steel and tape were right as to quality. I have found weak points."[22] As much as Sundback (and perhaps, as we shall see, even more so Colonel Walker) might wish to account for problems with the early samples of the hookless as caused by faulty materials, it quickly became evident to its inventor that his design was problematical. The principal problem was simple; as the inventor testified, "the plain corded tape on one side of the fastener would wear out in practical use."[23] It is easy to imagine Sundback's frustration at seeing his elegant and imaginative solution to the fastener problem foiled by so simple a difficulty. It is equally easy to picture, however, that the cloth tape and the cord that provided a beaded edge would be abraded constantly by the steel clamping jaws of the fasteners. In the act of opening and closing, especially, as the slider jammed the cloth and cord in and out of the jaws, the cotton simply would not hold up. A half century or so later such a design would hold more promise, with such tough fibers as nylon available to resist the rubbing steel and with more forgiving plastics for the clamps (indeed, this general design of fastener was resurrected using polymers on both sides, with great success in limited uses). In the early twentieth century, however, such options did not exist. As much as Sundback might wish that better cloth or less brittle steel would make the invention viable, he could see that such was not the case.

The problems of the hidden hook were never solved, and the fastener never made it into production. Yet its appearance signaled a momentous turn in our story. The abandonment, however momentary, of essential elements of Whitcomb Judson's designs marked the technical and commercial struggles in Hoboken as an effort that went beyond simply the improvement of one inventor's marginally workable idea. It was, it becomes clear in hindsight, the creation of a new technology. Gideon Sundback's novel product marked him, for the first time, as a true inventor, not simply as a skilled engineer who knew how to organize and improve the working out of others' ideas. Finally, the readiness with which those in the company, especially Lewis Walker, turned to the experimental device as a source of new energy and new direction indicated that there was, even after almost two decades of difficult and often futile work, a determination to see the matter through to success, whatever it took.

More specifically, the hookless fastener performed the great deed of luring Lewis Walker back to the fight, in time for it to become his life's work. Now in his mid-fifties, the Colonel had been largely absent from the Hoboken scene for the battles that had consumed first Peter Aronson and then Gideon Sundback. To be sure, Walker was a careful man, with his own money and with that which he had personally cajoled from others, and thus never completely lost sight of what was going on. But his personal interests were not easily transferred to the banks of the Hudson, and the trip to New Jersey was not one he relished. He kept himself as much as possible in Meadville, where he had other concerns, largely stemming from his original work with the Delamater fortunes. But once he saw Sundback's hidden hook, he was, it seems, almost transformed. Sundback himself spoke of the effect that it had on the Colonel: "From then on I wasn't lonesome." Walker's letters increased in frequency, and personal inspections of the work became almost routine. In spite of Sundback's frank misgivings, the Colonel perceived the new invention as the excuse and the means for starting afresh. He

quickly began making plans to shift the company away from the
Plako to the Hookless and, equally significantly, to reorganize
the effort both financially and physically. He apparently wanted
to take charge, and that could be done only in a new environment
more to his liking.[24]

Organizing and reorganizing companies were the chief things
that Lewis Walker did for a living, so the idea that the struggling
enterprise in Hoboken could benefit from a shake-up must have
come naturally to him. As early as 1911 he had begun to explore
the possibilities of refinancing the company, although he seems
not to have put much energy into the effort. Perhaps the expiration of Judson's original patents in 1910 and the impending
expiration of others made him cautious. Sundback's invention,
however, changed the situation and lit a fire in the Colonel that
never went out. By early 1913 he was laying plans, putting the
finger on new investors, and preparing the people in Hoboken
to make a move. At first he proposed to set up shop in Erie, about
thirty miles north of Meadville and a city not unlike Hoboken in
many ways, with its fine harbor, good rail connections, and
diversified manufacturing tradition. Even its large German-born
population evoked something of the New Jersey city's character,
and its rapid growth in the first decades of the twentieth century
made it an attractive site for new enterprises. It was not long,
however, until the Colonel decided on another course of action,
one tying his fate even more tightly to that of the fastener: The
new company would be moved to Meadville itself.[25]

In the spring of 1913 Walker put into motion the machinery
for disbanding the Automatic Hook and Eye Company and
establishing in its place the Hookless Fastener Company. Beginning in April, Automatic's books showed the Colonel's careful
and methodical methods, as records were made of the total debts,
including back salary and interest owed to long-departed officers,
such as Frank Russell and Victor Delamater. The moneys owed
to and from the long-moribund Universal Fastener Company
were calculated, and all the patent rights still outstanding were
consolidated. An inventory was made of the company's equipment and other capital, and arrangements were made to sell
all of Automatic's interests to Lewis Walker for fifty thousand
dollars. To finance part of the arrangement, the Colonel submitted bills to Automatic amounting to thousands of dollars, in

payment for traveling expenses and other services rendered to
the company as far back as 1903. Also in April, Walker joined
with W. S. McGunnegle, president of one of Meadville's leading
banks, and Theodore Lamb, a relative of his wife's who lived in
Erie, to form the Hookless Fastener Company. A charter for the
new firm was issued in mid-May, and the steps required to
liquidate Automatic continued. Among these were the purchase
of outstanding shares in the company at fifty cents a share. This
constituted a considerable loss for many investors, although no
doubt there were those pleased to see even that return on a
speculation that they had long since written off. While Walker,
good attorney that he was, took the proper steps to bring these
shares in and give the investors their due, some question can be
raised about how enthusiastically he performed this duty. He
continued to receive letters for several years from people who
wondered what had happened to their sometimes decade-old
investment.[26]

It seems that Walker was careful about following the proper
forms in taking over the fastener, but there is room for wondering
if he really scrupled at cutting corners on the transactions. His
large bills to Automatic for services as much as ten years old,
along with the other charges he made to the company for travel
expenses and the like (no one else seems to have submitted such
expenses), suggest that he was not above milking the Hoboken
company. One story told around Meadville for many years suggested that numerous people saw this side of the Colonel. As the
story was recounted by one of the modern company's patent
attorneys, during the period before 1913, when Walker's involvement in the company was minimal, he took advantage of a short
period of profitability to pay a visit to Hoboken, at which time
he explained to Sundback that he simply wanted to present him
with a specimen of the fine apples from the family's North Dakota farm. Sundback, for his part (the story goes), was perplexed
by the visit but a few days later received the Colonel's request
for five hundred dollars to cover the expenses of his visit.[27]

One exchange of letters that has survived leads to the conclusion that Colonel Walker was perhaps less than thorough in his
efforts to compensate Automatic's stockholders. Almost two
years after the stock purchase had been effected, in May 1915,
he received a letter from the Hoboken company's most famous

investor, James O'Neill. At sixty-eight, one of America's greatest actors was in the twilight of his career. His younger son, Eugene, was just beginning to carve out his own exceptional niche as a playwright. Many years later, in *Long Day's Journey into Night*, his unflinching portrait of his family, Eugene drew a scathing image of his father as a miserly tightwad, yelling at his sons for not turning out the electric lights. The other side of this miserliness (which biographers suggest the son exaggerated) was a penchant for investing in schemes that promised easy wealth. Of his father, Eugene once remarked, "He was an easy mark for anyone with a spare gold mine, zinc mine, coal mine, silver mine, pieces of real estate, etc.—and he rarely guessed right." Perhaps he had a more direct interest in his investment in Automatic Hook and Eye, however, for the Plako was touted as the perfect tool for the actor needing quick changes, and O'Neill's style of melodrama was always dependent on effective costuming. Be that as it may, in 1915 O'Neill wondered what had happened to his investment. He wrote the Colonel that he had tried to visit the old factory in Hoboken, only to learn that it had moved almost two years before. Why wasn't he told of the move? he asked. Walker's reply was a bit lame, saying that earlier letters had been returned but that he would be happy to exchange the Automatic stock for a proper amount of Hookless. It seems strange that letters did not get to the actor, for O'Neill's lavish home in New London, Connecticut, had been his address for more than thirty years. It is unfortunately easier to believe that Walker, who always projected himself as the consummately organized lawyer and businessman, was a bit sloppy (and tight) when it came to compensating Automatic's investors.[28]

The front page of the *Meadville Evening Republican* of July 23, 1913, carried this headline in boldface: IMPORTANT NEW INDUSTRY DROPS QUIETLY INTO MEADVILLE AND WILL BE PRODUCING BY OCTOBER. The story continued with the prominent announcement that the business was "well-established . . . with a promising future" and would be headed by Colonel Lewis Walker. The Colonel was interviewed for the story but, it was reported, insisted "that very little be said regarding his own connection with the business." The reporter confided to his readers, however, that "it has been very largely through his [Walker's] personal application and complete knowledge of automatic machinery that the hookless fastener has been brought to its perfection and the business established on a basis that has been profitable for several years." This would undoubtedly have been news to one of the figures identified in the story as "Gustave Sundbeck, Hoboken, N.J., mechanical superintendent." It was further reported that the company would be moving into the building on Race Street recently vacated by the McCroskey Reamer Company. In the forty- by seventy-foot two-story wooden building there were to be employed about twenty-five workers, "mostly expert mechanics." When the question was asked why the company was moving to Meadville, the answer, undoubtedly gratifying to the *Evening Republican*'s readers and consistent with their own view of their town, was "the wish to locate in a community where there is a minimum of labor troubles, where there are ample express facilities, . . . and where the members of the concern and its employees may enjoy the comforts and advantages of pure air and water, good schools and wholesome influences, such as are afforded in Meadville to perhaps a greater degree than in almost any other city of like size in the country." In spirit, as well as in time and place, Meadville in 1913 was very close to the Zenith of Sinclair Lewis's *Babbit*.

The newspaper story informed readers that the company would "manufacture the device known as the Plako Fastener, a mechanical fastener for garments, corsets, shoes, curtains, mail pouches, parcel post packaging, etc." By the time plans for the Meadville move were complete, Sundback, the Colonel, and everyone else concerned could see that the hookless was not a quick fix for the company's fortunes. While it was too soon that summer to give up on the new design—Sundback actually filed a second patent application at the end of June—most of the real work was directed toward resuming production of the Plako, with whatever cost economies that the new location and some new machinery might afford. The move itself cost both money and time since several months were required to get the new shop into production. In early August the *Evening Republican* reported that "Gustave Sundback" was in town to prepare for installation of machinery in the new plant of the "Wireless Fastener Co." and that "the concern will be in operation before snow flies." Sure enough, by mid-September the paper could report that "with orders on its books that will tax the capacity of

•

H

O

O

K

L

E

S

S

86 the plant," Colonel Walker's company had begun manufacturing and was looking for factory workers. Ten workers had moved from Hoboken to head the various factory departments, and it was expected that a total of forty or fifty would be employed once everything was in place. Already, the paper said, the company's product, a "mechanical lacing," was "in very large use throughout the country," and continued growth could be taken for granted.[29]

However confident the public image of the new Hookless Fastener Company might be, behind the scenes things were not so settled. The colonel struggled to put the best face on things, but with mixed success. In the fall of 1913 he began receiving sometimes testy inquiries from Frank Russell, now busy with airplane building in Massachusetts but still trying to keep an eye on his modest investment in the fastener. Walker replied that setting up the new plant had been a difficult proposition and that some time would have to be allowed before benefits of the move would be apparent. Sundback was said to be hard at work designing and building machines for making the hookless, but energies still had to be focused on keeping up production of the Plako. In November Walker reported that they were "turning out 1000 fasteners daily," which would have been a remarkable output. One problem still plagued the company, however, and that was the old one of selling.[30]

One of the consequences of Lewis Walker's decision to take command of the fastener was that he began, for the first time, to attend to the matter of how to sell his product. His involvement in this question became direct and forceful; while the technical fate of the fastener was in the hands of Gideon Sundback, its commercial future would be largely created by the Colonel. At the outset of the Meadville enterprise, Walker attempted to shape this primarily by exhorting his salesmen to greater efforts. This still meant, as it had for several years, lighting a fire under Willie Wear. In his letters to Russell and others, Walker gave vent to his exasperation with Wear, although it was sometimes hard to determine whether the frustration came from the belief that the master salesman was not trying hard enough or from a feeling that the whole business of hustling in the Wear style was just a bit infra dig for a respectable firm. In the last analysis, he seems to have concluded that he had little choice but to go along with

Wear, and in fact, over the next few years the Colonel constantly
cajoled, threatened, pleaded, and goaded Wear to keep up or
increase his sales.

The correspondence that documents this effort offers a remarkable look not only into the characters of the two men, so
uneasily dependent on each other, but also into a much-neglected
aspect of what was often involved in the expansion of the technological world. On the one hand, there was the prototypical entre-
preneur-businessman, whose belief in the inevitability of
progress was tied to a determination to make such progress serve
personal ambitions that were both expansive and respectable.
On the other side, there was the hustler, whose own personal
ambitions were no less real or driving but were acted upon on a
different scale, in the day-to-day battle of wits and sharpness
with individual men and women. There are, to be sure, those
technologies that seem to require little or none of these ambitions
to succeed, but it takes but a glance around oneself to realize that
much of our made world has taken shape because individuals
have bent it to serve their own ends—ends that may have little
to do with technology but that have everything to do with being
human.

At first Colonel Walker appears to have treated Wear in
much the same way as Alger Russell had in the past: admonishing
him that the interests of the company required steady sales.
Dismayed at apparent inactivity (he wrote Frank Russell that
Wear "has been loafing at home for five weeks"), Walker sent a
remarkable and long letter to Wear (in Alpine, Texas) on December 2, 1913, detailing the efforts that had been made to increase
the profitability of the business and emphasizing that the technical side of things was as well run as it could possibly be. "Mr.
Sundback has studied the 'Fastener' problem for seven years until
he has developed into a special and highly qualified *expert* in all
the delicate and intricate questions involved in the manufacture
of this specialty." The new factory, he went on, was now
equipped to produce 350 gross (50,400) of fasteners per month
(considerably more than the 1,000 per day he'd spoken to Russell
about three weeks before), and a minimum output of 250 gross
per month was required for profitability. The skilled work force
and the materials suppliers had to have a steady demand. Wear's
responsibilities were clear: "The volume of sales is up to you."

Besides, Walker went on to say, ". . . in the doing of this you will make more money than we can possibly make from the result." Walker pointed out to Wear that in 1912, a year in which the profits the company made from the Plako totaled $751.73, Wear had reported to the Colonel that he had purchased $2,000 worth of diamonds, property in Kansas City worth an equal amount, and two automobiles. Walker closed by saying, "We have done absolutely nothing to prepare for the sale of these goods except to tell you what we can produce and to pass the sales problem *up to you*." This entire discussion was particularly remarkable for its failure to mention the hookless fastener. The Colonel was, in fact, never, over the next couple of years, completely candid with Wear about the company's product development. It is thus hard to infer from this if he had given up on Sundback's invention at this point.[31]

In one other area the Colonel was apparently also not candid with Wear. He seems not to have told him that he was recruiting a new sales manager. The *Meadville Evening Republican*, however, on January 26, 1914, reported at the top of page one, that Henry E. Marschalk, who had spent many years selling phonographs, had joined Hookless to organize the company's sales force. Marschalk, however, seems to have been far better at self-promotion than at sales. In May, Walker wrote Russell that "we tried out a new sales manager who proved an absolute failure" and lasted only two months. The Colonel did not delegate responsibility for Wear, and the relationship between the two continued its delicate course. From Los Angeles the salesman wrote (on fine new stationery announcing "PLAKO—Wilson Wear Patents, Meadville, Pa.; distributing offices: New York City, Toronto, London, Paris") back to Meadville on February 9 that sales had picked up considerably, despite the fact that California was difficult territory. This was, Wear reported, at least in part due to the fact that in "almost every town I have been to in California, I have met people who said there was an old cripple tramp peddling that stuff around here some time ago." He emphasized the need to go with "salesmen of the highest stamp." He promised that he would make the Plako into a big business and that the people in Meadville would have to work to keep up with him. The Colonel had to acknowledge

Wear's success, reporting to Russell that net profits were running almost one thousand dollars per month.[32]

In the spring Wear made his way back east and settled for several weeks in Erie, bringing the Plako (for the first time, it would seem) to its home territory. A couple of days after the U.S. marines had seized Veracruz, Wear wrote the Colonel that "I am going to leave a gross Fasteners in Penna. for every Mexican that Uncle Sam kills in Mexico." Walker apparently wanted Wear to do what Marschalk had failed to do: train an army of sales agents that could handle the Plako by the thousands and tens of thousands. Wear had difficulty with this; there was one thing he did well and only one—selling. He tried earnestly to win Walker's respect, but the Colonel clearly had trouble regarding the fast-talking salesman as quite cricket. In one letter from Erie, Wear plaintively sought to get Walker to understand what a man like him had to do for a living:

> It is impossible for a professional man like yourself, accustomed to handleing [sic] big business in your line, to realize the nasty little propositions a man is up against in the selling of this PLAKO business. . . . Regarding the profits we are making on the sales of PLAKO to which you refered [sic] to in our recent interview, will state that it is a postive [sic] fact that I have not made a dollar clear money since I quit giving all my time to selling the Fastener and under took the training and getting others lined up in this work under the new system of selling. . . . The previous profits having been spent for Automobiles and Diamonds and other Necessary expenses. . . . Thanking you for your kind indulgence in reading this letter. . . .[33]

Wilson Wear wore a five-carat diamond ring on his hand, the mark of a successful man of the road, but anyone who would lump automobiles and diamonds together as "Necessary expenses" would always have trouble getting the serious respect of a man like Colonel Walker.

Odd couple though Willie Wear and the Colonel might make, they needed each other, and they knew it. More significant for our story, Gideon Sundback needed them both. Or rather, the creation of a new technology required not only a clever and ingenious engineer (whose technical triumph was yet to come) but also the determined and ambitious push of an entrepreneur who was wise in the way of organized enterprise and the audacious hustle and pushiness of a master salesman, who was willing, day after day, to convince people he might meet that the twentieth century required a novel thing and that their own lives, as well as their times, would be the better for taking that novelty upon themselves. Such faith, whether peddled door-to-door by a Willie Wear or broadcast throughout the land from the pulpits of professors and pundits, is as indispensable to technological change as invention itself.

C

H

A

P

T

E

R

Novelty in a New World

4

"As an example of how impossible it is, even with simple things, to forecast the future, I have often thought of how infinitesimally small would have been the chance of any man or group of men, except the one who actually had the idea, planning to invent the common zipper."[1] When, at the end of 1943, Bell Laboratories' head Frank Jewett sought an example of an improbable invention, he turned readily to the zipper. Even half a century later there is still something decidedly unexpected about the zipper's design. It seems to embody an ingenuity that goes beyond the "normal" invention. Perhaps this is due to its combination of simplicity, intricacy, and efficiency—all put to the service of a very small yet often vital task.

Look at a zipper—a metal one, with "teeth." The pull and the slider are not so very different from Whitcomb Judson's original "guide." The individual fastening elements, however, are quite different from anything he thought of; they constitute the essence of Gideon Sundback's key invention. If you look closely at these, you will see why the "teeth" are called scoops

•

Z

I

P

P

E

R

in the technical parlance of zipper makers. Each piece of metal protruding out from the cloth tape is characterized by a hollow on one side (typically, but not necessarily, the underside) and a bump on the other. The fastening consists simply of bumps nesting into hollows, with the individual scoops carefully staggered on each side of the fastener, so that a scoop on one side will fit snugly between two on the other, its hollow receiving a bump from one, and its bump in turn fitting into the hollow of the other. This is a remarkably simple principle, taking far more effort to describe than to appreciate visually. But now pull at the sides of the zipper. Pull hard. Nothing happens. The strength of the nested scoops is considerable, acting as they do together, anchored at one end of the stack by some kind of stop, at the other end by the slider. Now, if you can, flex the zipper: Bend it; twist it; fold it. Again, nothing happens to the fastening. A loose zipper, not attached to anything, can even be tied into a knot with no effect. Simple though it may be, the modern zipper is still, half a century after Jewett's admiring remarks, a marvel of ingenious and effective design.

As is the case with most very clever ideas, it is not really possible to trace the thoughts that led Gideon Sundback to his invention. If he kept written records of his experimental attempts to make a better fastener, we do not have them, and there is some reason to doubt that he wrote down much anyway (years later a patent attorney upbraided him for not keeping notes). It is not even possible to be certain about when he made his discovery, for many months seem to have passed between the time he identified his new approach to the problem and his application for a patent. When asked to describe events almost twenty years later, Sundback said that it took only about three months for him to realize that his first hookless fastener, with its metal clamps and beaded cloth tape, was a failure. While the Swede was generally unperturbable, one can imagine his agitation at this point. After all, it was on the basis of this invention that Lewis Walker had taken on the company's burdens and assets and moved it to Meadville. Sundback spoke of "lying awake nights trying to find a way out," turning over old ideas ("I had an innumerable number of them") in his head, and retracing the steps of past experiments. He refused to tell the Colonel that the clamp fastener was a loser until he had something better to show

N
O
V
E
L
T
Y

I
N

A

N
E
W

W
O
R
L
D

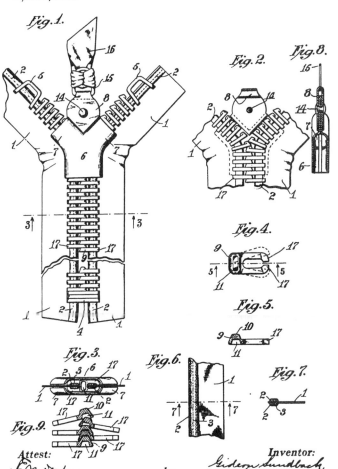

G. SUNDBACK.
SEPARABLE FASTENER.
APPLICATION FILED AUG. 27, 1914.

1,219,881.

Patented Mar. 20, 1917.

Fig. 1.

Fig. 2.

Fig. 8.

Fig. 4.

Fig. 5.

Fig. 3.

Fig. 6.

Fig. 7.

Fig. 9.

Attest:

Inventor:
Gideon Sundback,
by Edwards, Sager & Wooster,
Attys.

Gideon Sundback's U.S.P. 1,219,881 was issued in 1917. It described the modern zipper and became the foundation patent for the U.S. zipper industry, withstanding many challenges in subsequent years. *U.S. PATENT & TRADEMARK OFFICE* him. In December 1913 he had his second hookless fastener. "When I had the first sample finished, I told Col. Walker and Mr. Lamb that #1 was a failure. I never knew anyone to take it so calmly. . . . I set to work to make improvements on the first model of #2 and also to build a machine."[2]

This "#2" was the modern zipper, and the cleverness of its design makes the absence of a clear record of Sundback's thinking at this point particularly frustrating. The best description that we have is from one of his later patent attorneys, T. L. Chisholm, writing more than two decades after the fact. Sundback had the opportunity to look over and correct Chisholm's account, and it is consistent with the few clues that the inventor left to his thought processes, so it is probably the best we will have. In looking over his past speculations about improvements to the fastener's design, the engineer chose to pursue an idea that was likened to two sets of stacked soup spoons, their round bowls facing each other. If a space was opened up between each spoon in the stacks, just wide enough to insert a spoon from the opposing stack, when the two stacks were brought together, the bowls of the spoons would nest inside each other. If subsequently the top and bottom spoons were held in place, then the two stacks

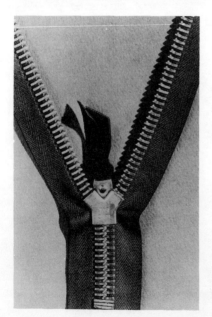

The Hookless #2 looked exactly like a modern metal zipper. Sundback's basic design underwent remarkably little modification after its introduction. The oblong shape of the "scoops" turned out to be particularly important in supporting the originality and workability of the design.

TALON, INC.

would lock together; no single spoon could be pulled out from
the assembly. If, Chisholm went on to say, the handles of the
spoons were split lengthwise down the center and a cloth tape
was inserted and fastened into the slit, then the spoon stacks
would constitute a fastener.[3]

According to Chisholm, Sundback actually constructed a
fastener along the lines of that in the 1911 patent of Katharina
Kuhn-Moos and Henri Forster, with rounded projections. Only
after doing this did he discover an important flaw in this design.
If the scoops ("soup spoons") were round, then the interlocking
stacks would be able to swivel, like a hinge. They would easily
pop apart (since they could be twisted out of line). Sundback
then experimented with the shape of his "bowls," eventually
making them rectangular rather than round. To understand the
alteration, look a bit more closely at a (metal) zipper. It will be
readily seen that the bump and the hollow on the scoop are not
round but are instead oblong in plan. In addition, note that the
bump begins at the edge of the scoop and rises gradually from
there. When, almost twenty-two months after he claimed to have
made his first version of the Hookless #2, Sundback and his
lawyers replied to the Patent Office's rejection of his claims of
originality on the basis of the Kuhn-Moos patent, they described
these two characteristics as crucial to the invention's practicality
and claimed that the Swiss invention "wholly fails to provide for
any lateral flexibility." In other words, that device would suffer
from the key defects of the Plako, except more so. In support of
this contention, Sundback and his colleagues actually prepared
samples based on the Kuhn-Moos design as well as their own.
With these, they stated, "The Examiner will notice that applicant's fastener doubles sharply on itself without disengaging the
projections, while the Kuhn-Moos fastener can hardly be bent
at all before the pins come out." In other words, Sundback's
fastener possessed the flexibility of the modern zipper, while the
Swiss invention did not. The examiners in the Patent Office,
and, after them, judges in patent suits, continued to require the
Hookless Fastener Company to explain and defend the distinc-
tion between Sundback's and Kuhn-Moos's inventions, and
eventually all the decisions boiled down to accepting the differences claimed here. Furthermore, the Patent Office and, more
important, the courts also agreed that these differences were

Katharina Kuhn-Moos und Henri Forster

Patent Nr. 55740
1 Blatt

The closest anticipation of Gideon Sundback's invention was this 1911 Swiss patent (number 55,740) issued to Katharina Kuhn-Moos and Henri Forster, of Zurich. Sundback successfully argued that the round shape of the nibs of the fastener elements would have made the device fold like a hinge and thus pop open. There is no evidence that the device was actually manufactured.

crucial, that, in the words of one appeals judge, "Seemingly, it [Kuhn-Moos] will not work."[4]

What is not clear from the record, however, is how much Gideon Sundback took from earlier inventions—Kuhn-Moos or any other to produce his own. Sometimes the technical literature and the patent record are so clear and well known that the safest assumption is that an inventor began with the closest prior invention and went from there. In this case, however, the issue is a bit muddier. Sundback never referred to other inventions in his own brief accounts. Kuhn-Moos and Forster took out patents in Germany, France, and Great Britain but not the United States. Certainly Peter Aronson, who was in France during this entire period of experimentation, was in a good position to know of Kuhn-Moos's and other European inventions, but there is no evidence that he communicated to Sundback about them. On the other hand, the patent examiner was very quick to reject all of Sundback's claims on the basis of the Kuhn-Moos invention, citing the British patent (14,358 of 1912); he replied to Sundback's original application only seven weeks after it was submitted. It took Sundback's attorneys almost a year to file their answer, and then it was under threat of a possible interference. An interference was a declaration by the examiner that two pending applications for a patent presented conflicting claims of priority (a patent is issued to the applicant who can demonstrate the earliest invention, not to the earliest applicant). A New York City inventor filed a patent application for "Opening and Closing Devices" that apparently echoed some of Sundback's claims quite closely. Since the Patent Office did not retain records of failed applications, it is impossible to examine this invention, but the interference posed no serious threat to the Sundback application. Further amendments continued to be called for by the examiner, however, and it was not until March 1917 that Sundback received U.S. Patent 1,219,881, which was held in subsequent years as the fundamental patent on the modern slide fastener.

When asked in later years, in the course of the patent suits that Hookless brought to defend his patents, just how he came up with his invention, Sundback provided a little more insight into his creation. Upon concluding that the spring jaw type of hookless fastener had fatal flaws, he attempted to figure just what he had learned about what worked and what didn't. Perhaps the most important principle that he came up with at this point was that he had to increase the number of fastening elements for a given length of fastener. The four per inch of the C-curity and the Plako would have to give way to ten or eleven. This naturally meant that the size of each element would have to be much reduced. In addition, the spacing between elements for the reception of an opposing element needed to be kept as small as possible, to ensure a secure fit. At the same time, Sundback realized that as a practical matter it was necessary to make the opening into which elements would be guided by the slider as generous as possible. As he pointed out, it was one thing to have a mechanism that operated when the fastener could be laid flat and the slider pulled absolutely straight; it was quite another to have one that worked in the real world, where the fastener was likely to be bent, and the slider to be twisted as it was pulled. Finally, Sundback emphasized on numerous occasions that his design was driven by manufacturing considerations from the outset. As he once explained, "It is easy to make a fastener even for universal use, provided you don't have to make the fastener, you can let your imagination run riot. When you design a fastener you have to consider commercial production or mechanical means of making a commercial product."[5]

None of the principles that Sundback outlined was particularly profound, but all evidenced a thorough understanding of the little mechanical world to which he had devoted himself. These principles were not the sort of thing a flamboyant inventor like Whitcomb Judson would have bothered himself with. They were, instead, the product of an engineer's mind, and the particular product of one engineer who had immersed himself in a problem that might have seemed trivial to most until raw, hard experience revealed the subtle traps that it posed. The more we learn about the processes of invention, the clearer it becomes that technological creativity is usually born out of such immersion. The "carrying out" that Diesel spoke of is often in truth indistinguishable from "the happy period of creative mental work" that he called the beginning of the inventive process. To make this "carrying out" fruitful, however, it is usually necessary for the would-be inventor to be so thoroughly absorbed by the "problem" that he or she is alert to every possibility, to the implications of every observation, to the subtle relationships and contingencies that make the difference between theoretical and practical ideas. Often even the apparently accidental discovery is really the product of the inventor's complete devotion to the problem before him. Charles Goodyear's discovery of vulcanization, for example, was not the chance observation of the result of rubber and sulfur spilled on a hot stove; it was the result of almost two decades of total dedication to the problem of making rubber useful and of knowing just what he was seeing where anyone else would have seen no more than an unpleasant, smelly mess. Gideon Sundback's invention was, of course, no accident. It was the outcome of seven years of observing, fixing, thinking, and experimenting. Frank Jewett was right: As surprising as the invention of the zipper might seem, it was in a sense the plan of "the one who actually had the idea."

On May 4, 1914, Lewis Walker wrote to Frank Russell to detail the continuing difficulties involved in bringing to a close the affairs of the Automatic Hook and Eye Company. "So much of the stock is lost and mislaid and stockholders have lost interest," Walker explained, that getting the minimum number in hand to close the company's books was particularly slow. He reported that details involving the new company, in Meadville, had caused their own headaches, although Wilson Wear's sales were up, a positive sign. He then reported to Russell:

> *Mr. Sundback has an entirely new fastener which for the present I am calling the "Hookless Hooker" for want of a better name. . . . Acting largely on Mr. Sundback's judgment, he knowing all the mechanical details necessary to perfect the Hookless Fastener as well as to develop and perfect the Hookless Hooker, we decided to suspend active work on the Hookless Fastener and to give the Hookless Hooker preference. Machinery for this latest fastener is much simpler, will require far less grooming and much less detail in the secondary tools and necessary machines for assembling and getting the fastener ready for market.*[6]

The term "Hookless Hooker" mercifully disappeared quickly, to be replaced by the colorless "Hookless #2." Since the public had never had a chance to see "#1" (the spring-jaw fastener), simply "Hookless" was adequate for the larger world, no doubt to the relief of the ever-so-thrifty Colonel, who must have shuddered at the thought of new incorporation papers, new stationery, and new stock certificates.

By the spring of 1914 Sundback had persuaded Walker that the new fastener was the superior invention and that whatever delay might be encountered by jettisoning several months of work on machinery for making the spring-jaw Hookless #1 and shifting to the #2 would be well worth it. It was not hard to make the case, as Walker had passed it on to Russell, that the new device would be far easier to manufacture. Sundback claimed to have had ease of machine production in mind when he designed the #2. He spent the spring and summer fashioning the machinery, but it was not an easy task. As he told the story, he had his first machine completed and ready to go on July 3 and confidently made plans for a glorious Fourth, only to discover that "the fool machine wouldn't work." The device made a couple of inches of fastener and then stopped. He had to redesign the mechanism and was not finished until the fall. The machinery was a special challenge, for not only was machine-based production essential to the technical and economic calculations behind the hookless fastener, but the small size of the scoops and the extreme precision with which they had to be placed on the tape essentially meant that hand operations had to be eliminated entirely, at least in the manufacture of the stringers, or chain, as the tape with attached scoops came to be called. While machine production was always a goal for the C-curity and Plako fasteners, hand fabrication had turned out to be the more practical and economical option. With this option essentially eliminated by the design of the Hookless #2, Sundback's considerable mechanical talents were tested to the utmost.[7]

His first successful design, in operation in the fall of 1914, used very standard machine technology of the day. The scoops were stamped from flat sheets and, in the same machine, punched to give them the proper shape, both for being attached to the tape and for interlocking with each other. Without leaving the machine, the tiny scoops were then attached to the tape. Even in this first machine, there was no handwork at all. When the machine was working properly, it could produce five hundred feet of complete fastener per day, which would normally yield at least five hundred fasteners (the standard Plako ran about ten inches in length; hookless skirt fasteners were probably about the same, but might be longer). The complexity of the machine was such that Sundback had to turn to Connecticut machine builders to construct the final models, and several months were required to "groom" them so that they operated smoothly and reliably. It was not until December, in fact, that Colonel Walker could report that they were "out of the woods" in having machine production operating as they wished. Apparently both he and Sundback decided at an early point that the new fastener would have to be made to very high standards. The new design, with its tiny parts and close tolerances, probably enforced higher-quality standards than they had hitherto aimed for; if the parts fabrication or placement were in the least sloppy, the new fastener simply would not work at all. Walker and Sundback, once the machines were working as they wished, always made a virtue of this quality requirement.[8]

Another contributor to the enhanced quality of the new product was the material from which it was made. All previous slide fasteners, from Judson's 1891 design to the Plako and the Hookless #1, had been made from steel. This was an economical metal that was sturdy and could be machined (stamped and punched, in this case) with well-known techniques. To be sure, it rusted and thus required protective coatings on the finished product as well as cautionary notes to users. The Hookless #2, however, did not require such a strong material and thus was fashioned from German silver, a nickel-copper-zinc alloy that did not rust and was stamped and punched in small pieces with great ease. This was considerably more expensive than the steel, and about the same amount of metal was used in the new fastener. Material costs, however, were never a key factor in production during the early years, and in the long run the much lower unit labor costs for the Hookless #2 would more than offset the materials. The new material, along with the hookless design, meant that no problem would be encountered in laundering the fastener, one of the difficulties Sundback had wished to overcome. The Colonel found the washability of the new fastener a particularly striking advance.[9]

Even before the machinery was completely satisfactory,

Lewis Walker turned his attention to the truly daunting task before him: how to sell the new hookless. By early fall he and his partners were certain both that the new fastener was a good product and that Sundback would be able to work out any difficulties with the machinery. The question of sales strategy now began to occupy the Colonel and dominate his discussions with the key figures in the enterprise. One obvious option was to sell just as the Plako had been sold, with Wilson Wear carrying on as before. But, as Sundback observed, "Col. Walker and Mr. Lamb were disgusted with this method of selling." The engineer was under the impression that sales of the Plako had been stopped, in spite of the fact that the hookless was not quite ready for market. This wasn't true, for not only did Willie Wear continue to peddle the Plako in much the fashion he had for years, but Lewis Walker urged him on in his efforts for at least another year. In October 1914, for example, just as Hookless was organizing a sales effort for the new fastener, the Colonel admonished Wear that he was running 210 gross behind his 1913 pace, and this "has upset all our calculations." He went on to say, "We are patiently and perseveringly getting out the goods, and while the last ten days' orders have greatly encouraged us, we are still willing to be further encouraged, and I can assure you we can supply the goods no difference how hard you crowd us." That fall the Wears had a son and gave it the middle name Lewis, after the Colonel. For his part, the Colonel wrote solicitously to Mrs. Wear and eventually encouraged her to help out in her husband's efforts. There was no word to either of them, however, of Sundback's invention, much less of any decision to abandon the Plako in its favor.[10]

Sundback was right in one respect, however, and that was the Colonel's insistence that the new hookless fastener would be handled in an entirely different manner from the Plako. In fact, Walker continued to refuse to let Wear have the hookless fastener at all. In August 1915 an exchange between the salesman and Walker showed how much distance the Colonel wanted to put between Wear and the hookless. By this time Wear had visited Meadville enough to have seen the new device, and like most who saw it, he was much impressed. Getting his hands on a few samples and an advertisement that had been printed up, Wear delightedly began his peddling and ordered a thousand more

Lewis Walker—"the Colonel"—as depicted in the Hookless Fastener Company's magazine, the *Hookless Scoop*, in 1926. *TALON, INC.*

Lewis Walker, Jr. (1881–1935), was his father's most dependable assistant. This photograph, from the *Scoop*, was taken about ten years after his stint in the garment district of New York City. *TALON, INC.*

Gideon Sundback was styled the Hookless Fastener Company's "Consulting Engineer and Inventor" in the 1926 *Scoop*. *SCOOP, TALON, INC.*

Wallace D. Walker (1887–1939) was the more dashing of the Walker brothers, and he spent much time on the road promoting the sales of the Hookless fastener. He attempted to withdraw from company activities for a time but took over duties from his ill older brother in the early 1930s and eventually the reins of the company after his father's death in 1938. *TALON, INC.*

circulars from Meadville. Walker hit the roof. He quickly wrote back to Wear (who was in Pittsburgh at the time) that "We don't care to have the Hookless Fastener advertised *now* except by the manufacturers" and said that there was still much experimenting to do before they would be ready to promote sales widely. Wear replied meekly that "I will take care not to make any trouble." The next month, not long after receiving yet another one of the Colonel's admonitions that sales were slipping but that the company was still depending on Wilson Wear to do his best, the salesman wrote back an almost plaintive letter—the last one to be found in the company files. He explained that sales had dropped off because "the new men that I have put on the job from time to time cannot stand the nervous strain." This was largely because "all the states have been so thoroughly covered with Plako 'it gets their sheep' and they lose their nerve when they come across the same fastener, as they always do in every town large and small." He continued, "As for myself, I expect to stay on the job and can sell as many Plako as I am now selling for the next thirty years and if I am ever fortunate enough to get a better fastener can sell four times as many and repeat orders besides. . . ." There is no record of a reply, nor that the Colonel ever let Wear handle the hookless.[11]

As 1914 drew to a close, Walker was anxious to put the C-curity and Plako and other reminders of failure and difficulty behind him. The week before Christmas he received a letter from an attorney friend asking about the worth of the stock that he had long ago purchased in the Automatic Hook and Eye Company of Hoboken. In reply, the Colonel wrote to tell of the healthy financial condition of the Hookless Fastener Company and of his confidence that "we have the best fastener that was ever made." He then admitted that "the profit will depend on our introductory campaign and how successfully we can get the public to accept the real fastener for the makeshift hooks and eyes that have been in use. How much time this will take, I am not prepared now to say." He explained the sales strategy that was then taking shape: "We have our plans to open up the question with the manufacturers, and have already received emphatic and satisfactory endorsements from the department stores that they will ask the manufacturer to put this fastener on a line of garments. . . ." The "emphatic and satisfactory endorsements" were at this point largely wishful thinking, but they were indeed the primary goal of what was to be a long and arduous campaign. The importance that the Colonel attached to this campaign was signified by the men he recruited to carry it out—his two sons.[12]

Lewis Walker's elder son, Lewis, Jr., was thirty-three years old, his brother, Wallace, twenty-seven, when they were called upon by their father to drop their careers, leave their families for weeks at a time, and devote the rest of their lives to their father's obsession. There could be no more forceful testimony both to the Colonel's determination that the hookless fastener should be his life's work and legacy and to the power that he wielded over his family and associates. Lewis, Jr., had parlayed an analytical yet practical mind-set and a degree from the Wharton School into a successful real estate business in Pittsburgh. The younger brother had also attended the University of Pennsylvania but had left before graduation. This had not interfered with his beginning to experience some success working with the steel industry in Youngstown, Ohio. Despite the fact that both men were well along in the pursuit of their own careers, they apparently had little hesitation in picking up and moving back to Meadville to serve their father's cause.[13]

Almost as much as Gideon Sundback's invention of the Hookless #2 and the machines to make it, the beginning of the Walker brothers' sales campaign marked 1914 as the central turning point in the zipper's story. The solution of the key technical problem of the slide fastener was necessarily accompanied by the redirection of energies to the problem of selling the result. This is a perfectly ordinary sequence of events in technological development, but for a couple of reasons the shift of focus from inventing to selling has special meaning for the history of the zipper. First, the selling of the zipper turned out to be a challenge equal in scope and duration to that of inventing it. The twenty years that passed from the time that Whitcomb Judson received his first patents to the moment that Gideon Sundback was able to present Colonel Walker with the Hookless #2 was matched by the two decades required to move the new fastener from the status of an interesting but largely unwanted novelty to a widely accepted part of daily life. The story of its selling is thus one that tells us much about how novelty is received and managed in the contexts of business, fashion, and culture. An additional reason that this story takes on special significance is that certain aspects of it are exceptionally well documented. In particular, the facts that the Hookless Fastener Company's chief agents were the Colonel's sons, that their father insisted upon full and regular written reports from them, and, finally, that much of their correspondence has survived give us an extraordinary and colorful glimpse into a poorly chronicled aspect of American enterprise—the sale of novelty.

The venue of the Walkers' work adds to the interest of their story and the documents they left behind. While in the fall of 1914 they began close to home, approaching manufacturers and stores in Cleveland and Pittsburgh, the scene of their work quickly shifted from the periphery to the center—New York's garment district. The Walkers' letters thus also provide an astonishing and novel perspective on one of America's most famous arenas of commerce. By the first decades of the twentieth century the New York City garment industry had emerged as one of the mainstays of the economy of the nation's largest city. In addition, because of its size and its location, it was at the center of many of the most important economic and social movements of the time. Labor conditions in the industry became a source of widespread concern as well as the tinder for the flaring up of one of the most radical labor movements in America. In the spring of 1911 the flames became literal, as a fire in the sweatshop of the Triangle Shirtwaist Company took the lives of 146 workers, largely Jewish and Italian immigrant girls. The tragedy focused attention on the sweatshops and on the conditions that supported the thriving trade. By this time garment making, particularly that done in New York, had become one of the underpinnings of retail commerce, epitomized by the grand department stores that had sprung up in every American city with any pretension to importance and prosperity.[14]

By the twentieth century, also, the New York garment trade had become a largely Jewish province, and in that way, too, it made a particularly distinctive impression on American life. As early as 1880 garment makers in New York City produced more than those in the next four cities combined, and the growth of the industry continued at an even more rapid pace, at just the time that Jewish immigration from Eastern Europe was becoming a flood. The greatest growth in the years around 1900 occurred in women's clothing, which had been slower to succumb to the ready-to-wear trade than men's and children's wear. By that year more than two-thirds of manufactured women's garments in the United States were made in New York City, and this manufacture was heavily concentrated in the Jewish Lower East Side of Manhattan. Not only did the work force in the garment trade have a high proportion of Jews, but the ownership and management of the trade were, if anything, even more decidedly Jewish. At first these were almost exclusively German Jews, whose families had begun to settle in New York in considerable numbers in the 1840s and 1850s, but in the new century the much more recently arrived East European Jews began to move up in the trade, and the garment industry became the single most important path to prosperity for them. According to historian John Higham, the peak of their influence was reached in the middle teens, at precisely the time of which we now speak.[15] Small wonder, then, that the two young men from Meadville were particularly struck by how foreign—in particular, how Jewish— was the business in which they had found themselves. They were uninhibited in reporting their responses to this new world and the strange people they found in it.

The Colonel, from the first days his sons were in New York, made a point of insisting "you take time to write me full details of each case you visit, together with names and a full account of just what was said and what took place. I want these reports to help me to a full and complete understanding and to educate me on the points brought out so I can take a hand in this game you are learning and teaching me at the same time."[16] Whenever the letters from Lewis, Jr., or Wallace slacked off, their father was quick to complain. "I know that you are not much of a letter writer," he wrote to his elder son, but "you will have to overcome your disinclination to put down all facts and get over the habit of waiting to report verbally."[17] Lewis, Jr., caught on to his father's wishes after a few such reminders, although in subsequent weeks and months the Colonel still did not hesitate to tell his sons when he thought a letter had been skimpy or to chide them for missing a day in writing.

The Colonel also did not hesitate to dictate the strategy that he expected them to carry out, especially in the first few weeks of the effort. "The fastener must be shown only to be applied," he stressed in an early letter. "Make fewer calls but work your educational campaign and deepen the impressions of the intrinsic merit and value of your fastener." This idea that the fastener would sell itself if only the boys showed it to the right people in the right way underscored the Colonel's unshakable faith in Sundback's invention. But it also emphasized his own naïveté about the garment industry's cautious approach to change. Perhaps reflecting his own small-town business habits, the elder Walker was sure that with introductions to the right people, his sons would have the necessary access to the "high class manufacturers . . . who will give you the right kind of a hearing." In reply to an early report from Lewis, Jr., about the difficulty of getting in to see garment makers, the Colonel remarked, "I am relieved to know you appreciate it is lost time to call on the 'Jews' unheralded and unknown. Also that hereafter you will avoid such experience and only open the fastener proposition under right conditions." In these early weeks the Colonel also offered advice on whether the fastener was to be pushed more at the level of stores or directly to garment makers: "Let us stick to the plan of working with department store support to get the makers of the garments to put fasteners at work. . . . If we can get a repeat order from McCreery's at Pittsburgh or some New York department store by the trial methods we have found how to get the demand to the manufacturers."[18]

For the next several years, at least, the Colonel's strategy developed along the lines he first suggested. Sometimes the emphasis would be a bit more on the stores, especially large department stores, with the pitch aimed at the buyers who could then let their wish for the fastener be known to the manufacturers. At other times the focus seemed to shift to the manufacturers themselves, from the largest producers of factory-made clothing to the specialty makers of such garments as theater costumes, sports clothes, or underclothing and on to the small-scale tailors and dressmakers, who were still seen as the dictators of fashion. Most of the time, however, the sales attack was carried out on a broad front, with approaches made to whoever would listen, was willing to take and try out a few samples, and seemed likely to influence others, either up or down the sales chain.

Lewis, Jr., and Wallace were, like their father, newcomers to the garment industry. Their letters thus reveal a learning process as, in the first few months especially, they felt their way around the strange new environment, eagerly picking up the customs and practices of this trade to which they were committing the future of their enterprise. The ethnic foreignness of New York's Lower East Side both enhanced the feeling they had that they had entered an alien world and gave them a ready explanation for practices and values that seemed peculiar to them. It was a time when most Americans would have found it easy to chalk up obstacles and surprises to "those Jews," and the Walker brothers were no freer from mental stereotypes and racial categories than their fellow citizens. The fact that they were reporting their work back not just to some boss at the company headquarters but to their father lent their letters an intimacy of detail and feeling that conveys their personal reaction to what they were learning and seeing to an extent rarely encountered in professional correspondence.

One of the first things the Walkers learned was that the world they had entered was not one in which strangers could make their way without help. From the start they had to make use of whatever personal contacts their father or friends could steer them to. In one of his first reports from New York (December

29, 1914), Lewis, Jr., reported: "We started out this morning together to see some manufacturers—all Jews—whose names we had. After *trying* to see three I called a halt. They didn't want to see us—just wouldn't so instead of going in wrong we left." The younger Walkers quickly learned that personal introductions were necessary, or else they would be taken simply for the kind of fast-talking hustlers that any East Side businessman knew not to waste his time on. "Looking over the days [*sic*] work," Lewis concluded in the same day's report, "I feel I have proven that to go in anyplace without some personal and explanatory introduction is the biggest mistake that could be made. You not only cheapen the fastener & yourself but you put both under a handicap that is nearly impossible to overcome." The best thing to do, of course, was to work as much as possible through family friends and business acquaintances. In his December 29 report home, Lewis describes a series of visits following their failure to get in to see the Jewish manufacturers. A Mrs. Tierney "was very glad to see us but I don't believe can do us much good." A Dr. Brash was able to introduce them to a "sample skirt man," who "is going to show it [the fastener] on his girls." Brash also promised to take them to see such promising targets as the "manager of the Hippodrome" and the "wardrobe mistress for the Schuberts' [*sic*]." Another family friend introduced Lewis to "a Mr. Stiles of Arnold-Constable Co. When I went there I didn't know they were one of the biggest & highest-class jobbers for dress-makers & etc. in the city." Here they met the head buyer and saleswoman, a Miss Regan: "She says it's splendid and she wants to know more about it. And believe me she will know." Even then he wasn't finished for the day. Traveling up Broadway, Lewis called on Leonard Nicoll, "one of the biggest custom tailors in New York." Thanks to a letter of introduction, he was able to make his pitch: "At first it was hard sledding but when I finished Mr. Nicoll was having it put on his own dress suit and his head tailor asked me for one for his everyday pants. Also I was asked for prices, delivery, etc." When Lewis emerged back into the cold evening of the street, he "was wet to the knees and completely played out," but he could hardly be blamed for a sense of optimism about their campaign.[19]

Time after time over the next few months the Walker brothers were to see that personal connections were the glue that held the garment industry together and that kept strangers separate. They did not find it that difficult to get an initial hearing as long as they had a note of introduction, a name that they could use as a reference, or some other means of tying themselves to the world in which they would always be the outsiders. The Jewishness of this world struck them immediately and was a cause of mixed concern, self-pity, and amusement. In an early letter Lewis, Jr., reported his brother's first reaction: "Wallace says he didn't know there were so many Jews in the world and all ready talks with his hands & has an accent like an Ikey." A week later the sense of culture shock had not disappeared: "Wallace went to the East Side & he says there were 500,000 Jews there in one bunch. When I questioned the statement he said he had counted them." Constantly references to manufacturers were put in terms of "the Jews," sometimes simply as a shorthand for the people they were meeting, sometimes with stereotypes attached. Very early, for example, Lewis, Jr., urged his father to move more quickly on getting patent protection for Sundback's work, for "these Jews who are seeing it now will probably take it to some mechanical friend and try to have it copied." Most often the allusion to the Jewish manufacturers was made in the context of explaining the difficulty that they were encountering as the result of the relatively high price of the fastener. Repeatedly the younger Lewis Walker reported that impressed or not as they might be at the fastener's performance, once sales talk turned to price, the manufacturers balked. Frequently the brothers expressed some suspicion that an effort was being made to take advantage of them, by manufacturers haggling over price or arguing for special treatment.[20]

The younger Lewis's description of his encounter with Nathan Schuss, "one of the largest skirt manufacturers here," illustrates well the spirit of some of their most important encounters. After two weeks or so of discussing the fastener with Schuss, who had taken the order for installing it in skirts for McCreery's department store, whose Pittsburgh store had given them their first tryout, Lewis summed up some of his impressions:

Schuss is perhaps as high class and exclusive skirt man as there is in the City, and his goods are all first-class and he deals with the very best firms throughout the country. For instance, I know that he showed the Fastener to Marshall Field's buyer, and I believe she ordered some skirts with the Fastener in. Schuss was very much disappointed not to get us down to a price proposition yesterday, and if he had come out flat-footed and said he believed in the Fastener and would use it on his own responsibility, we would have quoted him an introductory price, but until he does that I feel it would be a mistake to sell him the Fastener and thus give him a chance to shut us out of his shop. He is about as clever and foxy a jew as we have run up against, and you know that this is pretty nearly the last word.[21]

When he went back a week later, Lewis discovered that conditions in the Schuss firm were not encouraging. The proprietor was not in, but one of the tailors complained "they are having a great deal of trouble with their shop people over the Fastener. He said the men were also wanting more money for putting in the new article, and that the Union was going to take the matter up." Lewis argued that in fact, the new fastener could be "put in easier than hooks and eyes, or snaps," and offered to prove it. The tailor was not willing to pursue the argument in his boss's absence. When Lewis got back to his brother, however, he learned that "Schuss is saying he has the exclusive right to use these Fasteners and is buying them for 7¢." He remarked to his father, "I am perfectly willing to let him rave."[22]

Colonel Walker's reaction to these reports—"The Schuss situation demonstrates all that is foxy and underhanded in dealing with an unprincipled Jew"—showed the extent to which he shared his sons' impressions of the people they were dealing with. From time to time his letters spoke of "the scheming Jew manufacturer" or made some other prejudicial reference to Jews. He remarked on how Wallace, especially, was "getting in with the Jews" and of how he hoped that they would be able to do business with some "Gentile manufacturer" instead of having to depend exclusively on the Jews.[23]

The world that the Walkers, father and sons, saw as strange and alien was, in fact, a new creation, one that even its creators were struggling to understand and accommodate themselves to. Abraham Cahan's 1917 novel *The Rise of David Levinsky* tells the story, from the inside, of the making of the world of the

Jewish East Side. Levinsky, who had fled Russia and landed on a Hoboken pier with only four cents in his pocket, scraps his way ahead in the garment industry, becoming a skirt and cloak manufacturer. After sweating in the shops himself for a time, he manages to save and borrow enough money to set up a small shop on Division Street, equipped with two rented sewing machines and depending on the cheapest labor he could find. Gradually he makes his way forward in the business, well aware that he is part of a larger movement that is changing the world around him. At one point he encounters a once-prosperous salesman, Loeb, who represents the passing order. Loeb sardonically inquires of Levinsky, "What is Division Street going to do next? Sell a fifteen-dollar suit for fifteen cents? That's a great place, that is. There are two big business streets in New York—Wall Street and Division." Levinsky catches Loeb's tone: "You don't seem to like the Division Street manufacturers, do you? I suppose you have a reason for it." "I have a reason? Of course I have," Loeb replies. "So has every other decent man in the business." To himself, Levinsky reflects: "The old cloak-manufacturers, the German Jews, were merely merchants. Our people, on the other hand, were mostly tailors or cloak operators who had learned the mechanical part of the industry, and they were introducing a thousand innovations into it, perfecting, revolutionizing it. We brought to our work a knowledge, a taste, and an ardor which the men of the old firms did not possess. And we were shedding our uncouthness, too. In proportion as we grew we adapted American business ways."[24]

It was precisely this changing world that confronted the Walkers, posing opportunities and obstacles at the same time. The men they met in the shops were not bound by old traditional ways of doing things. Their trade itself, especially in women's garments, was relatively new. The Eastern European immigration that David Levinsky represented had coincided with the emergence of cloak and skirt making from a small-scale home-based affair into one dependent on sweatshops and factories, which could range in size from the three men with which Levinsky started on Division Street to the four-story factory and showroom that he was able to open a few years later on Fifth Avenue. In so doing, Cahan's Levinsky reflected, "we had Americanized the system of providing clothes for the American woman of moderate or humble means. The ingenuity and unyielding tenacity of our managers, foremen, and operatives had introduced a thousand and one devices for making by machine garments that used to be considered possible only as the product of handwork." Little wonder, then, that the Walkers were often met with an open curiosity, a willingness to take a few fasteners and try them out. In their first few months in New York they were able to get dozens of dressmakers, tailors, and skirt manufacturers to experiment with the strange new device. Because so many of the owners and shopkeepers had worked their way up from the shop floor, they were generally talking to men who knew what they were being asked to do, who could visualize both the possibilities and the problems that the hookless fastener posed for them. These were men who had gotten where they were at least in part through a willingness to consider new ways of doing things.[25]

This initial openness, combined with the personal charm of the two young men from Meadville, made the first few months in New York a time of great promise, as buyers, store owners, tailors, dressmakers, and manufacturers received the brothers cordially, looked at the fastener with an open curiosity and appreciation of its cleverness, and consented to experiment with everything from fancy skirts to baseball trousers. Once they realized that introductions and contacts were almost indispensable to getting a serious hearing, Lewis and Wallace pulled every string they could to open doors. Old family friends and recent acquaintances alike were pressed to provide a name, a letter, some indications of favor that would bring them face-to-face with the owner of a store or the manager of a factory. The experiences they reported back to the Colonel made it clear that the two were personable men who could make a good impression on a wide range of people. Their first visit to the New York branch of Wanamaker's department store was a good example of how their charm could be translated into initial good impressions. An old family friend, a Mrs. Stowell, accompanied the two to the store, explaining that the key to eventual success lay in an approach to one Miss Walls. This formidable woman had been "the last American buyer out of Paris," fleeing the German threat a few months before with some prized fashions in an automobile bound for the safety of the French coast. So valued was she by John Wanamaker that Miss Walls was reputed to be

"the highest salaried woman employed in the dry goods business
in America." Apparently this heroine of fashion and merchandis-
ing was a quick study, and after a brief introduction to the
hookless fastener, according to Lewis's report, she called in her
"head sales women, buyers, fitters & etc." to order them to try
the novelty out wherever the Walkers suggested. "She says it is
the greatest & best thing apparently that she has seen in years"
and promised all the help she could give. Miss Stowell, the family
friend, was dazzled by this reception, remarking to Lewis after-
ward that he should assure his father that the New York campaign would not need his help; if Miss Walls and Wanamaker's
went for the fastener, their fortunes would be made. She "also
looked at Wallace and told us not to ask the young ladies out to
lunch & etc.—said it wasn't necessary." From time to time Lewis
referred to his bachelor brother's way with the ladies, suggesting
that it was an asset that should not be scoffed at. These first
weeks gave the Walkers a sense that the eventual triumph of their
campaign was assured by the combination of a valuable novelty
and their increasingly assured presentation of it.[26]

For all that, the going was increasingly frustrating. Although
the men and women of the garment industry might be willing to
hear them out and even to experiment on their own products,
they were not ready to commit themselves in the way that the
Hookless people wanted. The reasons for their hesitation were
not difficult to discern, although there were some hurdles that
the brothers must have found particularly irritating. One that
showed itself quickly was the Plako. The old fastener, the pride
of the Automatic Hook and Eye Company and still the product
that Colonel Walker expected Willie Wear to hawk by the gross,
was known in the garment business, and its reputation was not
good. In the early stages of the New York campaign, Lewis, Jr.,
wrote several times to complain of their association with the old
product. He quickly stopped using the stationery of the Hookless Fastener Company that he had brought with him from Meadville, pointing out to his father that the stationery's boast of
Hookless as "Sole Manufacturers of the Plako Garment Fastener" was "nothing to be proud of." Other letters reported how
annoying it was to run into the Plako. On the initial interview
with a theatrical costumer, Lewis reported, "She had seen the
old fastener and we had trouble getting her interested." A month

later, at an uptown women's clothier, he noted, "As usual ran into the Plako here—it's getting to be a regular nuisance and nightmare." Several weeks later, visiting a large cloak and suit maker on East Twenty-sixth Street, he reported again: "Right away I ran into the fact that they had tried the old Fastener and were thoroughly disgusted with the idea of anything that was like it." Lewis finally felt compelled to order from Meadville several dozen Plakos, to be carried around to compare with the Hookless, "so that it could be proven to some doubting Thomases that this is not the same as they had seen before." This experience certainly justified Walker and Sundback's belief that the Hookless should be treated in a very different fashion from their old product.[27]

There were more fundamental problems, however, than distancing themselves from the Plako. Time after time Lewis, Jr., or Wallace would get the ear of a manufacturer or buyer, would cajole him into making some skirts or trousers with the fastener, and then find that they were no longer welcome. A typical experience was that with the skirt makers L. Shidlowsky & Company, on West Twenty-first Street. Both Lewis and Wallace visited during February. On February 2 they gave the firm's designer a dozen fasteners, for a "fair trial." On the fourth Wallace discovered that the firm was showing off the fastener to visiting buyers, "3 or 4 of whom have asked for F. in personal skirts." The next day Lewis gave away still more samples. But then, on February 8, their primary contact at the company, a Mr. Sheldon, worried because the fastener had caused problems in the shop, came by to talk to the brothers. The designer claimed that it could not be put into tightly sewn plackets economically and further declared that the union men were split evenly about accepting the fastener. The next day Sheldon reported that two customers who had had experience with the Plako objected to the new fastener. Finally, on February 17, Wallace reported that Sheldon was not able to sustain the company's interest in the fastener and that its experiments had been very minor and insignificant. To cap it off, "his father objected to it because Sheldon spent too much time discussing [the fastener] with customers." There was no further contact with the company. This was a depressingly familiar story; initial interest, even enthusiasm, from an individual won over by the brothers' charm and faith in their product and, perhaps, by the intrinsic cleverness of the device, followed by a few days or weeks of experimentation, only to result in resistance from more practical sorts and a final collapse of interest. The careful records the Colonel kept of the boys' work showed that they had visits with forty-five firms or individuals in New York during February, many of them several times. The March list showed fifty-eight New York firms and individuals, as well as others that month in Boston, Chicago, Philadelphia, and Trenton, New Jersey. While some of these were worth pursuing in the coming months, most were fruitless.[28]

Whatever other problems the Walkers might encounter, whether the shadow of the Plako or the resistance of designers or shop workers to dealing with a newfangled device that simply complicated their lives or simply the indifference of some to innovation, the central problem was one they recognized early: price. After they had been in New York barely more than a month, Lewis wrote to his father to try to explain to him the full dimensions of this difficulty. The Colonel had set a price of twenty-five cents for the fastener, and the boys were quick to tell him that this was sure to sink their chances of success. Hooks and eyes—the primary competition in dress plackets—cost a garment maker five to seven cents, including the cost of application. "We go to a manufacturer," Lewis complained to his father at the end of January, and "he likes the fastener but there isn't one single reason for him to use it for his own benefit except on a few model skirts. . . . He has to fight his designer & his whole workshop is upset without him having a single way to benefit any person but *us*." The same problem beset them in the stores: "[H]ere again we upset the whole routine of the establishment without giving anything in return—except Fasteners which are to all the workers only more trouble for them." In an almost plaintive tone Lewis emphasized: "We are asking for something all the time & giving nothing. I'm not listening to the Jews alone but Miss Walls, Miss McK., Miss Carroll & other *white* people too numerous to mention and they are unanimous in their opinion that the price will knock out its introduction. . . ." While these observations came early in their campaign, they summed up the situation that was to confront the Walkers all the years they were in New York.[29]

For the next week or so the letters back and forth between

the brothers in New York and their father in Meadville hashed out the price situation. The Colonel stressed that even with Sundback's machines working at their best, the cost to make each fastener worked out to about fifteen cents. The initial pricing of the fastener at twenty-five cents thus seemed a reasonable one, especially considering the work involved in the initial sales effort. Nonetheless, he was persuaded by his sons' arguments to allow them, when they thought advantageous, to offer an introductory price for the article at cost. It simply had to be recognized that manufacturers who were willing to make some kind of commitment to the novelty had to be rewarded with the best possible conditions for its introduction. One thing that Walker was not willing to grant, however, was an exclusive contract to any manufacturer or seller. He thought it was imperative that his company retain control over the distribution of its product; if an exclusive contract were given to someone for a particular application, this would leave the company at the mercy of the contractor for the fastener's fate in that direction. While the brothers accepted their father's reasoning here, they pointed out that this restriction handicapped them in many negotiations since most manufacturers willing to gamble on the new device, and the premium price it commanded, wanted some assurance that their gamble would not simply open the door for their competitors to take a market they had struggled to develop. The best that Hookless was willing to do for them was to assure any pioneers that the company would guarantee them the best price and the first supply.[30]

The campaign with the manufacturers and the department stores dragged on for many months. The initial optimism that the Walker brothers had brought to their work faded, although their faith in the hookless fastener remained unshaken. The Colonel kept his hand on affairs, discouraging his sons' suggestions that he come to New York or that they or one of their contacts would benefit from a retreat to Meadville. The problems that they identified in the first weeks in New York—trouble with applying the fastener, resistance from designers and workers, skepticism about its real usefulness or salability, and, above all, concern about the price of the item—remained resistant to simple solution. Only gradually, however, did they come to realize that these problems were, to a degree, intractable, that they were

faced with something more than just the initial resistance that
any novelty could expect to meet.

The hardiness of their optimism and of their faith that the
garment market would crack if only the right force were applied
at the right point is illustrated by an episode in the summer of
1915. In mid-July, Wallace encountered Charles M. Goldberg,
a supremely self-confident hustler who claimed to know the
garment industry inside out. "He was greatly attracted to the
Fastener," Lewis wrote home, "and said that he could undoubtedly sell the output of our factory in a comparatively short time.
Of course, we have heard all this before," but the boys were
apparently still susceptible to the charms and promises of a fast-
talking saleman promising to lead them out of the wilderness.
That Goldberg claimed to be a top-notch clothing designer himself and thus able to convince other designers, the most difficult
audience they had to face, made his self-promotion hard to resist.
For his part, if we are to believe Lewis's first report, Goldberg
was completely won over by the hookless fastener: "He says as
far as he is concerned, if we only get one of the good manufacturers handling the Fastener correctly and putting it on properly,
that the others will absolutely have to go into using it." He
promised that he could "swing in line" a couple of the major
garment makers right away, and the boys were obviously captivated. Lewis tried to strike a more level-headed poise in his
report to the Colonel—"If he only does 1/20th of what he says
he can, I will be more than satisfied"—but Goldberg's optimism
was a heady tonic for the frustrated salesmen.[31]

Over the next several weeks Lewis wrote home to tell of
Goldberg's activities. While the Colonel's responses were typically cool and cautious, the hustler's bravado, both about the
fastener and about his own capabilities, was hard for the sons to
resist. "I had another very interesting session with Mr. Goldberg
this morning. He has been out seeing some people and seems to
be very much worried for fear we cannot turn out enough Fasteners to take care of his orders he has in sight. I told him we turned
out 1000 a day at the present time, but he said that would not
amount to anything when he got started." Goldberg's thirty-
four years of experience in the garment district did indeed give
him the capability of opening doors that the brothers had found

120 closed. Even more important, the man's experience at the design
table and the workbench allowed him to argue the case for his
• product in ways that had been impossible for the Walkers. For
z example, upon visiting one of the largest manufacturing houses
in New York, Goldberg tried to persuade it that the price diffi-
I culty was in fact nonexistent, that the manufacturer would save
money—15 to 25 percent of its costs—by using the fastener.
P Lewis, Jr., was startled at this claim: "I asked him how this
P could be, and he explained that in a great many cases the Mail
Order Houses have to allow considerable for damage done to
E Skirts & suits that have been torn by a Hook and Eye, or Snap,
when a woman tries it on after getting it home; she may even
R wear it several days and then put in the claim, and they either
have to allow it or she sends back the garment, or refuses to pay
for it." Goldberg made the argument that the hookless fastener
would be much more unlikely to be damaged or to cause problems. The manufacturers listened.[32]

In the face of his father's continuing skepticism and caution,
Lewis continued for several weeks with tales of Goldberg's ability to get into the shops, of his mastery of everyone from owner
and designer down to the union people on the shop floor, of his
continuing optimism about getting one big manufacturer to go
along and the inevitability of others following. The Colonel's
position was that Goldberg simply couldn't be that important,
that he "fails to appreciate the fact that the working quality and
intrinsic value of the Hookless Fastener itself are the influential
factors that will secure its use by the New York manufacturers."
In part, the elder Walker's attitude was born of his own stubborn
optimism: ". . . whether Mr. Goldberg ever sells any Fasteners
for this company or not, it is just a question of time and labor
until the manufacturers of New York use the Fastener." After a
couple of weeks' work, Goldberg's optimism was hardly damp-
ened. He himself wrote the Colonel to warn him that the factory
needed to get ready to fill a flood of orders. A week later Lewis,
Jr., remained impressed by Goldberg's circle of acquaintances—
"he certainly seems to know about one-half the Jew population
of this town"—but he had to report some problems. Goldberg
began to ask for payment despite his initial claims that he would
expect nothing until sales came in. Lewis and Wallace consented
to "lend" him twenty dollars a week, for they valued him too

much to turn him down completely, but they did remind him of the clear terms of his commission agreement (he asked for, and got, one-quarter cent per inch on his sales). Lewis explained to his father: "[H]e is working well even if growling about the money. He is a typical Jew and I am delighted he is, for that's what we need."[33]

Disillusionment began to set in toward the end of August. On the twenty-third Lewis reported back home that Goldberg was insisting that the price of the fastener was simply too high, that ten cents for a twelve-inch fastener would make it possible for manufacturers to take it seriously. Once the manufacturers had committed themselves to the device, the Hookless people could then put the price back up to a profitable level. The brothers were quick to point out to Goldberg that this was a very different tune from the one he had played only a month before. While they were willing to consider discounting the fastener for its introduction, they deferred to their father, who always opposed such an approach. The arguments with the insider got more heated as the month wore on, as the brothers began to see that even with all his advantages and skills, Goldberg was being stopped by the same things that had stood in their way ever since arriving in New York eight months before.

On August 28 Lewis's letter, written with some emotion, attempted to sum up the frustration of their position. He pleaded with his father to put himself into the manufacturer's position to understand the central difficulties of adopting a novelty: "From your point of view—ours I should say—it's all right; from the manufacturer's—it's not. He don't care a rap about how good it is or how much it benefits his garments if it increases his cost one penny or causes him any trouble with his contractor or employees—and as it is *it does both*. It makes no difference if he is getting one or ten thousand fastenings where before he only had three or four. That don't [*sic*] interest him one second." Likewise, buyers were naturally resistant to anything that increased the cost of their product: "It would show in their net profits and every dep't is checked very carefully. Another thing—why should they fuss and argue with a manufacturer and pay more too—to help us sell our fastener. What if it is good— they've sold garments with hooks & eyes & snaps and believe they will continue to do so."[34]

These were truths, it was now clear to the brothers, that would remain, whatever magic they might seek from a man like Goldberg, or an influential buyer like Wanamaker's Miss Walls, or any of the dozens or hundreds of men and women they had met, and in many cases impressed, in their stay in New York. A novelty's way in the world is not made through cleverness or reliability or function. It is made through a combination of all these things, as well as through the discovery of distinctive applications or uses that will allow it to establish itself independently of the customs and competition of the workaday world. In other words, as the Walkers and Sundback and all their colleagues were to learn in the coming years, their novelty would make its way not by direct confrontation with the garment makers and designers and buyers but by seeking out small but distinctive applications that would slowly and steadily carve out a niche all its own.

C

H

A

P

T

E

R

Zip

5

The campaign to introduce the hookless fastener into the everyday clothing of men and women went on for the better part of twenty years before its original goals were met. It was not until the decade of the 1930s was about half over that the garment makers, in New York and elsewhere, regarded the fastener as an ordinary and generally accepted feature of adult clothing. By that time, however, the zipper was a well-known device, used by millions throughout the industrialized world. Its uses, though, were not necessarily those anticipated or initially promoted by its makers. Instead the zipper insinuated itself into daily life by more indirect means. In first one product, and then another, the device carved out a niche as a handy and dependable mechanism, one that could occasionally convert a humdrum thing like a tobacco pouch or an overshoe into a paragon of modernity.

That the act of invention is a creative one is almost a tautology, although our culture is surprisingly resistant to the notion that the creativity that goes into making a new technology is **123** every bit as much an expression of the human imagination as that put into a painting or a symphony. What is even less well understood is that technological creativity does not cease with the production of the artifact. Making a place for the artifact is likewise a challenge to the imagination—sometimes an even more daunting one. The difficulty in appreciating this creativity has a number of roots that are worth reflecting on. One problem lies in the fact that even more than modern invention, the successful introduction and integration of a new technology into society are not the work of an individual or even a small group of men and women. This is not simply "marketing," the work of salespeople and product developers (although they are certainly important). This is, rather, the product of the ideas and efforts and hunches of everyone who comes in contact with a novelty and proceeds to try it out, show it off, tinker with it, accept it, comment on it, or otherwise consider where it fits into his or her world. This is a sort of collective creativity that is something that modern industrial and consumer societies do all the time but that is hardly recognized for what it is: the means by which we constantly reshape the world around us. Another reason we fail to recognize the creative effort that goes into the acceptance of a novelty is that the very fact of success obscures the act. Once a novelty has been accepted and ceases to be a novelty, it tends to become a necessity, and the idea that finding a place for it was a creative challenge seems nonsensical, a foolish questioning of the order of things. To be sure, we know that historically we once did without, but we also readily assume that the lack was readily perceived once the new technology became available and that filling it was simply the working out of a sequence of events determined by technological needs and opportunities, played out against the background of the economic and social order. One of the great values of the story of the zipper is that it makes it apparent that such a deterministic view of our material world simply makes no sense.

Productive creativity requires not only imagination and skill but also faith. The creators need to believe in their capacity for making something new and valuable, and typically their success depends on others' sharing that belief. This was certainly true for the Hookless Fastener Company in the years before it became a profitable enterprise. At the center of the religion that sustained the fastener was, of course, Lewis Walker. The Colonel turned sixty in June 1915, although the letters between him and his sons in New York made no mention of this birthday. The Hookless Fastener Company was not his sole preoccupation at this point in his life. The lure of gadgetry ran strong in Walker, and he was involved in the Russ Automatic Labeling Company, which was trying to promote a machine for rapidly applying the labels to canned and packaged foods. His legal work continued as well, and even the Delamater farms in North Dakota were still cause for long train rides west. He enjoyed vigorous health and was clearly pleased with his own little universe. On one side of his comfortable house on Grove Street was the house of his eighty-year-old mother, and on the other side dwelled his ninety-six-year-old mother-in-law. Nonetheless, the fastener was the center around which his world and ambitions revolved. His dedication of his sons to the task of promoting it was the strongest token of that fact. It is hard to say how the Colonel regarded the young men whom he repeatedly referred to in his letters to others as "the boys," but his personality had room for a deep, if reserved, fatherly affection. Still, the letters between Walker and his sons, revealing as they are of the enterprise in which they were joined, are striking for the consistency with which they put aside personal concerns. Typically the Colonel would end a note to Lewis, Jr., by reporting that his wife and young son were getting along fine. "Martha and the boy are well," he would say, sometimes adding a small detail here and there. But more often than not, when either Lewis, Jr., or Wallace suggested that one or both of them visit Meadville, their father discouraged such a break from the New York campaign. The Colonel's dedication to the fastener bound not only him but those around him to its advancement.[1]

The most important of the apostles of the Hookless religion was Theodore Lamb, the relative of the Delamaters who practiced law in Erie. For the first several years of the company's existence Lamb mailed checks on a regular basis to the offices of Hookless, purchasing a few hundred or even a few thousand dollars' worth of stock at a time. He was one of the original directors of the Meadville company, and his interest extended beyond putting money in the business. He peppered the Colonel with ideas about possible applications and marketing opportunities, and he received in return reports about the progress of the manufacturing and selling efforts. The visits of "Cousin Theodore" to Meadville were frequent, both to see members of the family and to keep an eye on company business. Sundback recalled later that Lamb's participation made his influence on Hookless affairs second only to the Colonel's. In fact, Sundback called him "the power behind the throne" since his steady stock purchases gave Lamb financial control of Hookless. The continuing flow of Lamb's checks was probably the primary thing that kept the company afloat in those first years since sales were clearly too meager to have supported not only Sundback and his shop but also the work of the Walker brothers.[2]

While the Colonel did not promiscuously hawk his company's stock, he was not bashful about approaching friends with the opportunity to join the Hookless enterprise. One other convert from this early period deserves mention both because he was to bring a new name into the company history and because his recruitment reflected Walker's methods. Alice Walker, the Colonel's daughter, made acquaintance with Thomas Franklin Soles (who always went by "T. Franklin") of McKeesport, Pennsylvania, a town just up the Monongahela River from Pittsburgh. Soles's father was a prosperous banker of the town, and the colonel saw him as a prestigious target for his campaign. The elder Soles was not particularly enthusiastic, but his son, beginning practice as a lawyer, was already acquiring the means to make his own contribution. In early 1915, as the fastener sales campaign was getting under way, Colonel Walker gently but steadily prodded "T.F." to take the plunge. He did so in a modest way at first, but at the same time Walker recruited the young lawyer to take on some of the company's legal work, and the challenge of making a success of the curious novelty took hold of him. He was to participate in the company's affairs for the next forty years, eventually becoming chairman of its board of directors. His climb upward was not hurt, one may surmise, by Alice Walker's marriage to his somewhat dashing brother, Louis. The Soles family in the next few years purchased 12 percent of Hookless's stock, and more than half a dozen others in McKeesport also put their money in. The recruiting of Franklin Soles illustrates the low-key but effective approach that

Walker took to assure a solid financial underpinning for what he
came to see would be a long haul.[3]

Until about the end of 1917 the sales campaign for the hookless fastener had little real success. The Walker brothers continued trials in the garment district, but the pattern of approaches
and of responses varied little for many months. They were getting
support from Meadville, where their father did not shy from
keeping a direct hand in things. Like his sons, he discovered that
life was a bit complicated by the legacy of the Plako. Every now
and then inquiries would come into Meadville asking about the
old product of Automatic Hook and Eye. The Colonel would
reply that yes, the Plako was still for sale, but solely through
Wilson Wear. If, however, the correspondent was interested
in "a wonderful fastener, made of the very best material as to
durability and quality that can be manufactured" and that "does
its work perfectly," then the hookless fastener was available,
provided it was intended for an appropriate use. The company's
policy remained firm: It would not sell the Hookless fastener
through sales agencies but only to manufacturers for specified
uses. Walker never wavered in avoiding any taint of Wear's
selling methods on the new product.[4]

Maintaining control over the selling of the Hookless was
not always easy, and the company's insistence on tight control
probably cost it a number of sales opportunities. Having strug
gled for about ten years with the C-curity and the Plako, Walker
was particularly sensitive about getting the Hookless into an
application in which it would look bad. His belief was that
one or two obvious failures, caused by improper installation or
misunderstanding of the fastener's capabilities, would become
widely known and condemn it before it ever had a chance to get
established. When, for example, Frank Lawrence, the company's
Boston contact, reported in mid-1915 that he was successfully
interesting a number of Boston-based rubber companies in
applying the hookless to overshoes, the Colonel advised Lawrence strongly that this was not a direction he favored. "The
present Fastener," he wrote, "was made for garments, as you
fully understand. The shoe application is an entirely different use
and one that subjects the Fastener to an entirely different strain
under conditions not contemplated in the garment use." In the

future, he suggested, a modified fastener could be provided expressly for "the wear and tear demands of shoes—that is, certain kinds of shoes." Walker's caution was probably wise, but we can appreciate the irony of his response to Lawrence's initiative, in light not only of the slide fastener's beginnings on Whitcomb Judson's shoes but also of the crucial role that rubber overshoes were to play in shaping Hookless's fortunes and image only a few years hence.[5]

For his part, Gideon Sundback was eager to accommodate new uses for his invention. While the complex production machinery undoubtedly took most of his time, he made a point of listening to complaints and suggestions brought back from the field and seeing what he could do to the fastener's design in response. Already by the summer of 1915 he had produced a Hookless #3, although it seems to have been of so little significance that it is impossible to find an application that used it (or to discover what the modification was). One striking feature of Sundback's original design was that there were no basic limitations to the length of fastener produced. As a general rule, Lewis, Jr., and Wallace were carrying about with them ten- and twelve-inch lengths, but both longer and shorter ones could be provided with no difficulty. We think nothing today of expecting a well-stocked notions counter to have a wide range of zipper lengths, but it is worth pausing to appreciate the aspects of Sundback's design that made such variations so easy to produce. The "ends" of a zipper are the simplest parts; the stops are just pieces of metal put into place anywhere one wishes to cut the zipper chain. This had not been true with the Plako, which appears to have been sold in only one length (ten inches). Other features of the Hookless fastener were not so easy to vary. The tape width or thickness, for example, might concern the manufacturer, depending on the material of his garment, the design of the opening, or the special needs of anything from shoes to corsets. Altering the cloth tape that was fed into Sundback's automatic machinery, however, could invite trouble and would certainly require careful monitoring, if not, in fact, modifications of the machine. Production was so modest at this point that Sundback was willing to experiment in such matters, but these requirements certainly made the engineer's life unsettled.[6]

A year after the Walkers had gone to New York, they were

still pushing hard in the garment district. While the obstacles
they had encountered from the first—resistance from designers
and workers, the fastener's high price, and the lack of any perceived demand—were still in the way, they were able to point
to almost thirty makers of women's skirts and suits who put the
Hookless fastener in their spring 1916 lines. They insisted that
no one had found fault with the device's performance. They
pointed to a number of occasions on which they attributed garment sales specifically to the presence of the fastener. Nonetheless, the number of fasteners being sold to the garment makers
was still small, typically from one or two gross up to a dozen or
twenty gross. The one area that held out sustained promise was
in sports and athletic clothing. The first firm that gave any regular
orders to Hookless was that of Friend & Shrier, New York manufacturers of sports clothes. They devised a riding skirt that used a
fastener in front and another in back. When the wearer dismounted,
the fasteners were closed to produce an ordinary street skirt, but
when she was riding, the fasteners could be opened for the purpose.
The firm's orders were only for a few gross at a time, and they
ended in 1917. A bit more steady and substantial was the business
provided by another New York sports clothing manufacturer,
Freidenrich & Company (later Freidenrich, Van Cott), which used
the fasteners in trousers for such sports as baseball and football.
From January 1916 the firm put in orders, often for one or two
hundred dollars at a time, every few months, but by early 1919 its
interest, too, seems to have waned.[7]

By 1916 the Walker brothers were becoming anxious to get
at least two or three major manufacturers to move beyond this
experimental stage and commit themselves to widespread applications. New sales strategies were proposed to give garment
makers willing to make such commitments short-term exclusive
privileges, allowing them to buy fasteners below cost. Similarly,
the brothers suggested choosing one store each in ten cities, no
farther south than Washington, D.C., and no farther west than
St. Louis, to focus on the retailing side of the problem. The
selected store would be given an advertising allowance and all
necessary assistance to educate fitters and salespersons in the
applications and virtues of the Hookless fastener. If such a strategy was accepted by Colonel Walker and tried, it didn't work.
The garment industry proved stubbornly resistant.[8]

The most important orders that Hookless Fastener received in this period actually came from a rather surprising source—Australia. In a transaction that was discussed very little in the company correspondence, although it represented the vast proportion (about 80 percent) of company sales from November 1915 to August 1916, H. V. White of Melbourne, Australia, was appointed the exclusive sales representative for the Hookless fastener in Australia and New Zealand. White promptly ordered huge shipments (no less than fifty gross at a time) of fasteners. While the company had considerable problem with the exporters, White's orders came in steadily for several months, generally ranging from fifteen hundred to four thousand dollars per month. This far outran any orders the company received before the early 1920s, with the exception of a couple of special wartime orders. What is mysterious is that the White shipments drew so little discussion in the correspondence of the Walkers or any other of the company's personnel. By early 1917 White seems to have given up his agency, complaining to the Colonel of the difficulties he encountered in selling the high-priced novelty. One suspects that the Walkers always regarded the White orders as a fluke, unlikely to generate the long-term opportunities they were trying to establish. Perhaps White, being in a far-off land, was allowed to sell the fastener by "the agency method," à la Willie Wear; in which case the Colonel would not have a lasting taste for the proposition.[9]

The only other foreign shipment made in these early years, to the Nissei Trading Company, was much smaller but had a much larger meaning for the future. The sale to Japan in mid-1917 was not made without trepidation. Lewis, Jr., spoke to an agent in Wanamaker's export department about the order and reported back that he was told "that the Japs intended, no doubt, to copy this Fastener, as they did everything else." When Lewis suggested that the company's machines would be impossible to copy, the agent said "he had heard that very often before." No other orders were sent to Japan, and perhaps none was received. From the moment that imports of slide fasteners into the United States became legal (with the expiration of Sundback's basic patent in 1934), Japan was the chief source.[10]

For all the frustrations of this period, the brothers were in fact accomplishing something very important. More and more

people were getting to know the Hookless fastener, both within
the garment business and outside it. From their earliest days in
New York, Lewis, Jr., and Wallace had been visited by enterpris-
ing salesmen and hustlers who heard about their product and
wished to see what they could make of it. The Charles Goldberg
who so excited their attention in the summer of 1915 was but
one of many who promised an inside track and a hustling talent
that would take the novelty where they wanted it to go. While
the Walkers soon learned to be wary of such promises, they
always politely explained the fastener to their visitors and encouraged them to find applications for it, provided they adhered to
the rules and restrictions the company set down. For example,
in April 1916, Lewis, Jr., received, on pink stationery in a very
ladylike hand, a letter from one Effie Wright Taylor, of Washington, North Carolina, who wanted the fastener for a use she
refused to disclose. She was, explained her note to Lewis, afraid
of being "left on the doormat" if she prematurely revealed her
great idea for the fastener's application. In the most gentlemanly
way he could, the elder son turned her down. The result of this
policy was rarely substantial sales but instead a slowly expanding
renown. One visitor for several months in 1915–16 was twenty-
four-year-old Jack Nadel, who tried to persuade the Walkers
that he was just the man to sell their fastener to the shoe and
boot trade, provided, of course, that he be given an exclusive
commission for this service. This was against company policy,
but Nadel received enough general encouragement to try some
promotional efforts. On April 16, 1916, the *New York World*
featured a little column, with a picture of the hookless fastener,
headed No More Buttons, Laces or Clasps. Nadel managed
to get this piece in, although the article left off the name of the
company or its product (Nadel explained to Lewis that he had
had appendicitis and thus wasn't able to review the piece before-
hand). The same was true of the item that he persuaded *Popular
Mechanics* to run in its May issue; the word "hookless" was
nowhere to be found, although there was a nice little picture of
a woman fastening her shoes with the device. Given the Walkers'
skittishness about such applications, they may not have been
thoroughly pleased by this exposure. It was, however, just such
increasing notoriety that was to rescue them eventually from
their doldrums.[11]

These doldrums were experienced against a background that was mentioned little in the letters of those first years but that in fact was to be an ever-more-insistent part of the scene. This was the war in Europe. The First World War broke out at just the time Gideon Sundback was getting his machinery running for the Hookless #2. At that time it was for the men working away in Meadville, as it was for most Americans, an event remote both in place and in its relevance to daily life. In New York it was barely more apparent to the young men beating the pavement in the garment district, although its effect on the world of fashion—particularly in the disruption of the system by which Paris designers dictated the modes of women's wear—could be felt by those sensitive to such things. By 1916 the disruption of trade and the competition for strategic commodities among the belligerents could be felt even in Meadville. The price of the largely copper German silver alloy that was essential to Sundback's product was steadily rising, and the supplies were getting less reliable. The costs of making the fastener—already too expensive for most of the markets that Hookless was pursuing—climbed. Sundback struggled to reduce waste and inefficiencies in the production process and experimented with alternative metals with less copper. The war, especially as the threat of direct American involvement loomed larger, seemed to present dire dangers for the fastener.[12]

It was the war, however, that rescued it from obscurity, though the Walkers were slow to see the possibilities. Several months after the United States had entered the conflict in April 1917, Wallace Walker, being subject to the draft (his brother was overage), signed up for officer's training, and 1918 saw him heading an artillery battery in France. Brother Lewis remained in New York, attempting to keep the company's prospects afloat in the midst of confusing business conditions. Most of his efforts were along familiar lines, combining approaches to manufacturers with a campaign in the department stores. The war's influence was not pervasive in either of these environments. In June 1917, for example, Lewis, Jr., surveyed the fastener's applications in Wanamaker's Philadelphia store, and the mention made of "officer's uniforms" and "aviation suits" were the only hints of wartime concerns. Nongarment applications seem to have been getting more attention: A mothproof wardrobe, a slipcover, and sleeping bags got tryouts. Perhaps the greatest enthusiasm, however, was shown for the prospects presented for the fastener's adoption by the NuBone Corset Company of Erie, a project that the elder Walker had pursued. The Colonel's attention, however, was more diverted by the effort to find alternatives to the New York garment makers. After a trip to the Twin Cities, Milwaukee, and Chicago, he wrote to Lewis that he believed "the spirit of the West toward the Fastener would be much more to our advantage than you have found it among the Jews in New York City."[13]

The war, however, was to make the garment industry an even less inviting target for Hookless than it had been. While the controls over the economy that were put in place in 1918 were meager compared with those used in the next world war, they were substantial enough to dampen the enthusiasm of would-be experimenters. The War Industries Board worked hard to diminish what it saw as wasteful competition in many industries, including clothing. Manufacturers of shoes, for example, were forbidden to introduce new styles or produce new lasts. The government waged a vigorous campaign to promote "simplified" clothing for both men and women. This was not an environment in which manufacturer or retailer could be comfortable with introducing a "gadget" for clothes.[14]

Even with his younger son headed toward the front, Walker was hesitant to see the war as a major influence on their efforts. The possible exception appeared to be in the development of aviators' clothing, for which large government contracts could be anticipated. In mid-1917 Walker informed his sons that Frank Russell was head of a government advisory committee for procurement of aviation supplies, and thus "we should go after this thing [aviators' suits] with all the force we can possibly command." A visit to Russell would no doubt be useful, but the Colonel passed on Sundback's advice that "when you get ready to talk to Mr. Russell, invite him out for a cocktail or dinner and be sure he has one or both before you open the subject." The flying suits continued to be an inviting target, with important results.[15]

There were also others who saw the war and its requirement for unconventional clothing and equipment as a business opportunity for which the novel fastener would be a helpful ally. In the early autumn of 1917 there appeared in the increasingly lonely office of Lewis Walker, Jr., on Thirty-second Street an experienced tailor and designer by the name of Robert J. Ewig. Ewig's first idea for the fastener was for a windproof "waistcoat" or vest that would be used by aviators. This proposal, like so many that went before it, was an idea that sounded better than it worked, and it would not be worth mentioning here but for one little feature, which seems to have been overlooked by chroniclers of the slide fastener's lore. Ewig, afraid that his novel design would be stolen by imitators, claimed to Lewis to have "copyrighted . . . it under the name ZIP." More than two and a half years earlier, soon after arriving in New York, the brothers had suggested to their father that they needed a catchier name for their product. One of the manufacturers they approached, Lewis, Jr., reported, told them that "the name Hookless Fastener is very poor—says the hookless means nothing & will not be remembered. Says that the Walker Fastener, Jones Fastener, Brown or another special name would be better. Just like Watermans pens, Pears soap & etc. I agree with him here—do more every day." Their father's reply had been unequivocal: "The question of the name of the Fastener is not important. When you think of a man by the name of Carnegie or Rockefeller winning millions under such a name, I think we take our chances with the Hookless Fastener Company. What's in a name anyhow? The name Hookless will stick and attract people's attention when you come to advertise. Anyway it is too late to tackle that question now; the ship is launched and her name is 'Hookless.' " The Colonel was never to be comfortable with "zipper."[16]

Ewig's contribution turned out to be a bit more substantial than a little-noticed hint at a catchy name. Another idea that he mentioned to Lewis, Jr., as he pushed ahead on his vest was for a money belt. Such an item, in which the fastener would be applied to a pocket suspended on the inside of a trousers belt, was to be aimed at soldiers and, especially, sailors (whose uniforms had no pockets). It took some time for Ewig to produce the item, but by the end of 1917, Lewis, Jr., was getting excited by it. On December 15 he wrote his father, "I am really afraid to say much about prospects of using our Fastener in Money-Belts, the reason being that so far I am unable to find any objections to it, and a great deal in favor of it." A few weeks later

Ewig produced the belts. Quickly some of the major New York stores took it up and, for a change, sold the belts as fast as they stocked them. It was a product that could be carried in an extremely wide range of outlets; from Abercrombie & Fitch to Liggett's drugstores, and its novelty value and functional virtues overcame price resistance with ease. Ewig found his Brooklyn shop (originally just a room at home) as busy as he could make it. Orders for the fastener came into Meadville at an accelerating rate—a gross every day during March, even more in April, reaching a peak in midsummer. Ewig's orders during 1918 totaled more than seventy-seven hundred dollars; he was Hookless's first major steady customer, and it was estimated that he sold a total of twenty-four thousand belts before his business petered out in the months after the armistice of November 1918. While his orders were much appreciated by the people in Meadville, Ewig's greatest service to them may have simply been putting the novel device on the waists of twenty-four thousand men who had never seen it before.[17]

Money belts were not the only means by which Americans were introduced to the new gadget during the war. With the intensification of American involvement in late 1917, military-related applications became increasingly inviting targets. Sundback produced a Hookless #4 in this period, primarily as a sturdier version of the #2. This, along with the capacity for making the fastener in longer lengths, equipped the Walkers with a device that had some appeal to the makers of such items as sleeping bags, aviators' suits, overalls, garment bags, and the like. The confidence with which they began to offer the longer lengths was the result not only of the ease with which Sundback could get the chain machines to produce desired lengths but also of increasing reliability of production. Like any "chain," the hookless fastener was only as good as its weakest link, and the more units in each fastener, the greater the likelihood that one would be imperfect, thus making the entire device junk. With several years of manufacturing behind him, however, Sundback could control the quality of his output to a degree that made fasteners as long as seventy inches (for sleeping bags) a reliable product. Another innovation that aided expanding application was what Sundback called "the one-handed slider," which was a more strongly constructed slider that allowed easier use, especially for opening the fastener. At first the hookless fastener had been opened just like the Plako before it: The user gripped the top of the garment (or whatever) and pulled the fastener apart by a tearing action. The sturdier slider allowed it to be used for opening as well as closing, introducing the one-handed zipper action that is such a fundamental part of our image of the device.[18]

The more convenient, sturdier device was particularly attractive to entrepreneurs seeking some way of making their wares sufficiently distinctive to catch the eye of the procurement offices in Washington that were seen as the real engineers of the wartime marketplace. While creating a product such as Ewig's money belt that would appeal to the soldiers and sailors going off to war was a good business proposition, those who seriously wanted to take advantage of circumstances aimed their pitch directly to the War and Navy departments. Just one well-placed sale there would make a wartime fortune. As mentioned before, some designers of aviators' suits were attracted to the fastener. The cockpit of a World War I airplane was a cold and drafty place, to put it mildly. Clothing that would protect the flier from the wind was important, and much ingenuity went into providing options that would appeal to the rapidly expanding air wings of both the army and the navy. Perhaps the most radical approach was that proposed by Boston's Simplex Electric Heating Company, which designed a suit in which electrical wires acted like those of a modern electric blanket, keeping the aviator warm as long as the current was on. The hookless fastener would provide a wind-proof closure for this garment much more simply than buttons. As the company proceeded with making prototypes, it was instructed by the Navy Department to provide them with the Hookless fastener. When, in mid-1918, the largely leather suit was put to the test, it apparently failed utterly to hold up under the physical abuse that the procurement officers subjected it to. It was reported, however, that the fastener had come through unscathed. This simply reinforced the opinion that someone in the Navy Department had that the Meadville company's device was worth keeping in mind.[19]

This opinion was no doubt behind an unusual entry in the Hookless Fastener Company's account book in June 1918. There, in a book that, except for H. V. White's Australian orders, had never seen an order for the fastener larger than Robert Ewig's $931.51 to supply his money belt operation in May, appeared an order for $3,550.05 in the name of the Everfloat Life Preserver Company. Lewis Walker, Jr., had worked patiently with the company's promoter, one Charles M. Waite, for several months to make certain the #4 fastener could be successfully applied to the new preserver and could withstand the tests the government demanded before giving its initial order for ten thousand. In July another fastener order came in for $2,084.95 from Everfloat, although no new government orders were forthcoming. Everfloat was not heard from after that summer, although Waite himself continued to find applications in the coming years. With this experience, the men in Meadville learned the fickleness of government procurement.[20]

Of much greater significance for Hookless's long-term prospects were the small companies that, by mid-1918, were beginning to provide a steady, if unspectacular, customer base. The NuBone Corset Company kept up a small stream of orders, as did a couple of raincoat manufacturers. Washington, D.C.'s Closgard Wardrobe Company found the fastener perfect for keeping its product closed to moths, and it used a weekly average of two hundred thirty-six-inch fasteners for years. The sole result of the Colonel's efforts to stimulate western sales was the business of Guiterman Brothers, of St. Paul, Minnesota, which pioneered in applying the fastener to one-piece overalls ("Unionalls" they were called). By 1920 they were using more than ten thousand twenty-six-inch fasteners a year. Several sporting goods companies began to carry the hookless on a number of articles. The Freidenrich, Van Cott Company used a modest number (a few thousand) every year for its athletic trousers and even tried them on swimming trunks. The Brockton, Massachusetts, firm of Stall & Dean made many of the same articles and felt compelled to compete with Freidenrich, Van Cott by offering the hookless. This was exactly the kind of competitive response that the Walkers had been looking for but actually had few instances of. Another sports-related application that opened up new realms was devised by the Jiffy Lock Company of New York, where Charles Waite, who had so successfully (but briefly) promoted life preservers, advanced the fastener's use in tennis racket covers and bathing suit bags. These were arguably the first sustained use in any kind of luggage, making use of the sturdier #4 model. The Meadville producers took note of the potential in this direction.[21]

In the foothills of New York's Adirondack Mountains, where the hills begin to give way to the broad valley of the Mohawk, sits the town of Gloversville. It was here that Sir William Johnson, in 1760, persuaded a group of glove makers from Perth, Scotland, to come and establish their trade, thus enhancing the value of the vast properties that Sir William had obtained from the Mohawk Indians. The deerskins that were the principal trade goods of the natives and trappers, the pure water from the creeks feeding into the Sacandaga River, plus the plentiful forests of the nearby hills, made the settlement first known as Stump Town a perfect place for leatherworking. In the course of the nineteenth century the glovers' materials diversified as deer became increasingly scarce, but their techniques remained dependent upon skilled handwork. The opening of the Erie Canal, running through nearby towns like Fonda and Amsterdam, gave Gloversville ready access to New York City and national markets, and the village, along with neighboring towns in Fulton County, established itself firmly as the glove-making center of the United States.[22]

Although the industry resisted mechanization, glovers were willing to experiment. Glove making was a craft-oriented activity that did not readily lend itself to consolidated factories, and the great number of independent shops—there were more than 125 in Gloversville in 1925—increased the incentive for the glovers to try new techniques. A variety of methods were devised to split leathers to avoid waste. At the end of the nineteenth century gloves and mittens knitted from wool joined the output of the Gloversville shops, and cotton was added to the list in 1916. Fastenings, too, were the subject of trials; the first snaps were originally devised in France to replace the awkward buttons on gloves. The glovers were also not slow to take advantage of new styles and new needs. As early as 1909 the *Glovers Review* remarked that "The 'Motor' seems to affect everything!" and went on to talk about the thousands of pairs of gloves, many in new colors and styles, being sold to both men and women solely for automobiling.[23]

The Locktite tobacco pouch was the first stable source of demand for the slide fastener. It used the fastener's novelty effectively to carve out a modest but secure market. Its Gloversville, New York, manufacturers took 70 percent of the Hookless Fastener output for several years.

TALON, INC.

It was in this atmosphere of innovation that the Gloversville Auto-Glove Company became, sometime in 1917, a steady, if modest, customer for the hookless fastener. It had not been a simple matter to apply the fastener to its product. The company's first query to Meadville was made in January, and Wallace visited the town only a couple of weeks later, reporting back that the company's proposed use "is not such a bad one." Still, considerable experimentation was required, especially since, as the Colonel himself pointed out, a glove required the smallest, lightest fastener they could produce, and in rather short lengths. The Gloversville firm of Wells-Lamont, for example, also began applying the fastener to gloves, providing the kind of competition that the Walkers were so eager to see. But much more important to the fortunes of Hookless, and the reason that Gloversville plays a special role in this story, were the responses of several others of the town's shops. In a 1920 summary of users of the hookless fastener it was reported that the Wagman Manufacturing Company and the Van Dreissche Company, both of Gloversville, were experimenting with using the fastener in handbags. This was an exciting proposition for the Meadville salesmen, although they hesitated to predict long-lasting success.[24]

The primary reason for excitement was the experience of yet another Gloversville firm, the F. S. Mills Company. As early as February 1918 the company was experimenting with a new product, a tobacco pouch equipped with the fastener. It was not until early 1919, however, that Mills gave Hookless an order, and for several months it looked like a modest, albeit still-appreciated, addition to the company's order books. By that fall, however, things had begun to pick up, and with ever-steadier sales it began to be apparent that this was a major break for the hookless fastener. By mid-1920 the orders for fasteners to be used on Locktite tobacco pouches and cigarette cases were averaging 25 gross *per week* (which works out to 187,200 a year), and the Mills people reported the belief that they had "hardly scratched the surface of the market." With every pouch was enclosed an insert promising the purchaser. "Opens and closes by simply pulling tip across the top. Once closed, no tobacco can leak out in your pocket. No buttons or strings to fasten." In addition, the insert boldly announced at the bottom, "*Locks Mfg. by* HOOKLESS FASTENER CO., Meadville Penna." So distinctive was the pouch with its hookless fastener that the Mills Company received a patent on it soon after it introduced it (U.S.P. 1,322,650). The Locktite pouch was precisely what was needed—an application of the fastener that clearly bested its competitors in terms of neatness and convenience, so much so that it could easily bear a premium price.[25]

The fastener makers were the beneficiaries of a significant shift in styles, predating the war but no doubt hastened by the new informality in dress and manners that the conflict promoted. Gloves, which through much of the nineteenth century had been as much a standard part of the code for polite dress for both men and women as, say, hats, were rapidly diminishing in importance. The Auto-Glove Company represented an important trend, especially in men's gloves, toward "utilitarian" gloves, specialized for particular occasions or uses, such as playing golf or riding or doing rough work. Only the most formal occasions insisted on dress gloves, and even these were often displayed (rakishly in a pocket, in the style of the Prince of Wales) rather than worn. This trend was less pronounced in women's wear, and indeed was reversed to a degree in the coming decades, but even here the industry could see that its heyday, when actress Lillian Russell had been famous for hundreds of pairs of gloves, many of them shoulder-length, had passed. Small wonder, then, that Gloversville shops should be looking for alternative outlets for the leatherworkers, especially products that would be distinctive in their own right.[26]

This fitted very well with the needs of the hookless fastener makers, who survived, and then flourished, in the next decade by providing a product so different and curious that it retained its air of novelty far longer than a more ordinary invention. In the coming years, therefore, the Meadville manufacturers would time and again find their destiny in the hands of men and women who saw their invention as a way of setting some mundane product—a tobacco pouch, a garment bag, a pair of overshoes—apart from its rivals. This was to keep a premium on the fastener's novelty, even after it had been on the market for twenty years (almost forty if one recognizes its beginnings in Judson's "clasp lockers"). The slide fastener was stuck in the future and both benefitted and paid dearly for this. The benefits became clear through the 1920s, as a series of applications came, and frequently went, by adopting the slide fastener as an easy route to the cutting edge of fad or fashion or simply as a way to make a product seem more up-to-date. The costs were perhaps not so obvious at the time, although the continued failure to break into the mainstream of clothing, even as prices were reduced, was surely cause for reflection by the Hookless Fastener men. An additional result was to attach a label to the fastener that would brand it as a symbol of the modern and the artificial, even as it began to work its way into common life. This label was to remain attached to the zipper and sometimes imbue it with a cultural meaning that its inventors and promoters could never have foreseen.

The ability of the Hookless Fastener Company to exploit the possibilities of novelty was always dependent upon its technical capacities. New applications, it came to be expected, would put new demands on the fastener, which would require that Sundback and his shop modify designs accordingly. And new orders placed a strain on the production facilities of the Meadville factory and on the economies that the engineer was constantly trying to effect. After the armistice postwar economic pressures, especially the inflation in both material and labor costs, continued to provide extra incentives for Sundback to improve fabrication technology. In 1919, after considerable experimenting, he created a novel means of making his fastener that was to halve production costs in less than a year and set the standard of fastener manufacture for decades to come. As recently as the fall of 1918 Sundback had seemed firmly committed to the machinery he had devised in 1914 and filed patents for in 1916. But the continued climb in metal costs made the wastefulness of a mecha-

Gideon Sundback's "S-L" or
"scrapless" machine for
manufacturing the zipper was a
remarkable and ingenious
mechanism for making a device in
which the careful fitting of small
pieces was crucial to successful
working. This early S-L machine
was photographed in the early
1920s.   *TALON, INC.*

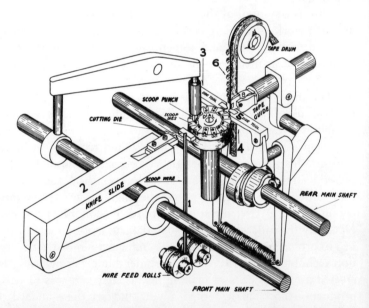

This schematic shows how Sundback's machine took special Y-shaped wire (I)
and cut the scoops from it (by the knife slide [2]), punched the scoop dimple and
nib (3), and clamped each scoop on the cloth tape (4) to produce continuous
zipper chain (6).   *TALON, INC.*

nism that made scrap of as much as half of the metal fed into it particularly irksome. Sundback's solution was a machine he called S-L, for "scrapless."[27]

The S-L was a brilliant design, which was modified but not fundamentally changed in the coming years. The key was the use of preformed wire rather than flat metal tape or sheet as the feed into the machine. This wire, generally nickel silver, was rolled into a Y section. As this was fed into the machine, a knife ("cutoff punch") cut a slice of Y and forced it into a turntable ("heading die"). This moved the slice under a punch ("pocket punch") that produced the nib and socket of the scoop in the leg of the Y. As the turntable moved again, the two arms of the Y were placed opposite the beaded edge of cloth tape. Another mechanism (the "clincher") then clamped the Y's arms onto the tape, which advanced an appropriate distance, and the scoop was in position. The machine was set to make what was called gap chain, meaning that a specified number of scoops was applied continuously to the tape, and then a length of bare tape allowed through, separating the lengths of individual fasteners (a later approach was to make "continuous chain" and then knock off scoops between desired lengths of fastener). The chain was next washed and sprayed with lubricant. Workers then drew two chains together and put on stops and the slider to produce the finished fastener.[28]

The S-L machine sacrificed some speed for reliability, but Sundback clearly thought the trade-off was worth it. The Hookless Fastener Company's control of the patent and technology of the S-L was to allow it to retain a considerable competitive advantage for some years after Sundback's fundamental fastener patent expired. To avoid the Sundback patents, especially in Europe, ingenious inventors devised alternative mechanisms, with different means of forming scoops, applying them to the tape, and making the final product. But the S-L, and the improved versions to follow, continued to be the basis of the Hookless Fastener Company's technology as long as metal fasteners were its primary product.[29]

The new machine was clearly a delight to the Colonel. Whereas postwar inflation had nearly destroyed the company's prospects for making a profit, Sundback's latest invention, combined with the sales to Gloversville, allowed Walker to paint a rosy picture to shareholders in July 1919. "Pioneer work in the

●

Z

I

P

P

E

R

development and introduction of an invention is always not only very expensive, but extremely hazardous," he declared, and the extra problems caused by the war made the company's task even more difficult. But with the return to more normal economic conditions and with the perfection of Sundback's machinery, he was confident that they could "turn our attention from a development policy to a more strictly manufacturing policy." No dividends were yet forthcoming, however, for more effort was still required to assure "the stability and permanency of the undertaking." This remained the Colonel's message for several more years, as he continued to perceive the establishment of "stability and permanency" as the company's paramount concern.[30]

Further technical development would continue to cost money, but Walker and Sundback were not satisfied with the limits of their product. In 1919 and 1920 Sundback designed two new models of the fastener. The #5 was a smaller size, meant to attract the still-resistant women's clothing market; the #6 was a little larger and sturdier, and Sundback continued development of an even larger size. This work gave would-be users considerably more flexibility in experimenting with novel applications. By mid-1920 the Colonel could report that steady customers were ordering the fastener for use in sports trousers, mattress covers, and tents, in addition to the still-important tobacco pouch, cigarette case, and wardrobe applications.[31]

As the list of steady customers grew, Hookless Fastener shifted its policy regarding "exclusives" and competitors. When the sales campaign in the garment industry began in early 1915, Walker was adamant about resisting his sons' suggestions that manufacturers would be much more ready to commit themselves to the fastener if they could be guaranteed exclusive access to it, at least for a period of time. By about 1919, however, it was clear that such resistance was self-defeating. So a policy was followed of recognizing certain manufacturers as "pioneers" for their particular applications and putting any other potential users on a "waiting list." This would suit everyone, the Colonel declared, as long as the pioneers "increase their volume of business and extend their trade to the extent of our capacity, and in a manner satisfactory to us." Such an approach, which was followed for years to come, allowed the men in Meadville to maintain the control they desired over not just who their customers were but just how they used the fastener. The company correspondence included numerous letters rejecting prospective customers because of this policy. Among the letters in 1921 was a rather poignant one from R. J. Ewig & Company, "Military Tailors, Washington, D.C." "I am very much surprised to note," wrote the man whose money belts had given Hookless its first real business, "that you cannot take on any new customers—I do not consider myself a new customer." The curt reply from Lewis, Jr., was simply to repeat, ". . . we cannot take any new orders at this time."[32]

The truth was that the company's capacity was being strained by the level of business that the postwar economy was beginning to support. In his statement to stockholders in mid-1921 Colonel Walker reported that despite continuing "unsettled conditions" in the economy, sales continued to rise steadily, to the point where the company's ability to meet its orders was at its limit; despite a doubling of capacity, the factory was "at least three months" behind in filling orders. While it was hoped that capacity could be increased in the next year at a rate of about 10 percent per month, this was hampered by the fact that Hookless made a practice of manufacturing all its own machinery. Sundback's control over his technology was complete, and he and the Walkers were reluctant to trust any of it to outsiders. Despite these limitations, Hookless managed to increase its production in 1921 from an average of between three and four thousand dollars per month to ten to eleven thousand dollars per month, both through the improvement of the chain machines and by moving manufacturing to a much larger building on Meadville's Cottage Street. The new factory was in the middle of Meadville's business district and housed both the production facilities and the offices of the company. Sundback's shop, along with the drafting department and the machine shop, took over the entire Race Street building, allowing that operation to function much more freely. Expansion required the training of considerably more workers, but the "soft" labor market made recruitment relatively easy. Walker reported that experienced workers were benefiting from the increased output through higher wages, although newer employees were receiving the lower rates prevailing in the poor economy. Not for the last time the Hookless

Fastener Company found itself expanding in a period of general economic downturn.[33]

The three years after 1920 saw the greatest proportional increase in sales and production in the company's entire history: from 1920's 110,500 fasteners to just over 2 million in 1923, with net sales rising at the same time from $26,470 to $401,549. With one important exception at the end of this period, this growth was sustained not by new applications but by the expansion of those pioneered in the years just after the war. The product line in 1922 consisted of three sizes of fasteners designated as # 4, 5, and 6. The #4 was a heavy-duty device used at this point solely for tent closures and made in relatively small numbers. The #6 was used largely for the overalls made by Guiterman Brothers and for a few other large items; it, too, was made in modest numbers. The #5 was the lightweight fastener that went into tobacco pouches, gloves, and sports clothes and was the sustaining product of the company.

The company's rapid growth was not without its problems, particularly in quality control. The Walkers and Sundback maintained the belief that the reputation of their product was sufficiently precarious to require vigilance in overseeing the quality of both the fastener and its applications. It was thus with some dismay in early 1922 that Lewis, Jr., reported that the #6 fastener was being returned to the factory as defective in growing numbers and that the same problem was beginning to crop up in the output of the much more crucial #5. He urged the formation of an independent inspection department and the clearer separation of the development operations (Sundback's shop) from those involved with day-to-day manufacturing. In these changes, as well as other managerial proposals, the younger Walker was, consciously or unconsciously, attempting to set his small but rapidly expanding company on the paths that were then proving so important for the large technology-driven corporations of the twentieth century.[34]

The sense of urgency that the younger Lewis Walker betrayed in his 1922 report was tempered by optimism about sales. Despite the recent near tripling of capacity to ten thousand or eleven thousand dollars per month, he suggested that were the capacity increased to twenty-five thousand dollars per month, there would be no problem selling the output. In only a few

months, by mid-1922, Sundback and the production force indeed
more than doubled production, and sure enough, sales easily
kept pace. In fact, by the time the Colonel was ready to make
his annual report in mid-1923, orders for the fastener had backed
up six months, and there was no choice but to increase production again, this time with another factory next to the Cottage
Street plant. Lewis, Jr., and Wallace, still in charge of sales,
could continue to be choosy about their customers, although
they took nothing for granted in keeping an eye on the quality
of applications. They also continued to keep their eyes out for
the kind of breakthrough order that would give the fastener
somewhat greater security for future growth than could be
sought in tobacco pouches and coveralls. In the midst of the
general growth of the early twenties, they found it.

The account books for the Hookless Fastener Company registered at the end of April 1921 a routine small order for $5.05
worth of fasteners to be delivered to the offices of the B. F.
Goodrich Rubber Company in Akron, Ohio. This unremarkable
order was followed by several months of silence until July, when
Goodrich made a query about the Meadville company's ability
to fill large new orders and the extent to which it might offer
discounts. This caused the younger Walkers to take notice, and
Lewis, Jr., made the relatively short train trip to Akron to see
what was up. The rubber people were not talking, however, they
simply wanted to know what Hookless could do for them. Since
the Meadville company was not, as we have seen, hurting for
business, it was not in the mood to play games, so it offered no
concessions and no promises. Nothing more was heard from
Akron for several more months.[35]

The mixed signals from Goodrich were, it seems, the result
of corporate indecision. A Goodrich engineer, Frederick H.
Martin, had espied the hookless fastener on a pair of gloves and
quickly had a brainstorm. The novel snug closure seemed a sure
thing for rubber galoshes, and their use could propel his firm
from being a minor player in the field of rubber footwear into
the front rank—if only he could persuade the powers in Akron.
This was not a simple task apparently. It was not made easier by
the fact that, as with so many other applications, this new use
of the fastener posed design and manufacturing challenges that
resisted easy solution. In early 1922 Goodrich again approached

the Meadville manufacturers, now revealing the firm's ideas and seeking not simply assurances about supplies but also assistance in engineering. Negotiations opened up again, and active cooperation between the two companies was applied to the challenge of making what Goodrich salesmen had dubbed the Mystik Boot a viable product. Applying the fastener successfully to rubber boots was not without difficulties. Shoes and boots always posed problems, for they usually put the fastener under a constant sideways strain, while it was also being frequently flexed, that could be particularly hard on the cloth tape of the fastener. In addition, when rubber was applied to the tape, it stiffened it to such a degree that the fastener's flexibility was impaired and the tape itself was weakened. This and other technical problems were confronted and overcome by the two firms, and by the end of 1922 Goodrich was ready to introduce the new boots and prepared the way with an extensive promotional campaign.

The new year was no more than a month old when it became clear that the novelty was a clear success. Only a week after Goodrich's first large monthly order—for $3,588—was put on the Hookless books, Wallace wrote his brother in New York to report on a visit from one of the rubber company's representatives. Goodrich was immensely pleased with the new product's reception and was anxious to secure all rights to the fastener's use in rubber footwear. Since it was a considerable strain on the Meadville producers just to manage the Goodrich orders, without abandoning their other customers (such as the steady friends in Gloversville), there was little danger that other firms would have any chance of getting in on the new fashion. In fact, later that year the Walkers departed from past practice and contracted to give Goodrich, at least for a time, exclusive rights to the fastener. In his report to Lewis, Jr., Wallace reported on another response in Akron to the new boots: "He [the Goodrich representative] stated that the sale of the shoe was certainly proving most satisfactory and that he was positive that same would grow to be considered a staple in the line even though people at the present time might consider it a novelty. He also advised me that they had changed the name of the shoe from the Mystik Boot to the Zipper, said name having been suggested by the president, who, on being presented with a pair of shoes fitted with the Hookless, showed boundless enthusiasm."[36]

B. F. Goodrich president Benjamin G. Work's boundless enthusiasm gave his Meadville suppliers more than a faithful customer. "Zipper" was quickly registered by Goodrich as a trademark for its new boots, but if there was ever a term predestined to be appropriated by the public for its own uses, then "zipper" was it. It is doubtful that the Walkers gave the slightest thought to poor Robert Ewig in Washington, who less than six years before had translated his own boundless enthusiasm for their product into dreams of the Zip vest, only to be diverted to the quick returns for his money belt. No, the term "zipper" probably appeared to them first as a strange quirk of Work's imagination, but one they would certainly go along with if it made their biggest customer happy. Yet not much later the brothers' routine wires to each other, requesting or confirming shipments, occasionally referred to "zips," even though this would never—even decades later—be quite proper for Hookless people to do. It is harder to document the public's more general adoption of the term. After all, for much of the mid-1920s, the most likely place they would encounter zippers would be in Zippers— Goodrich's boots, which managed to take 70 percent of Hookless's output during these years (up to 1927). By the late twenties, however, once the fashion for the boots had waned, the term "zipper" had set itself solidly in the American language. More so, it would seem, than the fastener itself.⁷⁷

"Growin' like the Deuce"

6

It is fitting that the 1920s, the decade of the flapper, the Charleston, and F. Scott Fitzgerald, should have been the decade in which the zipper emerged into the public consciousness. The flamboyant years of speakeasies, Teapot Dome, and Billy Sunday were the years in which Americans first encountered this metal contraption in their overshoes, in their pocketbooks, and, rarely, in a pair of trousers. This was the decade in which the great technologies of the twentieth century became also technologies of the common man and woman. The years after World War I saw electricity transformed from a miracle into a commonplace, the technological underpinning for everyday work and life everywhere except the remote countryside and farm. The automobile truly claimed its place as the vehicle of the twentieth century. The great production revolution of Henry Ford's assembly line was joined by the marketing strategies of Alfred P. Sloan's General Motors, in which different nameplates—Chevrolet, Buick, Cadillac—were carefully groomed for their targeted customers, and all were made rapidly obsolete, at

least to the fashionable and even the merely up-to-date, by annual
model changes. Even more extraordinary technologies, formerly
hardly more than fables to most people, began to appear and
even become common. Airplanes had shown both their possible
deadliness and their potential for revolutionizing ideas of distance
during the First World War, and the first rudimentary forms
of air service emerged in the following decade. The war had
transformed radio, too, from an exotic, complex instrument of
specialists into the means for projecting anything that the mind
might imagine into the ether. Broadcasting began in the new
decade, and the boom in radio was an economic as well as a
technical phenomenon. Almost three-quarters of a century later,
the 1920s still symbolize a time of often breathtaking change and
a willingness to break with the past.

Years that saw great changes not only in technology but in
popular tastes and styles, in modes of dress, in the literature and
music of the American people could only be encouraging to the
entrepreneurs who had discovered themselves so confounded
by the conservatism of dressmakers, tailors, department store
buyers, and their customers. In the 1920s the Hookless Fastener
Company finally encountered prosperity, and by the end of the
decade its founders were on their way to becoming wealthy men.
The production of fasteners grew at a prodigious rate, exceeding
an average annual increase of 87 percent from 1920 to 1929; the
profits of the company grew even faster, more than doubling,
on average, each year of the decade. In 1920, a total of 110,500
fasteners came out of Meadville, fewer, in fact than the number
of Plakos that had been manufactured in 1913 and hardly enough
to make much of an impact on any aspect of American life. Total
Hookless production in 1929, however, exceeded 17 million zippers, still modest by later standards, but enough to make a mark
on at least some small realms of fashion and habit, and the
company reported profits of nearly one million dollars for that
predepression year. As one final measure of the success of their
enterprise, the Meadville manufacturers faced their first direct
competition before the decade was out, and they were forced to
defend both their patents and their markets.[1]

The success of the 1920s, however, had its limits, and in
spite of their obvious progress, it was clear to Sundback and
the Walkers and other observers that their circumstances at the

The term "Zipper" was introduced by B. F. Goodrich with the 1923 debut of its new galoshes, featuring the Hookless fastener. Goodrich took over the bulk of Hookless output for the mid-1920s, but the name for its product, extended to the fastener itself, turned out to have an even more durable impact.   TALON, INC.

decade's end were not ideal. Indeed, occasional rude reminders intruded to signal that the future of their technology was not secure, nor was it fully in their control. The great growth that they experienced in these years was actually based on a narrow and, it turned out, precarious foundation. The string of impressive years of growth, for example, was broken in 1928, when zipper sales declined 31 percent (and profits were off more than 61 percent) from the previous year. The cause for this was greater grounds for concern than the fact, for the drop was seen as due largely to the appearance, for the first time, of direct competitors and, perhaps even more seriously, the fickleness of their market. Mild winter weather and apparent saturation of the single market that was sustaining their prosperity—rubber boots—reduced the demand for fasteners precipitously. This drove home a great truth: The hookless fastener's success was almost solely in the role as adjunct to something else. When Goodrich's Zipper Boots sold, the fastener sold; when they did not, the fastener didn't. It was certainly not unusual, nor is it still, for a novelty to be

dependent upon some other product for its success—driving
gloves will sell widely only as long as open-air touring cars are
common; plastic knee protectors are successful only as long as
skateboards or roller skates are in fashion—but such dependency
is risky business, as the warm winter of 1927–28 revealed to the
zipper makers, and it was not, in any case, suitable for the
ambitions of Colonel Walker and his colleagues. The men who
had charged into New York's garment district with such optimism and drive would hardly be satisfied a decade later simply
as suppliers to the Akron boot makers.[2]

When, on July 1, 1924, Lewis Walker made his annual report
to the board of directors of the Hookless Fastener Company, he
had been engaged in promoting the slide fastener for almost
thirty years. This was not an anniversary that he remarked upon,
as far as we know, but it is certainly worth noting here. Of
course, when the Colonel had joined Whitcomb Judson and
Harry Earle in Chicago to form the Universal Fastener Company, his own role was modest. For almost ten years he saw
himself as little more than an investor, and Judson's fastener was
to him but one of a number of interesting opportunities that
seemed worth a small-town lawyer's dabbling in. For the next
twenty years, however, the fastener had taken ever-greater portions of his time and energy until it had become his life. It was,
more than anything else, a remarkable, inexplicable, faith on the
Colonel's part that had sustained the invention through the
flawed devices of Judson's creation, the difficult manufacturing
in the Hoboken factory, the creative years of Sundback's experiments with designs and machines, and, finally, the frustrations of
markets—possibly huge markets—that simply would not yield.
While this faith is not to be explained as the product of rational
calculations, it was clearly the kind of thinking that is behind
much of the change that takes place in our material world. It was
sustained by a complex mixture of ambition, stubbornness, and
self-delusion. It was also supported by the values of a culture that
approved of material ambitions harnessed to creative enterprise,
even when the products of that enterprise seemed to most people
largely unneeded and even unwanted. The proudly bourgeois,
capitalist society of the nineteenth and twentieth centuries fos-
tered exactly the kind of devotion and effort that Lewis Walker
poured into the fastener. This society did not promise success

for such efforts—that was up to the decision, without appeal, of the market—but such entrepreneurialism was visibly and widely recognized as valuable and honorable work, and for a man like the Colonel, in a place like Meadville, such approbation was sufficient to sustain a life's work.

Walker's 1924 report depicted a company in the throes of expansion, with the difficulties and exhilaration that this entailed. Despite having added considerable new factory space in the last years, the company was working to double its capacity, for the first time building a factory of its own (rather than leasing older structures). The healthy earnings of the company continued to be put back into buildings and machinery, although its first modest dividend had been paid the previous year ($.013 per share). In spite of this rapid growth, Walker reported that after the new factory was in operation, he anticipated still more expansion would be called for. For the time being, "the use of the Hookless Fastener in diversified applications has been curtailed," since it was impossible to increase production any faster. In the longer term, continued innovation would be needed, particularly to improve production techniques and machinery. The new status of their enterprise was also marked by another significant turn of events. "For the first time in the history of this company," Walker informed his shareholders, "we are threatened with competition from a manufacturer with a fastener device that we believe is an infringement of the inventions of the Hookless Fastener Company." Legal action would be pursued if this competition threatened business. Patents or no patents, the Meadville company would no longer have the field to itself.[3]

In the 1920s the story of the zipper finally becomes more than the story of one company (or, to be more precise, one series of companies). Not only did some Americans observe the success of Hookless and Goodrich and wish to emulate it, but the opportunities overseas beckoned to others. As long ago as Harry Earle's visit to London to promote the "Universal Fastener" in the late 1890s it was apparent that such a clever invention ought to be able to earn pounds, francs, marks, and pesos as well as dollars. Peter Aronson's more extended stay in Paris a decade later did in fact introduce the Plako—le Ferme-tout Américain—to a small European audience. At about the same time European

inventors in increasing numbers began to make their contributions. While the 1911 patent of Katharina Kuhn-Moos and Henri
Forster was never brought into production, another Swiss inventor in that year, Denner-Meier, was more successful. In early
1912 the firm of Vorwerk and Son, in Wuppertal-Barmen, placed
on the market its *Universal-Verschluss*, based on Denner-Meier's
patent. Sold with much the same aim as the Plako fastener (primarily for women's skirts), this device seems to have suffered
much the same fate, meeting with some initial curiosity but then
generating either dismay (at its failure at inopportune moments)
or uninterest. World War I disrupted development in Europe,
and the economic disruptions of the postwar years offered further discouragement.[4]

The patents of Gideon Sundback provided the basis for most
European zipper efforts. As compensation from the Hookless
Fastener Company for his inventions over the years, Sundback
retained all non-American rights to his patents, and he lost little
time in trying to exploit them. In late 1917 Sundback asked a
Swedish-American friend, J. T. Bruhn, to make some approaches
for him on a trip to England. Bruhn naturally encountered great
wariness in war-tired Britain and had little success at first. Immediately before returning to the United States, however, he was
called upon by a man he had met on the ship coming over,
one Charles S. Colton. Colton had been intrigued by Bruhn's
description and samples of his product and had made some inquiries at the Admiralty. It is likely, in fact, that the fastener had
already come to the attention of military and naval purchasers.
A London sleeping bag manufacturer, C. Campart, had been
using a few in its products, to apparent approval of military
customers, and a number of the same things being sold to the
American military—flying suits, equipment covers, and the
like—were beginning to make an impression. What Colton heard
at the Admiralty apparently encouraged him to pursue the possibilities of getting Sundback's rights himself, and he opened negotiations with Bruhn. In March 1918 Sundback signed an
agreement with Colton. Before Colton's Ready Fastener Manufacturing Company was under way, however, a more substantial
foundation for European efforts appeared.[5]

Kynoch's Limited was a respected member of the host of
companies that made the name of the city of Birmingham synon-

156

•

Z

I

P

P

E

R

ymous with metalworking. Like its neighbors, it had largely directed its efforts to war matériel since 1914, but by late 1917 Kynoch's managers were looking beyond the war. The company's technical expertise lay in the area of metal stamping, and it had established a good reputation for its production of shells and other important munitions work. This brought it to the attention of the Admiralty, which played a role in bringing Kynoch's and the Sundback interest together. The munitions work also caught the attention of Britain's most important explosives company, Nobel, which included Kynoch's in its acquisition in 1918 of several other companies to form Nobel Industries Ltd., the forerunner of the giant Imperial Chemical Industries combination. The slide fastener had the virtue of having proved at least moderately attractive to military procurement officers; hence it was possible even before the war's end for the firm to get permission to set up production. Colonel Walker was happy to cooperate with Sundback's overseas ventures, since he never aspired to move beyond U.S. markets. Beginning in the late summer of 1918 the Hookless Fastener Company recorded sales to Kynoch's of more than twenty-five thousand dollars, largely in the form of chain machines of Sundback's latest design. In 1919 production on a very modest scale finally began in the Birmingham suburb of Witton. The beginning was slow, but by 1924 Kynoch's Lightning Fastener Company was tasting the same prosperity of its American forebear. One of the Kynoch's managers reported to Colonel Walker that the company was on double shifts, "and even by doing so we are unable to meet the demand for fasteners."[6]

The agreement between Sundback and Kynoch's initially covered all rights to the fastener outside the United States, and the British did not lose much time in attempting to exploit these possibilities. In 1924 they began operations of the Canadian Lightning Fastener Company, in Brownsburg, Quebec, using some of the machinery that had originally been shipped from Meadville to Birmingham. The Canadian company was not, however, to remain long an offshoot of the British. A few months after its start-up Gideon Sundback took possession of it, giving to Kynoch's in return rights to the use of further inventions not included in their original agreement. Sundback also received all the Western Hemisphere rights to his patents (outside the United States, of course), which in succeeding years he proceeded to exploit with some success. In the spring of 1925 Sundback became president of the Lightning Fastener Company and quickly moved to give it his own stamp. He first shifted operations from Quebec to St. Catharines, Ontario, adjacent to the city of Niagara Falls, an eighty-mile drive south of Toronto and only a few hours from Meadville. He soon invited numerous Meadville colleagues to invest in the Canadian firm, so that shortly Lightning and Hookless possessed a coziness in ownership and control as well as in technology. Sundback remained the chief source of the Meadville firm's technological inspiration and expertise, but as the years went on, he became more preoccupied with his foreign ventures. Lightning was able to take advantage of the earlier firm's pioneering marketing and soon thrived with sales to Canadian tobacco pouch and overshoe makers.[7]

Kynoch's also lost little time in exploiting the Sundback patents in Europe, and these it maintained some control over for many years. In France, it will be remembered, the C-curity and Plako fasteners had made an appearance as the Ferme-tout Américain, and Peter Aronson's efforts to promote and manufacture this continued until the war. Kynoch's sold its Ready fasteners in France from their first appearance in 1919, but in 1921 some employees of French automobile maker Citroën began to negotiate with the British for the means to set up production on the Continent. These negotiations were protracted, however, with several different groups trying, and failing, either to satisfy Kynoch's conditions or to raise sufficient capital for the enterprise. Finally, in December 1924, the Société Anonyme Fermeture Éclair (SAFE) was organized, and a factory began operations in the ancient French city of Rouen that spring. Its first sales were predictable, to a maker of tobacco pouches and to a supplier of curtains and covers to the automotive industry. Production in Rouen grew rapidly—increasing to more than two hundred thousand feet per year by 1926. Sales, unfortunately, did not keep up, amounting to between half and three-quarters of the output. The rubber overshoe—zipper boot—boost received by the people in Meadville never seems to have reached France, and French sales never matched those in Britain or Germany except for the rather unusual period of the Nazi occupation, when the Rouen factory was used to make up for diversions of German production into other areas.[8]

The fastener met with more sustained popular success in Germany, only to run afoul of the checkered history of the German economy in the decades after World War I. On the heels of Peter Aronson's French efforts before the war, a German firm promoted the *Universal-Verschluss*, but this did not survive the war years. When Lightning Fastener's product made its way to Germany in the early 1920s, it evoked some popular comment. The Germans were particularly ready to think of the device as a clever, even mysterious product of technological wizardry. In 1925 the Nuremberg firm of Deutsche Amac-Vergaser-und-Apparatebau successfully negotiated with the Birmingham zipper makers for the German license, and by the next year it had begun modest production. The attractiveness of the product in the German market was signaled by the rapid appearance of competition, and the confused German patent situation made it more difficult to restrict than elsewhere. In Berlin a company called Reissverschluss-Vertriebs began making fasteners using alternatives to the Sundback machines and apparently produced a somewhat inferior product. They must have had some impact, however, for the term *Reissverschluss* became the universally accepted German word for the fastener, despite the fact that the more successful Nuremberg company put its product on the market initially as the *Original ZIPP Blitz-Verschluss*. With this name it attempted not only to carry on the Birmingham company's theme of "lightning" (*Blitz*, also French *éclair*) fasteners but also to capture the new term "zip," which had already made its unauthorized way across the Atlantic. It, in fact, called itself the ZIPP-Werk, although the term "zipper" did not become part of the language. The sales pattern was also much like the American experience, moving quickly from small leather goods (including the ever-crucial tobacco pouch) to rubber boots and informal clothing. By 1929 the output at Nuremberg was almost 15 percent higher than Birmingham's, and new customers had to be, as at Meadville, turned away for lack of capacity. Competition noticed, new patent dodges were devised, and by 1930 at least eight new companies had entered the field. The major firms felt compelled to create a patent pool, which functioned well to control competition for about ten years (with the Sundback patents still being at the heart of it).[9] At just this time, however, the depression's devastating effects on the German economy hit Nuremberg and the other producers in the cartel. The sales in 1932 and in 1933 from the ZIPP-Werk, for example, were less than 45 percent of those of 1930—a slump not experienced by the other European companies or, as we shall see, by Meadville. At the beginning of 1931 most of the German producers joined a cartel (Kartel der deutschen Reissverschluss-Industrie) in order to protect profits in the rapidly shrinking market. But it was, in fact, the Nazi-led rearmament of the German military, beginning in 1934, that provided the real lift in orders for the fastener makers. The prosperity of ZIPP-Werk even outstripped the spectacular over-all performance of Germany's *Wehrwirtschaft* (war economy) in the mid- and late 1930s. While national production and income doubled between 1932 and 1937, sales from the Nuremberg factory increased fivefold (again making it Europe's largest producer) and grew rapidly until 1940.

During this period the German zipper producers demonstrated their considerable technical originality as well. They developed important alternative machinery to that used by the Americans and were leaders in the experiments with nonmetallic—plastic zippers. With the onset of World War II pressure to convert production completely to war matériel was resisted with some success, and even after 1941, when military priorities became paramount, the ZIPP-Werk producers were allowed to make up some of their reductions by increasing output at the Fermeture Éclair factory in occupied Rouen. Given the zipper's dependence on increasingly scarce and strategic copper-based metal, this was an exceptional experience; in Birmingham, for example, 1943 fastener output was less than 15 percent of 1939's (the comparable figure for Nuremberg and Rouen combined was better than 42 percent). While the allocation of resources in the Third Reich was often not a model of rationality, the favored place of the zipper is worth pondering. From the moment of its introduction in Germany, the *Reissverschluss* impressed people by its sheer cleverness. It quickly became a symbol of the ingenuity of modern technology, and its use was itself a badge of modernity. The maintenance of zipper production was a consistent part of the Nazi regime's effort to shelter the German people from any sense of deprivation during the war years. It was thus perhaps particularly fitting that in Germany's prostration at war's end, entire zipper factories, so the story went, were taken apart and shipped to the Soviet Union among the Red Army's prizes of war.[10]

Elsewhere in Europe the Birmingham-based entrepreneurs extended their efforts. Even before production had begun at Nuremberg, an Austrian maker of safety fuses, perhaps well known to Kynoch's Nobel partners, began modest fastener production near Vienna. Bickford & Company was almost fifty years old when, in 1926, it decided to diversify by taking on, in partnership with Lightning, the zipper. Its growth was very modest for the first ten years, but after the Nazi Anschluss of 1938 it came within the orbit of the thriving German industry and, like its German partners, was able to maintain a relatively high level of production until the very last year or so of the war. In Spain the Lightning subsidiary S.A. Azamon began zipper production in Barcelona in 1933, although its growth was fitful until the early 1950s. Lightning did not confine its expansion to Europe. Under the umbrella of ICI's Australia-New Zealand company, ICIANZ, operations were introduced down under in 1932, although output continued to be very small until after World War II.

A number of European efforts went ahead without benefit of Kynoch's. In Switzerland an engineer by the name of Martin Winterhalter brought his experience as a manufacturer of novelties to bear on the problem of bypassing the Sundback patents. He patented his Rinne-Rippe (groove-rib) fastener in 1924, altering the shape of the zipper scoops just enough to get by, at least in Switzerland and Germany. His Ri-Ri factory at Mendrisio rapidly became one of Europe's most productive zipper operations and a source of considerable technical innovation, including metal cast zippers and, in the 1940s, the first molded nylon fasteners. In Czechoslovakia the world's largest producer of snap fasteners, Waldes Koh-i-Noor, took up zipper production on the heels of forays made by its American subsidiary. Jindrich (Henry) Waldes had a lifelong and deep-seated interest in clothes fasteners of all kinds and had opened in Prague in 1916 the world's first museum devoted to the subject. It should be no surprise, therefore, that the slide fastener held a special fascination for him. He, too, was an experimenter of some accomplishment. The Koh-i-Noor Kover-Zip was a zipper with cloth bonded to the outer face of the scoops and was one of the first responses to the perceived need for a zipper that would afford a complete color match when applied to a woman's dress or man's trousers. Perhaps because of the fact that Koh-i-Noor already had a well-established American outlet for its snaps, the Czech company became the first importer of zippers into the United States after such imports became legal upon the expiration of the basic Sundback patent in 1934.[11]

Much more important, however, as a source of imported zippers to the United States was yet one other venue for zipper manufacture—Japan. By the first decades of the twentieth century Japanese industry was known in the West for its vigorous capacity to take advantage of relatively cheap labor to organize the manufacture of small articles to compete with European and American businesses through a lively export trade. It will be remembered that the Walker brothers were warned as early as 1919 that the sale of their product to Japan would likely result in quick imitation. Actually, it was not until 1930 that zipper manufacture began in Japan, and growth was slow at first. The orientation of Japanese manufacturers toward hand fabrication did not serve them well, and their early product quickly gained a reputation for poor quality. In 1933 the export of zippers to nearby Asian markets began as a means of supplementing the extremely limited domestic demand; this was extended to Central and South America the next year and to the United States in 1935. The shipments to the United States rapidly turned into a flood, as the Japanese manufacturers found it easy to undercut the prices of American producers; in the shorter lengths they were able to price their product at less than half the American article. At first, poor inspection practices allowed an excessive number of poor-quality fasteners to make their way to American customers, but the Japanese entrepreneurs were quick to correct the situation. One of the most important of these was Tadao Yoshida, who began his San-S Shokai company in Tokyo in early 1934. Starting with the small-scale handwork orientation that typified the early Japanese industry, Yoshida emerged as an entrepreneur of exceptional ability, taking advantage of the weakness of competitors and building the scale of production. The

162

•

Z

I

P

P

E

R

company thrived on the export market; only about 10 percent of Japanese production was consumed domestically. This was not an unusual orientation in Japanese industry, but for zippers it was absolutely necessary, since traditional Japanese clothing had no use for such a fastener. Even after the United States increased the duties on imported zippers to 66 percent of value, Yoshida and the hundred or so other small-scale Japanese producers continued to thrive.[12]

By 1938 some form of zipper production could be found in nineteen European countries, with five of them—Germany, Great Britain, Italy, Belgium, and Switzerland—producing exportable amounts. The number of German firms (including annexed Austria) had climbed to twenty, thirteen different companies were operating in Britain, and twelve in France. Total annual European production was estimated at about 105 million feet, which was impressive, although only about half the U.S. output. Even more striking in comparison with the American experience, it was estimated that annual consumption of zippers in Europe (excluding the USSR) was about three inches per capita, in contrast with American figures approaching twenty inches. The zipper was a worldwide commodity before the beginning of the Second World War, but it was still in America that its destiny truly lay.[13]

Another measure of the flourishing of the zipper during the 1920s was the effect that it had on the communities in which it was made, particularly on the town of Meadville. During the decade the town and Crawford County shared in the optimism and prosperity that characterized much of America. Farming and dairying provided a sound base for the area's economy, and its inheritance from the nineteenth century continued to give Meadville's industry a substantial foundation. The locomotive shops of the Erie Railroad, taking advantage of the location midway between New York City and Chicago, gave the town not only considerable employment but also a level of technical expertise out of proportion to its size. As a result, Meadville had become a modest but important center of toolmaking, with products ranging from the hand tools of the McCrosky and Champion DeArment companies to the vises of the Yost company, the large machines of the Barrett Machine Tool Company, and the sometimes huge castings of the National Bearing Metals plant. The old Keystone View Company, which had supplied America with the parlor stereoscopes that had been such a craze at the end of the last century, had adjusted to the times to become an important producer of optical testing equipment. The Spirella Company, the "largest made-to-measure corset plant in the world," employed several hundred more Meadville workers, and the City Ale Brewing Company, along with the distillery that made Meadville Rye, slaked the thirsts of many of these workers, as well as others beyond Crawford County. This was an environment in which the zipper makers could grow as fast as their capital and their markets allowed.[14]

Grow the Hookless Fastener Company did. Meadville's *Tribune Republican* dutifully chronicled the decade's progress. Most visibly the company's move into new buildings and employment of more and more workers gave the town's newspaper something to talk about. At first, the quarters of older firms were taken over by the newcomer: In the summer of 1921 Hookless occupied a former glove factory on Cottage Street in the center of town; at the end of 1922 another Cottage Street factory was taken to house the Hookless machine shops; this was augmented by the construction of another building on Cottage Street in 1924. At this point the *Tribune Republican* reported that Hookless employment had reached three hundred, including many "high grade expert mechanics." Less than two years later the Cottage Street plants were judged inadequate, and the company made its most important move: the acquisition of the four acres and three buildings soon to be vacated by the Meadville Theological Seminary (which was moving to Chicago). Within a few months of the property's purchase, construction began on a large factory to augment the old seminary buildings. By the end of 1926 the newspaper reported that the plant was almost complete and that the number of Hookless employees had almost reached six hundred.[15]

In January 1927 the move to new quarters was front-page news. The *Tribune Republican*, which was, in the style of many an American small-town paper, the voice of the local chamber of commerce, reported the company's expansion and prosperity with enthusiasm. The celebrations of the move were accompanied by banqueting, speeches, and songs, one of which was reprinted by the paper:

Meadville's Song—"The Zipper Boot"

This Hookless crowd is hard to beat,
Zipper Boots, Oh Zipper Boots,
They built a plant up on Arch Street,
Zipper Boots, Oh Zipper Boots,
They used three acres of floor space,
It certainly is a bang-up place,
They're way ahead, they'll win the race,
Zipper Boots, Oh Zipper Boots.
(to the tune of "Maryland,
My Maryland")

Subsequent verses celebrated such people as Gideon Sundback, Lewis Walker, and others in the company, but the most striking message was perhaps the acknowledgment that the company's fortunes were fundamentally tied to the "Zipper Boots" being made a few hours away in Akron. The Meadville celebrants could not have known that these boots were then at the height of a popularity that was quickly to wane, putting their own prosperity in peril.[16]

It was at this time, too, that the company's optimism found another outlet, the *Hookless Scoop*, a factory magazine that served as a vehicle for everything from pep talks by management to social announcements, gossip, and jokes. Good-natured ribbing of fellow employees was combined with historical sketches (somewhat inaccurate), statements of company policy (technical suggestions accepted by the engineers would earn payment—five dollars in the examples given), advertisements from Meadville merchants (including such things as "Hookless Fastener" diaries, pencil cases, and autograph albums from Gill's Book Store), reports from various departments on everything from the basketball teams to the recuperation of a hospitalized employee, and snatches of poetry and song, many by one Doris Paige from the Drafting Department ("The Hookless Fastener Company is growin' like the deuce / A makin' Hookless Fasteners for

The 1926 *Hookless Scoop* depicted the "girls" of the inspection department.
Zipper factories, from the beginning, depended heavily on the work of low-wage
women, particularly for final assembly and inspection.   SCOOP, TALON, INC.

Everything in Use . . ."). The *Scoop*, the Christmas bonuses, the
celebrations of continuing expansion all contributed to the sense
of benevolent paternalism that Colonel Walker and his associates
worked hard to make part of Hookless's public image and private
style. The rapid growth of the mid-twenties made it clear that
the recruitment and retention of workers would be one of the
challenges that the Meadville company would have to meet head-
on. The small-town environment in which it operated, combined
with the traditionalism of the Colonel's own approach to management, dictated the perpetuation of a low-key, almost folksy
style for the company long after expansion might have seemed
to make it irrelevant. No doubt the large number of women
("girls," in company parlance) working in the plant made it easier
to sustain this style in the coming years. Just as in the first days
in Hoboken low-paid women had been employed for the hand
assembly of the C-curity and the Plako, so, too, in Meadville
they tended to have many of the remaining handwork jobs—
fitting sliders on finished chain and inspecting and packaging the

final product. This was an employment pattern still to be seen in zipper factories around the world.[17]

The growth and prosperity of Hookless in the mid-twenties had, as even the "Zipper Boots" song suggested, a narrow base. This was not necessarily by choice, as the expansion of the company was probably as rapid as the Walkers were comfortable with, although it just managed to keep up with Goodrich's requirements and those of other customers to whom it felt an obligation. Throughout these years, as the fastener became more widely known and became more closely associated with commercial successes like Goodrich's Zippers and the Locktite tobacco pouches, the junior Walkers received more and more queries from eager customers. The obligations to the purchasers in Akron and Gloversville and the limitations of the Meadville factories dictated a very restrictive response to these. Numerous other actual or prospective makers of tobacco pouches, for example, wrote to Meadville, only to be told that Locktite took all of the available supply. Even for the kinds of applications that they once tried so hard to promote, the Walkers had to turn down prospects. The DuBois Overall Company was told that no additional supplies for men's trousers were available; the Globe-Superior Company had to be told that the #5 fastener it wanted for work and play clothing was simply not available; the Atlas Underwear Company received word that a competitor was getting the entire allotment for men's and boys' underwear. Experimentation was also discouraged: Lewis, Jr., had to tell the Vanity Fair Silk Mills, for example, that none of its fasteners was, in his opinion, dainty enough for women's silk underwear. Other customers that were turned down included makers of auto seat covers, women's athletic bloomers, pencil cases, and many other items. The Walkers were proud of the variety of applications that they believed had been opened up by 1927, but their fundamentally conservative approach to the growth of their industry made the supply for their proven customers the first priority and imbued them with considerable caution about experimental applications.[18]

Naturally, with the spectacular success of Goodrich's galoshes, the desire of competing overshoe makers to use the new gadget was particularly strong. The increase of Goodrich's share of the galosh market from 5 to 16 percent in the matter of a few years came at the expense of other rubber companies, both large and small. The Hookless response to these other firms was clear-cut; its agreement with the Akron company simply forbade sup-plying any other manufacturer. The incentive of the competition in this case, however, was so great that this state of affairs was simply not acceptable. If Hookless would not supply other over-shoe makers with slide fasteners, then another company would have to. These were the circumstances that gave rise to Hookless's first real competitors, as well as to the company's first battles to defend its patents. At least five established rubber-shoe makers strove to devise slide fasteners of their own, each of them mindful of Sundback's patents on Hookless's device and the machinery for making it. The quickest response was perhaps that of the La Crosse Rubber Mills Company of Wisconsin. Soon after the appearance of Goodrich's Zippers, La Crosse made inquiries to Hookless, only to be rebuffed. The company then quickly looked around for an alternative and found it in a device made by a small-scale Connecticut hardware manufac-turer, George E. Prentice. Prentice resurrected an idea that had appeared in several nineteenth-century European patents—a fas-tener consisting of two helical springs that could be brought together by a slider, much in the fashion of Sundback's Hookless. Prentice's E-Z Lok fastener did not hold very tightly, but at least it gave the La Crosse Mills a superficially convincing facsimile of the gadget on Goodrich's boots. Only a couple of years later, however, in 1926, Prentice recognized that the inferior perfor-mance of the E-Z Lok was not a sound basis for longer-term success and began producing a fastener virtually identical to the Hookless, a strategy that served it well at first, despite the pre-dictable lawsuits from Hookless.[19]

Meanwhile, larger rubber companies were not standing idle. When their business was refused by Hookless, four of the best-known rubber-shoe makers—Converse, Hood, Firestone, and U.S. Rubber—attempted to produce slide fasteners on their own. Converse and Firestone could make little headway, and Hood soon was absorbed by Goodrich. The only success was that of U.S. Rubber's subsidiary, the Shoe Hardware Company, which began manufacture in 1926. The effect of Prentice and Shoe Hardware on Hookless's market was rapid. The downturn in business in 1927–28 was due not only to the drop-off in sales of Goodrich's galoshes but also to the appearance of the competition, both in fasteners and in galoshes. By 1928 competitors were taking almost 40 percent of the total slide fastener market, by one estimate. This in turn spurred other entries into the business. The one that must have galled Walker and company the most was the Lion Fastener Company, set up in Meadville by Noel J. Poux, a former Hookless employee. Poux's effort brought home another lesson to the industry's founders: As difficult as the creation of their technology and their markets had been, neither was hard to duplicate once known.[20]

The Hookless men responded to the situation in a variety of ways. Just as the colonel had promised back in 1924, the company was ready to defend its patent monopoly in court, and suits were filed against both Prentice and Lion. The company's sales activities were increased, the efforts to experiment with and develop novel applications were given new life, and technical innovation was promoted as never before. The result was not only the recapture of its markets (by 1931 Hookless had 80 percent) but a much more rapid spread of the zipper into the uses that made it in the following decade a common article of everyday life and at the same time the symbol of modernity. As is not infrequently the case in new industries, the emergence of vigorous competition was the catalyst that moved the slide fastener from novelty to necessity.[21]

There were many signs of the new aggressiveness in Meadville. The reports by management to the stockholders of Hookless in the summer of 1927 were filled with indications of a new competitive push. Already there was a new effort to wean the company away from reliance on Goodrich's boots. The proportion of sales to Goodrich still hovered around 70 percent, but important new customers were now appearing. The most promising of these was the H. D. Lee Mercantile Company of Kansas City, which purchased more than a million zippers the first half of 1927. Some of its products, such as those for firefighters, used as many as five zippers, and the company let it be known that it expected soon to overtake Goodrich as Hookless's primary customer. This did not happen, and the kind of clothing that Lee manufactured did not represent any kind of breakthrough for the fastener, but the company was still the first big clothing manufacture to use large numbers of zippers steadily. The eager-

In 1928 the Hookless Fastener Company adopted this trademark for its product. It changed the corporate name to Talon, Inc. a decade later. *TALON, INC.*

ness of Hookless to develop and publicize new uses for the fastener mounted as the decade drew to a close.

For the first time the Hookless Fastener Company began advertising widely, investing in a regular series of ads in the *Saturday Evening Post* and preparing broadsides and a glossy catalog to boast of the great range of applications of the fastener. Another part of this effort was adoption in early 1928 of a distinctive new trade name. Time, custom, and the pushing of colleagues wore down the Colonel's resistance to a catchier moniker for their product, so the Talon fastener came to market, complete with a striking new logo of an eagle in full attack. The new name had the additional advantage, important now that competitors were on the market, that it would easily fit on the pull tab of the zipper. Whereas the *Saturday Evening Post* ads in 1926 had been relatively modest quarter-page black-and-white depictions of luggage, sweaters, and children's pencil cases, by mid-1928 they were full-page colorful and artistic promotions, claiming, "You see the Talon Fastener everywhere you turn." Despite the 1928 decline in sales, the sales and advertising campaign was seen as a success since the list of customers that stood at only about 100 in 1927 had expanded to about 250 by the end of 1928.[22]

The campaign to defend the Hookless patents was also pursued aggressively. The Prentice E-Z Lok fastener, while avoiding

170

•

Z

I

P

P

E

R

using Sundback's scoops, used a slider much like that of Hook-less, and this drew an infringement suit from the Meadville company. Since the basic form of the slider was not much changed since Judson's early inventions, patent protection for which had long expired, it was not surprising that Prentice was largely successful in defending itself in this case. When, in 1926, however, Prentice abandoned the coil design for one much more like the Hookless, it found itself back in court, and this time it had much more trouble defending itself against Sundback's basic hookless patent. Not for the first—or the last—time the competing company drew upon the Kuhn-Moos patents to claim that the Sundback design lacked originality. The inventor himself devoted much effort to the case, for not only was the Hookless monopoly at stake, but the validity of his own patent position worldwide, with consequences for his Canadian enterprise as well as for the various ICI-Lightning efforts, was at risk. In U.S. courts several decisions were rendered in various Hookless-Prentice suits, stretching into the mid-1930s. Sundback successfully argued that the design of his fastener—especially the shape of the individual scoops—was sufficiently distinct from and superior to that of the Kuhn-Moos patent that his patent was indeed valid. Further argument was required to show that the devices of Prentice (and others) were in fact infringing, but the courts largely agreed. Prentice kept up its own legal efforts, however, extending beyond the expiration of the basic Sundback patents. Further suits thus argued more arcane matters, such as the means for manufacturing the Hookless sliders, that were covered by later patents. Hookless's victories in these cases were not total, and Prentice was able to fend off and eventually pierce the Meadville monopoly.[23]

In Canada Sundback himself filed suit against Prentice and its Canadian partner, the Colonial Fastener Company, and after a prolonged struggle, which took him and Lightning all the way to the Privy Council in London—the seldom-used final venue for Canadian justice—the validity of Sundback's patents on zipper machinery throughout the British dominions was emphatically upheld. This decision discouraged competition in Canada and elsewhere, and in Europe at least it seemed to foster the development and use of alternative machinery. The new machines often, it was conceded even by their users, produced zipper chain of lesser quality than that made by the Sundback machines, but they allowed price competition and even the development of an export market to the United States.[24]

Another patent case pursued by Hookless had a somewhat more personal edge. Noel J. Poux was a native of the Crawford County community of Frenchtown, and his father was a merchant in Meadville who taught French on the side (Gideon Sundback had been one of his pupils). The son was a man of mechanical bent who naturally sought out the rapidly growing Hookless Fastener Company as a place to apply his talents and expand his technical knowledge. Serving as a member of the Hookless engineering staff did not provide the creative Poux with enough room for his ambitions, so in 1929 he left Hookless and, with the assistance of some of the company's tool- and diemakers, as well as capital from one or two former Hookless backers, established across town the Lion Fastener Company. One can imagine the dismay and even anger with which Walker and company viewed the appearance of this local rival, and they were not slow in seeking to shut it down through patent litigation. This was particularly urgent since Lion clearly possessed all the technical expertise necessary to produce quality fasteners and was prepared to do so at a lower price than Hookless. Furthermore, Poux was not simply a copier; he was a bright and imaginative engineer in his own right, and his arguments in court, both against the validity of Sundback's patent monopoly and in favor of his own originality, were often striking and persuasive. Separate cases were pursued against Lion in defense of Sundback's fastener designs (going back to his original Hookless patent of 1917) and of his various machines. Neither one of these cases resulted in total victory, but enough of Sundback's patent claims were upheld, after five years of courtroom battles, to force the upstart out of business. In a remarkable gesture, Hookless forgave the damages awarded by the court and took back the turncoat workers, including Poux, whose mechanical talents were once again put to work by the Colonel's men.[25]

By the end of the 1920s the world of the zipper makers had become a large and complicated place. Their humble little product was making its mark on a wide range of businesses and manufactures, in both Europe and America. The makers of everything from galoshes to overalls had to pay attention to the novelty. From Kansas City to Prague there was a new element added to the calculations of manufacturers, designers, retailers, and buyers as they performed their designated functions in the cycle of production and consumption. To be sure, for most it was a very small element in the commercial calculus, easily ignored or relegated to the minor status accorded to odd and unusual things. Even so, the zipper had begun to alter little parts of the everyday world and to provide to its makers a sufficient return to justify almost four decades of faith and persistence. Despite competitors, the real shapers of the zipper's fate were still the men and women in Meadville, and the modest success they enjoyed at decade's end was simply not enough for them. Their decades of work and belief were not adequately rewarded by the place their product had won for itself in such things as overshoes and handbags. Experience had already shown them that such outlets were unsteady platforms for permanent prosperity, and the worlds yet to conquer were so much larger and richer that the twenty million fasteners sold in 1930 were evidence not so much of success (though they were proud of how far they had come) as of the distance yet to travel.

C

H

A

P

T

E

R

Bye-bye Buttons

7

From the perspective of a Talon salesman looking back at the end of the decade, "there had really been no 'selling' " before 1930. Before that time the important applications of the zipper—from money belts to tobacco pouches to galoshes—all had come from outsiders spotting the gadget and pursuing it for their own ends. To be sure, Sundback and others in Meadville sometimes gave crucial assistance in solving technical glitches, but the important ideas were those of the final product manufacturers. This had to change in the new decade; Hookless salesmen and technicians had to seek out new uses and markets vigorously. Their efforts superficially resembled those of the Walker brothers more than a decade earlier, but the circumstances were dramatically different. Instead of attempting to hawk an unknown, untested novelty to a very skeptical industry that they did not understand, the men selling the Talon fastener were probing in a variety of different directions, armed with a device (actually, with several different models and sizes available, a series of devices) that had been proved both technically and commercially in highly visible and well-known applications. Nonetheless, some of the challenges had not changed that much: There was still the problem of price, the problem of fashion, and the belief that the success of the venture would not be secure until the larger-scale clothing market finally opened itself up.[1]

By the end of 1929 Hookless sales had fully recovered from the setback of the previous year. This was made possible not by recovery of the galoshes market but by the exploitation of other outlets that had earlier been opened but not fully developed. The most important of these was in ladies' handbags. The possibilities of using zippers for purses had been apparent to the Walker brothers back in the days when they were pounding the pavement in New York City, for Manhattan was the center of the handbag industry in the United States. The first steady customers in this area were some of the Gloversville companies, for which purses and pocketbooks were natural offshoots of glove making, but getting the New York City makers to adopt the novelty was harder work. About 1920, after the fastener had proved itself in tobacco pouches, Wallace Walker was able to get the firm of Wilkinson to take on a small number of fasteners on a regular basis, but the relatively high price of the fastener and the fashion-consciousness of the handbag market limited the device's appeal, just as in most clothing. An external circumstance intervened, however, to give Hookless a much firmer foothold in the New York market. In 1923 the handbag framers of Manhattan, strongly organized in a union, went on strike, demanding considerably higher piecework rates (up to sixteen or even twenty dollars per day). The manufacturers resisted, and when it became evident that a slide fastener could be installed in a handbag by a seamstress without the benefit of a frame at all (in the manner of the soft-sided tobacco pouch), demand took off, at least for a period. Application of the fastener began in higher-priced bags but eventually made its way to fifty-cent handbags; this was a remarkable penetration for a device that was never cheaper than ten cents itself. For the remainder of the 1920s there remained room in the popular styles for zipper-fastened handbags, and a small but steady export market to Europe sustained demand. By 1931 handbags constituted the largest single outlet for zippers— 35 percent of the total supply (more than all clothing applications combined). Here, too, however, the zipper makers were at the mercy of fickle fashions, so that in 1935 the demand from this source plummeted in one year from more than eleven million to four million. The problem of a sustained, stable demand would not be solved in this direction.[2]

As the twenties ended, the intensity of the sales effort for the zipper increased. Perhaps the most visible sign of this in Meadville was the replacement of Lewis Walker, Jr., as sales manager in 1929 by Sam Kinney. Kinney was an experienced marketer, having once worked for the *Ladies' Home Journal* and organized sales campaigns for everything from automobiles to furniture. He brought to Hookless a new, systematic approach to marketing, supported by a carefully recruited team of young, college-educated salesmen, many of whom were distributed around the country to assure close contact with important customers. Much of this work was accomplished against the background of the deepening economic crisis of the Great Depression, but this seemed to have little effect on Kinney's job. The new manager later reflected on the challenge he faced in this period, identifying three conditions that shaped his strategy: (1) The slide fastener was (still) higher in price than the traditional devices it replaced; (2) manufacturers would always be reluctant to adopt a device that complicated the production process; and (3) the applications of the fastener were, by 1930, so various that advertising promotion for specific uses would only affect a fraction of the market. The implications of this last condition, as Kinney saw it, were that advertising could not be used to change significantly the public's demand for zippers, and thus manufacturers would have to be the primary targets of sales efforts. Furthermore, Kinney believed that "instead of invention of new uses, the great problem for this company [is] to find a way to introduce the slide fastener principle to the large staple industries where it can contribute valuable functional service." This meant, he never had any doubt, the clothing makers.[3]

This, of course, was hardly an original insight, but Kinney's attack on the problem was far more sophisticated than that of the Walker brothers some fifteen years earlier. He recognized that clothing was a highly segmented business, with different manufacturers (and, to an extent, retailers) aiming their efforts at specific, defined markets. He thus sought to determine just which segments of the market were most vulnerable to the appeal of the zipper, given the constraints of high price and manufacturing conservatism. One of Kinney's campaigns, which caught the eye of marketing experts, illustrates his approach, showing the lengths to which the fastener promoters thought they had to go to persuade customers in the depression to accept their novelty. It also serves as an extraordinary example of the way in which a technology's path into the world is shaped by ideas and motivations quite foreign to its creators.

About 1930 Sam Kinney gave one of his assistants, Jack Keilly, the task of promoting children's wear applications. This was not a new area for Hookless. By 1929 the list of small-scale applications for children's clothing and accessories was long: Playsuits were a natural extension of the overalls that had been made for years by Guiterman Brothers, in St. Paul; the Zip-On Manufacturing Company began promoting its own distinctive zippered suits in 1926; Kansas City's H. D. Lee Mercantile Company made a children's version of its Whizit coveralls; and the Snuggle Rug Company of Goshen, Indiana, had made a zippered baby robe since the mid-twenties. Like so many other applications, however, the number of fasteners absorbed by these manufacturers was modest, and Kinney believed a more aggressive push in this direction would pay off large dividends. Keilly and Kinney calculated that children's clothing would be more susceptible to utilitarian arguments for the fastener and less stymied by fashion-consciousness. Up to a point they were right. First Keilly attacked the market for leggings—the close-fitting articles that were used to keep children's legs warm and clean and could be worn under trousers or skirts. Traditional manufacturers resisted (as usual), but when the New York fabric and corduroy manufacturers Hallett and Hackmeyer were persuaded to enter the market themselves, armed with the Talon fastener to make their offerings distinctive, the market turned around with astonishing speed. When, in late 1931, the Hookless salesmen tried to prepare a window display to contrast the old buttoned legging with the Talon-equipped article, they reported that they simply could not find any of the old ones for sale! It was this episode that probably convinced Kinney that the children's clothing market represented an unrealized potential worth extra effort.[4]

Kinney and Keilly had some important allies, and it is their unwitting role in the zipper's fate that makes this episode so striking. In 1923 the U.S. Department of Agriculture established its Bureau of Home Economics, and in that largely female domain flourished a group of activists intent on bringing messages of efficiency and professionalism to homes throughout the land, targeting age-old habits and errors in everything from nutrition to furnishings to clothing. This last area was the concern of one Ruth O'Brien, who came to the bureau in 1924 and proceeded to pursue an agenda of both research and public education, investigating the behavior and uses of different fabrics, attempting to standardize sizes, especially for children's clothes, and providing advice both for home sewing and for wise purchasing of ready-made wear. In this category, children's clothing was a relatively new entry, for the low cost of children's garments, combined with relatively simple styling and the need for frequent alteration (for the growing child), as well as firmly entrenched traditions of child rearing, kept this form of clothing a home product rather than a market item even after factory-made clothing had become dominant in the adult world. Changing tastes and perceptions of women's roles, as well as the growth of both manufacturing and retail opportunities, served to alter this situation in the years after World War I, so that by the mid- and late 1920s, the market for infants' and children's clothing was a rapidly growing segment of industry. O'Brien's Division of Textiles and Clothing attempted to shape this industry and the tastes of its consumers.[5]

These efforts were in turn influenced by currents of thought that in the 1920s were changing the way that children and child rearing were perceived. Two key terms representing these currents were "child study" and "behaviorism." The Merrill-Palmer School opened in Detroit in 1920 as a new kind of nursery school, in which education of the young child was meant to be placed on a scientific foundation. Its influence and that of emulators across the country directed the attention of both educators and parents toward new theories of human development and psychology. The most important of these was the behaviorism boldly advocated by John B. Watson. By the time that Watson published his *Psychological Care of Infant and Child* in 1928, elements of the behaviorist influence on child rearing and education were already widely apparent. Merrill-Palmer's Ellen Miller, for

1...2...3...
and she's dressed herself

These completely buttonless garments are easily fastened . . . even by a two-year-old . . . because of the tiny Talon Fastener

All set for play in this washable cotton suit with tiny Talon fastener.

THE SELF-DRESS IDEA
A new convenience in children's clothing . . . welcomed by mothers and youngsters alike!

The Self-Dress idea is not a style . . . not a fad . . . it's a basic improvement in children's clothing.

Talon-fastened clothes teach self-reliance and sturdy independence to the youngsters in a practical way they'll like.

50   *In using advertisements see page 14. When writing to advertisers please mention* THE PARENTS' MAGAZINE.

The sales campaign for children's clothing featuring zippers reached its height in the early 1930s. The appeal to the current teachings of child psychologists was one of the most original of the fastener makers' marketing efforts. This sort of advertisement appeared in *Parents Magazine* **and** *Woman's Home Companion.* TALON, INC.

example, wrote in 1927: "The child's clothing should be so fashioned that he can dress himself." The distance that children's fashions had to go before that point could be reached was illustrated by Miller's study of small boys, in which it was observed that an "average of more than seventeen buttons had to be fastened each morning" in the course of dressing, and some of these buttons were unreachable by small arms and hands. The solution, it was suggested, lay in "simplification"—using fewer and larger buttons and using such alternatives as elastic where possible. The primary goal of this was, in Miller's words, "to allow the learning child some measure of success." O'Brien herself wrote that "psychological terms formerly the exclusive property of the learned profession itself are now becoming part of every mother's vocabulary," with the resulting message that "the independence and mental growth of the child should be stimulated by providing him with clothing so designed that he can dress and undress himself."[6]

While child study and the education of mothers were important to the effort to reform children's clothing, an even more immediate target was the clothing manufacturers. These men (and they did tend to be men) had to be won over for the reform to succeed. Perhaps the most important convert was George F. Earnshaw, owner of a Massachusetts knitting mill and one of the most influential of the new breed of children's garment manufacturers. Earnshaw embarked on a crusade for a reform of what children wore, denoted by the slogan Self-Help. His Vanta line of clothing, highlighted by the "sunsuit," an overall-like garment of Earnshaw's own invention, was directed, according to one observer, toward "producing the modern, standardized, 'scientific' baby." The key to this was the elimination of buttons and pins. Earnshaw focused on the fasteners of children's clothes as the key determinants of either dependency or liberation: If a child could get his clothes on and fastened without assistance, then independence, self-reliance, and rapid psychological development would follow. He was no doubt influenced by an additional sales angle, illustrated by the remarks of a home economist that "the problem of finding garments which tend to promote rather than preclude self-care has been especially agitated by those in charge of nursery schools and institutes of child welfare, largely because of the work involved in caring for the many children at one time." The twin goals of fostering independence in young children and relieving some of the labor and attention they required of their care givers were to become the central features of both an educational campaign and a sales pitch into the mid-1930s.[7]

Since self-help clothing was largely (though not exclusively) a matter of simplified fastenings, it is not surprising that the style came to the attention of the Hookless salesmen. Indeed, the possible role that zippers might play in this regard had caught the eye of Ruth O'Brien and her assistants in early 1928, when they ordered a small shipment from Macy's notions department (there is no indication that they contacted any of the manufacturers directly). Psychologist John Carl Flugel wrote in 1930 that the zipper might be important in reducing the difficulty of dressing, especially if a smaller version could be produced. Hookless's 1926 contract with Zip-On showed that the potential of the children's market was not neglected, but the company's ability to make headway in that direction was indeed hampered by the lack of a suitably small fastener. The smallest of the three sizes available in 1929, #5, was still too large for delicate or small-size clothing, but the introduction of #3 in 1931 changed the situation, and the sales pitch out of Meadville changed accordingly. Hookless's general manager, W. L. Gilmore, anticipated "a considerable volume in children's clothing" for 1932, because of "our being able to furnish a small fastener." According to one of the company's applications engineers, however, it was not until 1933 that the #3 fastener was deemed reliable enough to make a strong push into everyday children's wear. Writing in the early 1940s, W. D. Craig remembered that sleepers were the first major target to open up the territory beyond leggings and playsuits. The primary manufacturer, Dr. Denton, would not budge, but some progress was made with smaller makers. Then Jack Keilly weighed in with his "Self-Help" campaign. This, too, apparently moved little until Keilly, accompanied by his four-year-old daughter, Joan, met one of the major department store buyers. The little girl was a walking advertisement for the virtues of zippered clothing, and the buyer, so the story went, was won over, and her chain of stores followed quickly. The children's campaign then moved into high gear.[8]

At its full extent, in the early 1930s, the selling of the zipper for children's garments was an astonishing marketing effort. Keilly pulled out the stops on every modern marketing tool he could devise, recognizing the challenge posed by the fact that applying a zipper to a little girl's cotton dress could easily double the price (from, say, 69 cents to $1.39—presumably because of manufacturers' premiums on the novelty more than the actual cost of the fastener). He detailed salesmen to train demonstrators in children's sections of department stores across the country. He and Joan traveled up and down the East Coast for demonstrations. Recognizing the questionable wisdom and propriety of such an occupation for a four-year-old, Keilly struck on the idea of a film that could be used to indoctrinate buyers and saleswomen. The pioneering New York outfit of William J. Ganz produced *Bye-Bye Buttons*, featuring rosy-cheeked little girls and boys getting in and out of their clothes with aplomb and independence, beaming mothers simply looking on with pride and pleasure. So effective was the film that stores began requesting copies for showing to their customers—this despite the fact that such showings would typically cost a store from $50 to $100 a week, simply to pay for the projector and operator. The best-known department stores in the country were among the customers: New York's Bloomingdale's, Boston's Filene's and Jordan Marsh, Philadelphia's Strawbridge & Clothier, Los Angeles's Bullock's, and Detroit's J. L. Hudson Company. Large posters were made from movie stills, and more images from the movie were put into a child's booklet that recounted the history of children's clothes in rhyme, with zippered Self-Help garments obviously representing the ultimate step in modernity. These cost the stores 2 cents a copy; Hookless had to print more than two hundred thousand to satisfy demand. One of the things that impressed advertising men about the campaign was how much of the cost Hookless was able to put on the retailers. Apparently, for a while at least, the attractions of the Self-Help message were so great that stores were eager to join in, even at their own expense.[9]

National advertising on radio and in magazines reinforced the sales pitch. The ads showed how thoroughly Hookless adopted the Self-Help message for its own purposes. "1 . . . 2 . . . 3 . . . and she's dressed herself!" went one popular piece, appearing in both trade and general publications. "The Self-

Dress idea is not a style . . . not a fad . . . it's a basic improvement
in children's clothing. Talon-fastened clothes teach self-reliance
and sturdy independence to the youngsters in a practical way
they'll like." "Now children *enjoy* dressing themselves," claimed
another advertisement, appearing in *Parents Magazine*, and another even more explicitly trumpeted: " 'They'll be self-reliant
children,' psychologists say, *'if they learn to dress themselves.'*"
In the same outlet one advertisement took the other important
tack of the crusade: "The Self-Help idea in children's clothing
brings new leisure to busy mothers! . . . Think of the time it
saves! No more running up and down stairs to fasten clothes!
No more missing buttons! No more repairing of ripped buttonholes!" The advertising message was reinforced by editorial material, which promoted in the same magazines the general Self-
Help message, pointing out its support by the Bureau of Home
Economics and the U.S. Children's Bureau, and adding that
slide fastenings were a useful design option for the right kind of
clothing.[10]

By some measures, the children's campaign was a success.
Hookless added, in one year, 250 retailers and more than 50
children's clothing manufacturers to its customer base. Another
zipper manufacturer reported that close to one-fifth of its business went to the makers of children's clothes. In 1934 it was
estimated that as many as a quarter million children's garments
were sold with zippers and Hookless counted more than 600
retail stores with these products, more than 100 of them with
separate sections to promote them. *Fortune* magazine reported:
"Today there is scarcely a well-dressed child who does not have
at least one zipper in his wardrobe." Yet, by 1935, the children's
campaign was under attack, and the market began to dwindle. It
slowly became clear at this point that this market, like so many
before it, would not be the source of stable and steadily growing
demand that the zipper makers wanted and needed. By the end
of 1934 children's clothing had fallen from representing 17.5
percent of the market for zippers to a little over 3 percent.
Applications engineer Gilmore recalled that "the designers of
little girl's dresses rebelled" and demanded more stylish approaches than the zippered Self-Help garments. "And the designers of little boy's suits said one-piece boy's suits were no good
because Junior insisted on separate pants like daddy's even if

they were only 16 waist by 4 inseam instead of 42 by 33." In addition, the whole Self-Help program came to a screeching halt when George Earnshaw threatened to sue for trademark infringement (he ran pointed advertisements to remind merchants that the Self-Help label had been registered in 1928). Hookless quickly backed down on that, making a go at "Dress Alone" as a sales moniker, only to be sharply reminded by Philadelphia's Nannette Manufacturing Company that this was its property. These setbacks were enough to halt momentum entirely, and by about 1937 the children's market had receded into relative insignificance.[11]

The zipper industry as a whole suffered little, however, for in the early and mid-1930s a host of applications was spreading, particularly in the clothing trades. Between 1931 and 1934 the proportion of zipper production that went into clothing increased from 34 to more than 59 percent, even as such early promising outlets as children's clothing and corsets faded. The base was still narrow, however: Of the 1934 clothing sales, 82 percent went for sports clothing. Here was yet another fashion that caught on and helped sustain the zipper for several years, before still another outlet took its place. Since the turn of the century the special clothing designed for outdoors activities for both men and women had been taking on greater importance, and with the proliferation of informal styles in the years after World War I, "sporting clothes" began to make the transition to "sportswear" in the modern sense. This had important implications for the zipper makers, since the mechanical, untraditional nature of their commodity made it much more readily acceptable in the kinds of clothes that would be used for riding, hunting, cycling, and other active sports than in ordinary street wear.[12]

While the early development of sports clothes was largely a British development, their transformation into a large class of attractive, informal street wear was an American trend. The effort began as an attempt to adapt British sporting styles to wear that was appropriate for spectators, and it was accelerated by the growing popularity and accessibility of such sports as golfing in the 1920s. The result was clothing that was looser and more comfortable than traditional wear as well as more stylish than clothes needed purely for sporting purposes. At the same time, American college students began to adapt some of the clothing initially developed for outdoor work, such as so-called mackinaws or lumberjacks, short woolen coats of the sort derived from practical wear for construction or railroad workers. Erstwhile plebeian fabrics like corduroy or canvas began to be found in informal outerwear, which could be accommodated to the still-bulky zipper by the more daring designers. Indeed, by the end of the twenties some of the weirder clothing experiments featured zippers prominently, as in a zippered gabardine coat with a lining that zipped in or out or a golfing jacket, described by *Esquire*, that could be rolled up into a zippered bag.[13]

The ability of the zipper makers to take advantage of the growth of this kind of clothing hinged on the continued development of the device. In the late 1920s Sundback and his colleagues in the Hookless Development Department perfected two important innovations, the lock slider and the separable fastener. Both ideas had been experimented with since the earliest days of the fastener—there was even a separable version of the Plako—but making them work reliably and smoothly turned out to be technical challenges. Since the galosh and handbag applications that sustained the company through the twenties did not require these features, their development did not receive priority until near the close of the decade. The separable fastener, in which both sides of the zipper came completely apart when open (common today, for example, in a zippered jacket), was spurred most perhaps by the fact that Colonel Walker always believed that the corset market would be an important one, and it would require a fully separable, easy-to-operate fastener. The pin-lock slider was a fairly simple modification of slider design, in which the slider pull was made with a catch that fitted into a notch on the slider itself, preventing the slider from moving. Because this required the user to remember to engage the lock and had other limitations, the Hookless designers continued to elaborate the idea, eventually developing automatic and semiautomatic locking sliders. In these, the slider design was considerably complicated, incorporating a spring that would engage a catch to stop the slider whenever the pull was released. The complications were considered worthwhile, however, for the chances of capturing the trousers and dress markets were thought to depend on having a fastener with little chance for accidental opening.[14]

The separating zipper came into its own not in corsets—

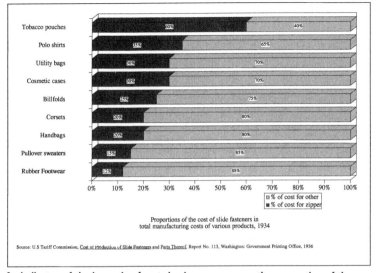

Proportions of the cost of slide fasteners in
total manufacturing costs of various products, 1934

Source: U.S Tariff Commission, *Cost of Production of Slide Fasteners and Parts Thereof*, Report No. 113, Washington: Government Printing Office, 1936

An indicator of the key role of costs in zipper usage was the proportion of the manufacturer's total costs for an article represented by the zipper. This chart, prepared from 1936 Tariff Commission data, shows that even at this date zipper costs could be as high as 60 percent, for an article like tobacco pouches, one of the most successful long-term applications.

which were rapidly heading toward oblivion— but in sports outerwear and sweaters. A Hookless salesman in Philadelphia by the name of Don Leslie had latched on to the knitwear industry of that city and persuaded designers that the zipper gave their product a distinctive flair. At first, in the early thirties, V neck sweaters, in which the most ordinary fasteners could be applied, proved the practicality of the fastener for knitted goods. When V necks became less fashionable, the Hookless salesman promoted the separating zipper as the perfect feature for so-called coat sweaters, which resembled the already established sportsman's jacket. While technical problems had to be successfully overcome to persuade manufacturers to adopt the new fastener widely, this posed no great difficulty. More significant was the problem of color. The standard Talon fasteners were available in either their original nickel silver or a version called NuGild, which gave them a golden or coppery sheen. This was satisfactory for jackets made of wool or leather, but for the lighter knit goods the metallic effect was considered unstylish. The zipper manufacturers had differing responses to the demand for better color matching between fastener and fabric. Hookless devised an enameling process that applied a coat of color to the visible front of the zipper's metal scoops. This additional processing added to costs, and the result was not always satisfactory, since rubbing between the slider and the fastener scoops could wear away the enamel in time. Perhaps the best alternative was that of the Czech-American Waldes Koh-i-Noor firm, which devised the Kover-Zip, in which the scoops of the fastener were covered by fabric matching that of the zipper tape. This, too, could suffer wear, but Waldes was able to sell it for less than the Talon enameled zippers, and the color match was as good as could be asked for. The demand for zippered sweaters waned in coming years, but the jackets became some of the garments most closely associated with zippers. Indeed, in leather, the zippered jacket was, in later decades, to take on a cultural meaning far beyond anything imagined by the zipper makers.[15]

The result of the experiments of the 1920s and the campaigns of the early 1930s in everything from children's clothing to sportswear was that the zipper by the mid-thirties was a well-known device, and the zipper companies were prospering, even in the midst of the Great Depression. Observers of the industry were struck by an annual output that exceeded one hundred million fasteners. They commented on novel applications, such as the ninety-five-foot zippers that W. & J. Sloane used to connect the sections of a gigantic carpet in one of the Waldorf-Astoria's ballrooms. And the apparent imperviousness of the zipper business to the economic slump was particularly noteworthy. WHO SAID DEPRESSION? headlined the *Brooklyn Daily Eagle* in a story about Meadville, which it characterized as riding a "Florida Boom" on the strength of the zipper industry. The application of the zipper makers for tariff protection from Czech and Japanese importers directed attention to what journalists called "a typical American industry," and one breathless newspaperman referred to the zipper as "the latest and perhaps greatest expression of our modern culture." Even the most enthusiastic journalists, however, noticed that the greatest challenge for the zipper makers was still not fully met; that of making the fastener a standard item for adult clothing.[16]

The manufacturers, in Meadville and elsewhere, were certainly aware of the unmet difficulty of developing the market that had beckoned so long. Chief salesman Sam Kinney and his crew in the mid-1930s decided that the long-term health of their business depended on a direct attack at the target, and so ensued the campaign that finally brought the walls of tradition tumbling down, eventually with a speed that not even the aging Colonel Walker or his most enthusiastic follower could have been prepared for. The battle was joined on two fronts, one for men, the other for women. Different strategies were necessary for each, but they were pursued simultaneously, and it is likely that they reinforced each other.

Kinney himself described the "battle of the fly," in which the manufacturers and designers of men's clothing were prevailed upon to change the fastenings on trousers. He underscored the significance of the effort for the industry; writing in the key year of 1937, he pointed out that Hookless would produce about one hundred million fasteners that year, which needed to be compared with the seventy-five million men's and boys' trousers (excluding work clothing and overalls) that would be sold. Obviously the addition of 75 percent to the demand for zippers was worth all the effort that the company put into it. Any successful campaign, however, would have to be sensitive to the intrinsic conservatism of the clothing industry—a lesson learned with difficulty and frustration by the young Walker brothers almost twenty years before. Kinney, however, was far more savvy than his predecessors had been. He knew, for example, that in menswear the manufacturers called the shots and the retailers went along. Changes in styles and new kinds of demand were not likely to be generated at the customer or store level. The manufacturers, for their part, were generally steeped in tradition and saw very little to gain from experimentation and novelty. Kinney realized that the effort had to be made to look less "experimental"; all potential problems in styling and production would have to be carefully worked out by the fastener people themselves.[17]

The technical problems of using zippers successfully in trousers involved both the fasteners and how they were applied. The lighter-weight zipper introduced in the early thirties made things much easier, for the older, heavier model that had been successful in overalls and work clothes was simply too bulky for the crisp lines of a man's suit. Making this lighter-weight zipper as reliable as its predecessors was imperative to Kinney's strategy, for even more than in other applications, any number of flawed samples in trousers could ruin the fastener's reputation disastrously. Then there was the problem of putting the zipper in. Traditional tailoring treated a pair of trousers as two fabric tubes that were then joined, and the fly finished by applying buttons. But putting a zipper in properly in an already-made pair of pants turned out to be a formidable task, one resisted at all levels of manufacture, from factories to the finest tailors. The zipper makers came up with a system of providing fasteners to tailors in separate halves; each half was applied to one leg of the trousers, and only when the two were joined were the slider and bottom stops put in place. This required an adjustment in thinking on the part of the zipper makers as well as the tailors, but it turned out to be a simple and eminently satisfactory system. Indeed, the Hookless salesmen claimed that the product of this method was typically trimmer and neater than button-fly trousers.[18]

Breaking down market resistance would take more than solving technical difficulties, however. Kinney and company attacked on several fronts. Major manufacturers were approached, given intensive sales pitches, and the firmest assurance that Kinney could muster that the zipper was not only attractive but reliable. Two major Chicago clothiers, Hart, Schaffner and Marx and B. Kuppenheimer, were the first nationally known men's suppliers to give the proposition a sustained try, although their initial orders were small. A Cincinnati house, H. A. Seinsheimer, was the next to move, with a measure more confidence. These experimenters discovered that the new fastener could appeal to the younger segment of their market, so college and high school boys became the standard-bearers for zippered pants. While this was a gratifying breakthrough, it had its drawbacks. Boys and young men as a rule purchased less expensive pants than their elders, particularly in the ready-to-wear trade, and thus the zipper was in danger of being associated with the cheaper end of the market—this despite the fact that putting zippers in trousers could raise their price as much as a dollar. Kinney attacked this difficulty head-on, sending his salesmen out to deal with the most expensive custom tailors in the country. Since some of these gentlemen would try the novelty only on a suit purchased by the salesman, this could be a costly approach (at more than $150 a suit!). Kinney claimed success, however, with thirteen out of the nineteen expensive tailors agreeing to endorse the fastener, a fact that he lost no time in getting into promotional material and advertisements.[19]

Success was still elusive, however, for it was not enough simply to figure out workable techniques for the tailors and manufacturers; they also had to be schooled in making those techniques work consistently in the real worlds of both custom tailoring and unionized factories. Every worker who was engaged in trouser manufacturing required some degree of training with the new fastener, for its use changed in sometimes subtle ways a host of approaches to cutting and fitting, not just the application of the trouser fly. Troubles were encountered with poor workmanship until Kinney realized that the manufacturers had to be supervised by the zipper makers for some time before their use of the product could be taken for granted. Kinney recalled later hiring thirty-four new inspectors in one week and training them to call regularly on the garment makers to make sure their techniques and their workers were not slipping. Labor unions raised other problems by attempting to force extra wages for zipper installation. The salesmen also had to deal with rumors that the zipper was a passing fad whose attraction was quickly waning and that it was potentially dangerous to users. Retailers were made to worry that they could be held legally liable if a man injured himself with the newfangled machine on his trouser fly. Stories were circulated about particularly embarrassing failures of zippers, and these acquired lives of their own. Only the most conscientious salesmanship, involving much follow-up work and educational activity, could overcome obstacles like these.[20]

In the middle years of the 1930s Kinney's salesmen made considerable headway on a number of fronts. Major manufacturers like Kuppenheimer committed themselves at least to making zippers available and moved slowly and steadily toward conversion of their entire lines. The college market continued to be favorable, and this began to have some positive effects on the broader market, especially as trend-setting campuses such as Yale and Princeton came to be seen as receptive. Most striking, perhaps, was the fact that the universally acknowledged arbiter of taste in men's clothes Edward, Prince of Wales, was reported to have adopted the zipper. In 1936 the prince became King Edward VIII, but before the year was out, he had abdicated and assumed the title Duke of Windsor. His influence on masculine fashion was hardly diminished, however, by the vicissitudes of the abdication. No doubt his daring choice of the new fastener influenced some of the tailors in Bond Street (and their customers), but it is something of a myth that the zipper's success in the late thirties was purely a matter of his whim. Kinney and others, not only from Hookless but from competing companies and those overseas, did their job well, and they continued to push.[21]

In early 1937 the Hookless Fastener Company became Talon, Inc., and the company embarked on an ambitious advertising campaign, peppering major magazines with promotions for the zipper in men's clothes. In outlets like *The New Yorker* and *Esquire*, as well as the more plebeian *Saturday Evening Post*, Talon and other manufacturers pushed the notion that the well-dressed, thoroughly modern man would consider nothing other than zippers in his trousers. This effort reinforced the continued approach to the manufacturers and major retailers. With a relative suddenness that startled the zipper makers, the gathering momentum of the generated demand came to a head in the late summer of 1937. Orders poured in in such numbers that the Meadville factories went to twenty-four-hour production, and the defiance of the nation's economic slump, which had been noteworthy before, now became astonishing. Talon rapidly overshadowed every other industry in the town, employing at the height of this boom more than five thousand workers in Meadville—out of a total population of less than nineteen thousand. The clearest turnaround was in the area of summer suits. *Men's Wear* magazine reported that it expected more than 20 percent of suits for the 1938 season would be equipped with zippers, compared with less than 6 percent for 1936. Talon salesmen were quick to portray the move to zippers as an unstoppable bandwagon, trumpeting surveys of men's clothing stores that appeared to give nearly total approval to the modern fastener.[22]

There is no easy way to account for this breakthrough. It seems to have been the result of the many years of pushing, demonstrating, and handholding on the part of the zipper makers

and sellers. It was also a logical, incremental next step in the slow
accumulation of experience with the fastener, on the part of both
manufacturers and consumers. By the middle years of the thirties
zippers were no longer strange to most people. Their presence
in everything from galoshes to handbags was readily accepted,
even expected. There were many garments in which zippers were
perfectly normal—overalls, playsuits, hunting jackets, and the
like. The fastener had proved itself in an even wider range of
articles, withstanding the strains of a corset, the rough laundering
of workmen's trousers, the impulsive pulling and jerking of a
young child. The questions of fashion and propriety posed the
last barriers, and they seemed to fall largely because they stood
alone and because the salesmen could successfully make the case
that only the most reactionary gentleman could have a problem
with a device so obviously useful, neat, and clever. The acceptance by trendsetters such as the Duke of Windsor was obviously
useful, but it was really the zipper's acceptance by ordinary men
and women in so many of the articles of everyday life that made
resistance in the realms of high fashion so fickle.

The case for this undramatic, but ultimately compelling,
explanation for the final triumph of the campaign of 1937 is
bolstered by the simultaneous victory on the battlegrounds of
haute couture. Unlike menswear, in which a fundamental conservatism posed the central challenge to change and to the acceptance of zippers, women's fashions were in the 1920s and 1930s
a field of constant change and even revolution. The movement
of hemlines, the shifts in profiles and silhouettes from full to flat
to thin and back again, the constant search for styles novel
enough to catch attention but not so radical as simply to have no
wearers made the world of women's clothing, particularly at the
higher levels denoted by the powerful term "Paris fashion,"
one in which change was in the expected order of things and
experimentation had almost lost the capacity to surprise. By
1937 zippers were not unfamiliar features in women's underwear,
sports clothes, or other informal garments, but these were restricted domains. The full acceptance of the zipper in the full
range of women's clothing hinged on its appearance in the Paris
styles.

Women's fashion, even—or perhaps especially—at the level
of haute couture, is sufficiently complex and variegated an area

to make generalizing about a single season a risky business. Nonetheless, in the August showings of 1937 one trend seemed to stand out: slimness. The narrow silhouette struck most observers as the key feature of the offerings of such couturiers as Mme. Paquin, Edward ("Captain") Molyneux, and Robert Piguet. A less prominent consequence of this trend was the introduction of zippers into realms that had hitherto eluded them. The lamé evening gown of Lanvin, the tightly draped dress of Maggie Rouff, and, most notably, the long winter coat of Molyneux all sported zippers. Molyneux's long coat, in particular, featured a zipper that ran in the front from neck to hem, making it a prominent feature of a very expensive garment. Other coats, from hip-length suit jackets to ankle-length evening coats and daytime coats, sported slide fasteners, and the feature clearly caught the eye of reporters and buyers alike. A reporter for *Life* magazine remarked: "Overnight, the zipper, which since 1913 had been an accepted functional gadget for smooth, secure closings, became important as a style element." The relation between the zipper and the rage for slimness was evident: "Fashion writers, grateful for something different to ballyhoo, invented a new mumbo-jumbo. 'Pencil-slim,' 'molded silhouette,' 'poured-in look,' became stock phrases. Behind them all was the suggestion that by the magic of the zipper, plumpish women could attain a svélt figure."[23]

This was not the first appearance of the zipper in the world of women's high fashion. In 1933 Charles James, who began his career working out of Chicago, made a splash by spiraling a long zipper all the way around one of his dresses. Two years later Paris's most flamboyant couturier, Elsa Schiaparelli, always looking for new ways to startle, even shock, her contemporaries, saw the possibilities of the fastener. These were not, however, possibilities that even the most sanguine of the zipper makers would have imagined. "Sciap" was inspired not so much by the zipper's mechanism or function, or by the lines that a zippered closure facilitated, as by color. The eye of the Italian-born designer was caught by a new product of the fastener makers, the first plastic zippers. In the desperate attempt to find means for providing colored fasteners that would readily blend into a garment, one of the most promising, though technically challenging, avenues was to abandon the metal zipper entirely and replicate

The new plastic fastening featured in the

Schiaparelli Autumn Collection

On shoulders, sleeves and skirts; to front, side and back openings and on pockets, the "Lightning" plastic zipp is fitted both for the decoration and for the smooth, swift fastening of Evening, Town and Sports wear.

Elsa Schiaparelli was not the first haute couture designer to experiment with zippers, but she was the most flamboyant. Her use of brightly covered plastic zippers, especially, encouraged wider experimentation with the fasteners, leading to their general acceptance by the late 1930s. *LIGHTNING FASTENER, LTD.*

194 the zipper design in a totally new material. By the 1930s the facility for precision-molding plastics, particularly the easily melted (and readily colored) cellulosics like celluloid or Pyralin, was well established. With the assistance of Du Pont, makers of the nitrocellulose Pyralin, the engineers in Meadville created a plastic zipper that took the brightest colors anyone could wish. In Great Britain, Lightning, aided by the plastics' makers of its parent firm, ICI, began producing a similar product. When Schiaparelli encountered them, she was clearly thrilled by the possibilities. The creator of "shocking pink" described the reaction in her immodest autobiography, *Shocking Life* (in which she generally referred to herself as "Sciap"). She put the introduction into the typically overdramatic context of a world "split just then between kingdoms, republics, and dictatorships" and a Europe distracted by international conflicts. "Fashion," she remarked, "even in the most difficult years, when it goes eccentric or foolish, undoubtedly retains some relation to politics." She added: "Sciap, catching the mood, showed regal clothes embroidered with pearls or daringly striped, but what upset the poor, breathless reporters most were the zips. Not only did they appear for the first time but in the most unexpected places, even on evening clothes. The whole collection was full of them. Astounded buyers bought and bought. They had come prepared for every kind of strange button. Indeed these had been the signature of the house. But they were not prepared for zips."[24]

Who could have been prepared for Sciap's zips? These were not closures, not discreetly placed plackets with zippers to open and close a gown conveniently; they were ornaments—and, in the Schiaparelli style, flamboyant, colorful ornaments. This was, after all, the designer who used Salvador Dali as a source of inspiration, who decorated her gowns with closed bureau drawers or bright maroon lips and made a hat that looked like a shoe. Schiaparelli was also eager to experiment with new technology. She was perhaps the first Paris designer to adopt synthetic fibers; the story was told of a synthetic Schiaparelli gown that was sent to the cleaners and dissolved in the dry cleaning fluid. Elsa Schiaparelli was undoubtedly a woman of enormous ego, so it would be wise to take with caution her claim that she set the fashion world acock with her zippers. Nonetheless, her 1935 gowns were the first to proclaim the decorative possibilities of the

new fastener—an appropriate statement from a designer already
famous for flamboyant buttons.[25]

It is hard to find any widespread effect of Schiaparelli's zippered gowns. By 1937, however, the fashion world seemed ready for zippers. Edward Molyneux's pencil-thin coats received much attention, and his use of zippers to accent the narrow silhouette was not lost on observers. Schiaparelli herself continued to promote the fastener, sometimes in less showy ways. *The New Yorker* commented that "she still uses Talon fastenings on clinging, crisp dresses with greater effect than anybody else." The zipper salesmen noticed and were quick to take advantage. Autumn advertisements for Talon fasteners in *Vogue* alternated between references to the usefulness of zippered corsets and girdles to keep shapes thin for the narrow silhouette and showing evening dresses and skirts with Talon fasteners in the plackets. The promotion for girdles had been carried on for some years, but the touting of fine gowns with zippers was something new. The advertisements sometimes mentioned cooperation with the Fashion Originators Guild of America, which kept a registry of designs. One arm of the guild, the Dress Creators' League, was a group of prestigious dressmakers who focused on the manufacture of garments in the junior miss sizes. Kinney wined and dined representatives of the league and got them to agree to use zippers widely in their lines for at least two years. He in turn agreed to Promote the zipper's use in their products with heavier Talon advertisements.[26]

The memorable result of this was Talon's most famous advertising. In such magazines as *Life*, *Ladies' Home Journal*, and *McCall's*, there appeared a striking series of ads, warning of the dangers of "gap-osis." This was a self-conscious spoof on the familiar Listerine mouthwash advertising that directed Americans' attention to the horrors of "halitosis." Pictures of women with buttoned plackets and prominent open spaces bulging between the buttons were accompanied by sets of eyes with dashed lines drawn inevitably to the gaps. "Today America lifts its eyebrow at 'Gap-osis,' " admonished one ad, while another told a story: "It started off like a real rush . . . orchids, football games, sixth row on the aisle and all that. Then suddenly p-f-f-f-t! It was all off! What happened? A true lover's tiff? No! Just 'gaposis,' the carelessness that kills glamour . . . the untidiness that

"Does your slip show? Haw, that's a good one!"

It's no laughing matter to have "gap-osis"—a show-off placket. Especially nowadays—when everybody's attention is on neat little waistlines. It's wiser to insist on smooth Talon slide fasteners in the plackets of dresses you buy. They're swift, secure. Never gap or pop...Then—to make certain you're getting a really satisfactory slide fastener—"take a second look" for the trademark "Talon"!

TALON SLIDE FASTENER • MADE BY TALON, INC. • MEADVILLE, PENNSYLVANIA

The "gap-osis" campaign, aimed at the women's clothing market, was an imaginative takeoff on the well-known mouthwash advertisements featuring the artificial disability halitosis. James Thurber, famous for his satirical depictions of the "war between men and women," was the perfect illustrator. TALON, INC.

makes men shudder." After some effort Talon was able to get James Thurber, one of the comic geniuses of the day, to adorn some of these ads with the distinctive Thurber men and women who had become symbols of the "battle of the sexes" in the 1930s.[27]

The year 1937 was the culmination of a struggle for technical refinement and commercial acceptance that had been waged for more than forty years. At year's end, there could be little question in the minds of observers that the zipper was on its way to becoming a permanent part of everyday life. It is fitting, therefore, that at this moment the one man who had made this achievement his life's work, who had witnessed its awkward and difficult beginnings in Whitcomb Judson's "clasp lockers," and who had never lost faith in its promise, should finally pass from the scene. Colonel Lewis Walker was eighty-two years old but still carried a vigor and energy that were the marvel of those around him. Since 1933 he had slowed down a bit, but he did not relinquish the reins comfortably. The sudden death of Lewis, Jr., in 1935 had been a great personal blow to the Colonel, but the old man had carried on, continuing as the chairman of the Hookless board of directors and overseeing its transformation into Talon, Inc. In October 1937 he helped along the extraordinary 250 to 1 stock split that had been necessitated by Talon's new prosperity, although the company kept its stock off the exchanges. Finally, in November of that year, he acknowledged the tolls of old age and asked that Wallace Walker be put in charge of the company's affairs. On January 24, 1938, Lewis Walker died, but by that time the old Victorian had put his own stamp on the twentieth century.[28]

In the final years of the 1930s the zipper at last insinuated itself into everyday American life. While the rest of industry continued to struggle fitfully to extricate itself from the greatest slump in history, the zipper manufacturers were engaged in a spectacular rise in production and sales. The total industry sales for the breakthrough year of 1937 was 139.5 million fasteners, which was not a great rise from the year before. The total sales for 1938, however, were 202 million (a 70 percent increase); and for 1939 the figure was 300 million. This growth slowed in 1940, but by the end of 1941 total zipper production in the United States had topped half a billion units.[29]

Just as significant as the overall growth of this period was where that growth took place. The records for Talon (which still accounted for about two-thirds of U.S. zipper production) show that while trouser makers took less than 3 percent of 1937 sales, by 1939 they accounted for almost 14 percent; dress and skirt makers took 14 percent in 1937 and more than 20 percent in 1939. The journal *Apparel Manufacturer* estimated that almost 80 percent of the dress and sport trousers made in the United States in 1940 were zippered—an astonishing and rapid transformation of a fundamentally conservative industry. The full scale

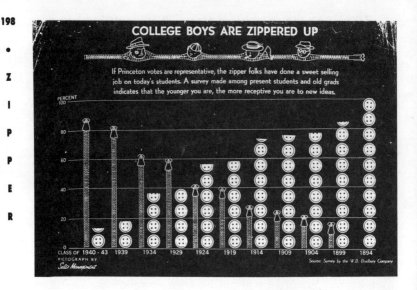

COLLEGE BOYS ARE ZIPPERED UP

If Princeton votes are representative, the zipper folks have done a sweet selling
job on today's students. A survey made among present students and old grads
indicates that the younger you are, the more receptive you are to new ideas.

PICTOGRAPH BY *Sales Management*

Source: Survey by the W.B. Bradbury Company

**The dramatic turnaround in the fortune of zippers in men's clothing is illustrated
neatly by this pictogram, which appeared in a marketing magazine in 1940.**
SALES MANAGEMENT, *OCTOBER 1940*

of this revolution was reflected in the results of a curious survey
reported in *Sales Management* magazine in the fall of 1940. Presumably taking advantage of the annual gathering of alumni at
Princeton University, the W. B. Bradbury Company queried
both current students and the members of the reunion classes
from 1894 to 1939 (that is, a sampling of alumni from classes
spaced five years apart) about what they were wearing on their
trousers. While not a single member of the class of '94, men in
their sixties, would admit to having the newfangled closure,
almost 85 percent of current students were sporting zippers. In
the classes between, there was a steady drop-off of button use as
one asked younger and younger graduates. The transformation
of men's and women's clothing that had been so earnestly sought
for more than twenty years by the fastener makers was completed
with astonishing speed.[30]

Just now, however, a new cloud that was to halt this fantastic
progress in its tracks appeared on the horizon. Even as the
Princeton students sported their new zippered trousers, the war
that had begun in Europe late in the previous summer turned

ugly. While the first few months after Hitler invaded Poland in September 1939 were characterized by a "phony war" in the west, with the coming of spring in 1940, the German armies turned toward France. On May 10 the Wehrmacht poured across the Dutch, Belgian, and French frontiers. The fall of France was quick work, and the British, after the desperate scramble of Dunkirk, hunkered down. In December 1940 President Roosevelt informed a reluctant nation that America had to be prepared to become the "arsenal of democracy." At the same time the administration began putting together the governmental machinery to rearm the country, coordinated by the Office of Production Management. Within months it became evident that the new emphasis on national defense would require controls over every aspect of American industry. By the fall of 1941 the implications of this for the zipper makers began to be clear.

As early as August 1941 the supplies of the copper alloy that fed the chain machines in Meadville and elsewhere stopped. Within weeks Talon sent eight hundred of its more than fifty-two hundred Meadville employees home—the first substantial reduction in the company's work force in more than a decade (the company was never to employ so many again). What the Great Depression had failed to do, the push toward war accomplished. The dependence of the slide fastener makers on valuable alloys was their Achilles' heel. By 1941 the production of zippers took 0.6 percent of U.S. copper production, 0.2 percent of all zinc, and 1 percent of total nickel output. These amounts were not negligible to the planners in Washington, but zippers, while perhaps a novelty no longer, had no priority in strategic thinking. Thus the people of Meadville, whose economy was now overwhelmingly dependent upon Talon, were threatened with a shutdown, a fate they were to share with such disparate sorts as the refrigerator makers of Mansfield, Ohio, and Evansville, Indiana, and the washing machine manufacturers out in Newton, Iowa. The irony of such impending economic disaster, with its ensuing unemployment, while the rest of the nation boomed under the stimulus of defense production, was not lost on observers.[31]

The zipper manufacturers fought back at first. Talon president William C. Arthur, who had taken over upon the death of Wallace Walker in 1939, went to Washington to argue his industry's case. By this time there were twenty-one companies making zippers in the United States (although some of them only assembled parts made by others). Arthur argued that the value that these producers got out of the metal they used was exceptional. For each $1 worth of copper, the zipper makers added $2,037 of value in fabrication. Further, more than one hundred industries could now be counted that used the product, some quite dependent upon it. According to Arthur, this represented twenty thousand manufacturers with a quarter million workers. To replace all the zippers now consumed would, he estimated, take 1.3 *billion* buttons per year, and buttons were already beginning to be in short supply. Others reported that metal shortages had also crimped supplies of hooks and eyes and snaps and that the machines that garment makers used to produce buttonholes were almost impossible to find. A New York garment maker was quoted as saying, "We can go back to string—if we can get it. But to me it looks like Gaposis on a national scale." There was little doubt in Meadville, however, that the boom was over. As the secretary of the local chamber of commerce said, "Meadville's never thought it was bigger than Uncle Sam, and if he tells us we've got to take it, we will. But we'll think it's as unfair as hell."[32]

Before the full effects of the metal cutoff were felt, the zipper manufacturers flourished. With demand fueled by the anticipation of shortages, 1941 turned out to be Talon's best year ever, with sales reaching thirty-one million dollars. But the strategic requirements finally bit, and zipper production plummeted. While another novel product that had begun to catch on right before the war, nylon stockings, became completely unattainable and a famous symbol of the sacrifices of wartime, the zipper did not disappear completely. Talon and some other makers avoided total cutoff by persuading the government that the military itself would sorely miss zippers if they were banned from production. Lighter and shorter zippers were made in order to stretch available metal supplies. In addition, research that had been under way for years to come up with alternative materials for zippers intensified, with some results. The plastic zippers that had made their first appearance in the mid-thirties were still expensive and were judged too liable to failure for military applications. Other metals were experimented with. Steel had always been economically attractive to the zipper makers, but the combination of its hardness, which was murderous on the cutting parts of the chain machines, and its tendency to corrode and rust made it impractical. Stainless steel was the object of experiments, but it was particularly hard on cutting tools and so was abandoned. Talon engineers devised ways to galvanize the zipper scoops (coating steel with zinc), and they produced some quantity of this so-called V (for victory) fastener during the war.[33]

It is a bit surprising that there is no record of Talon's exploiting another metal, aluminum, with which Gideon Sundback had experimented some twenty years before. This metal's light weight and resistance to corrosion would seem to make it a natural for a slide fastener, but in fact, it posed real technical challenges, since it required careful alloying lest it be too soft to withstand much wear, and the finished product tended to be weaker than other zippers. Aluminum also required redesigned machinery for fabrication and finishing. Talon engineers apparently judged the problems posed by aluminum to be more trouble than they were worth, perhaps in part because this metal, too, was a strategic commodity. Only toward the end of the war did they turn to aluminum. Under different circumstances, however, aluminum was seen as the right material for the job. In Japan, where the government had restricted copper supplies to Tadao Yoshida's zipper shop in the late 1930s, the energetic entrepreneur made aluminum his vehicle for staying in business, which he was able to do even through the war years, becoming the military's chief zipper source. Yoshida actually flourished during these years, until his factory was completely destroyed by American bombs in 1945. The aluminum fastener, too, was to flourish, completely overtaking all other zipper materials in the years after World War II.[34]

American zipper makers were not able to sustain production as Yoshida did. By the end of 1941 zipper production had largely shut down throughout the industry. Talon was able to continue making a few plastic zippers, but these were expensive and had not acquired wide acceptance. As early as February of 1941 one of Talon's Meadville factories began making precision gauges for the machine shops of the makers of war matériel. While the chain machines ground to a stop, being unsuited for anything other than making zippers, the skilled mechanics who designed and built them were ideal producers of other critically needed machines. Talon boasted that its tool room could perform jobs requiring precision within one five-thousandths (0.0002) of an inch, and its six factories turned out bomb and shell fuzes, aircraft fasteners, mine detectors, parts for antiaircraft guns, hypodermic needles, and a variety of other gun and aircraft parts. The armed forces soon came back, asking for zippers, too, finding all sorts of places on airplanes and submarines where they were useful and expecting them on uniforms for everyone from paratroopers to tank drivers as well. The zinc-jacketed steel zippers were provided in response to this demand. In addition, the plastics expertise that had been acquired for the new zippers was put to broader use, and Talon became a supplier of molded plastic parts for war equipment—and an important source of poker chips for servicemen. By the late summer of 1943 the sense of urgency that had driven the early war effort had waned, and controls on civilian production began to be loosened. In May 1944 the Slide Fastener Manufacturers Association put together an exhibit for the War Production Board presenting the argument for the overall savings to be realized from unrestricted zipper manufacture. In trousers, it was claimed, two million yards of cloth could be saved by using zippers rather than buttons; in handbags the savings could be as much as nine and a half million yards; and in dresses, the projected savings were as high as twenty-five million yards of cotton and other fabrics. The zipper makers were allowed to resume nonmilitary manufacture, although there was no full recovery until 1945–46.[35]

The different responses of the belligerents to the problem posed by the zipper's dependence on strategic metals presented a curious set of contrasts. In the United States and Britain zipper production was curtailed drastically, and zippers joined the long list of consumer items that the home front just simply didn't see during the years of war. Yoshida in Japan, thanks to his savvy in beating out competitors and his willingness to experiment with materials like aluminum, was able to shift from dependence upon exports to becoming the military's supplier of the increasingly popular fastener. In Germany the zipper's popularity was already established, and thus the manufacturers were the beneficiary of the Nazi government's strenuous efforts to provide the public with such goods as would give them some semblance of normal life. For these years the zipper's fate, like that of so much else, was shaped by the combined decisions and values of entrepreneurs, bureaucrats, and the popular will. These, in turn, not only were products of business sensibilities, political and military exigencies, and fashion but were also shaped by deeper meanings that, from time to time, a technological novelty can acquire and foster and that for the zipper had, by the end of the 1930s, become widely manifest.

"Alligators of Ecstasy"

8

That we invest our technologies with meaning is neither novel nor surprising. At least since the Renaissance, when the first clocks were seen more as models of the workings of a divinely ordered universe than as timekeepers, both makers and users have seen much more in their machines than practical mechanisms. In the eighteenth and nineteenth centuries the machines that were remaking the economic and social order, such as steam engines and locomotives, drew both the admiration and the ire of poets, novelists, and essayists, not simply for the changes they wrought but also for the values that they seemed to incorporate. At the opening of the twentieth century this intellectual tradition found an eloquent spokesman in Henry Adams, who brooded on the meanings of the great dynamos that seemed to dominate the machinery at the 1900 Paris International Exhibition. As the century wore on, the new technologies that made it look, feel, and behave so differently from the past—the automobile, the airplane, radio, and the like—all drew their own literary detractors and admirers and those who saw in these machines and

devices the symbols for the order and disorder that characterized
their century.[1]

The zipper was different from the other technologies that evoked such responses. It was, after all, a small, even trivial, thing that no one could claim was remaking the world on any scale. It hardly compared with steam engines or electricity or air travel as a technology that portended great (and possibly evil) things. Yet in its smallness and simplicity the zipper managed to embody important messages about the way the world was organized and functioned. With remarkable speed it took to itself certain values and implications that were broadly recognized as parts of the twentieth-century order. Like other technologies that seemed to incorporate values, the meanings of the zipper derived both from what it did and how it did it. It seemed to pose challenges to traditions and harmonies that men and women everywhere in the industrialized world saw breaking down around them.

It's worth pausing for a bit in our exploration of the zipper's rise to look at the great variety of means by which the zipper's messages found expression in Western culture. These means ranged from high culture to low, from the province of the novelist to that of the cartoonist. In the course of all this, the zipper's messages became complicated yet remarkably durable and direct. To comprehend both the complexity and the durability, it will be useful to abandon the consistent chronology with which the zipper's story has been followed up to now and to range freely over the last seventy years or so, tracking down the voices and the signs that gave the otherwise trivial fastener surprising expressive power.

Unlike large technologies, zippers could hardly be the subject of intellectual discourse, the focus of anguished meditations on modern life. Such statements, even if they had occurred to writers, would have seemed laughable if made in a straightforward manner. Thus it is not surprising that the zipper's meanings should find expression in the realm of satire. A bit more surprising is the speed with which the zipper attracted the satirist's attention, as well as the locations of that attention. It was not in America, where the device was born and pushed so hard, that it first became the object of the combined respect and derision that characterizes satire's bite, but in Europe. The zipper caught the

eye of two of the early twentieth century's most successful prac-
titioners of ironic and critical literature, Kurt Tucholsky in Germany and Aldous Huxley in Britain. The one, only a few years
after he could have first encountered the device, made it the
subject of one of his humorous yet caustic commentaries on
modern commerce; the other, whose fame spread much more
widely, insinuated the zipper into the novel that was to sustain
his reputation for the rest of the century. Ironically, Huxley's
zippers, while certainly noticed by his contemporaries, made a
statement that is lost on the modern reader since his novelty is
now simply an accepted part of the order of things. In this fact,
too, obviously unintended by the author, lies some of the deeper
meaning of the zipper's literary experience.

Before he took his own life in 1935, at the age of forty-
five, Kurt Tucholsky wrote about twenty-five hundred articles,
poems, reviews, and stories. He won fame in the troubled 1920s
as the Weimar Republic's greatest satirist, but he became increasingly disillusioned with the promise of German cultural or political life, and during the period of his greatest fame he lived outside
the country most of the time, first in Paris and later in Sweden.
Born in Berlin of a comfortable Jewish bourgeois family, Tucholsky rejected most things Jewish and bourgeois and even *Berliner*.
He wrote most of his stories under various pseudonyms, one of
which was Peter Panter. In 1928, only a couple of years after
manufacturers began producing zippers in Nuremberg, a Peter
Panter story appeared that sought to answer the question of its
title "What Did the Inventor of the Zipper Look Like?" (*"Wie
sieht der Erfinder des Reissverschlusses aus?"*)[2]

Panter begins by painting a picture of the man who could
invent such a curious thing. "I think of him as an elderly man,
a mixture of contentment and peevishness. Happy when his wife
is out of town, vexatious in all other situations in life. He has
thin, white hair, even though he's not all that old; slightly lame
in one leg with a perceptible limp, discreet spectacles, a low
turndown collar like his grandfather used to wear." He is, naturally, an American, but of German extraction, and his name is
Sam. Sam, we are told, is a bookkeeper in a garden supply firm,
but he enjoys tinkering with things at every spare opportunity,
to the dismay of his plumpish wife. At the moment he is lying
awake in bed, thinking about the unsatisfactory clasp on his

wife's purse. He has a sudden inspiration, and the next morning,
Saturday, he proceeds to work all day at his bench, "knocking
and hammering and twisting with pliers. Then he goes out to the
garden shed and does some beating on the small anvil, gets the
soldering tools spluttering, and is very busy." The following
Monday Sam demonstrates his invention to a businessman.
" 'You pull here,' says Sam, 'see, and here, like this.' " There is
no reaction at first, but then the man tries the device himself,
"taking hold of the small leather article with tiny bits of metal
sewn onto it. He pulls. Not a sound is heard in the small room."
The businessman finally reacts: "Yes, it does have possibilities.
Some possibilities. How much do you want for it?" There are
some negotiations. Sam dictates a crude description of the invention and sells his idea for a "fat check."

The businessman hurries to the Patent Office, and his company is "firmly convinced that the chance of a lifetime has presented itself." But then the youngest manager asks a simple
question: "How does it work?" Silence. Sam's description tells
them how to make and operate the zipper but doesn't explain
why it works. Calls made to Sam's house are to no avail since
Sam "has gone off with a blonde, slender, beautifully manicured
girl—to Paris. At least, that's what the books say, and the film.
Sam has a briefcase full of dollars; the girl has a heart (and other
attributes) of celluloid." Ignorance of why the zipper works
poses no obstacle to success. "Before long the first pouches fitted
with zip fasteners are on the market, and they create a sensation.
Everyone wants to own a zip fastener. They fit out tobacco
pouches and ladies' bags and small cases and attaché cases. A
pity that all ladies' clothes cannot be fitted with them!" But:

*nobody can puzzle out how it does it. Nobody knows why,
oh why, does it work. Nobody. Manufacturers may make
it, but they really don't know exactly what they're making.
I don't know. You don't know. None of us knows. And
while you are reading this, the only person who does know
is sitting on the corner of the Boulevard des Italiens and rue
Helder in Paris, selling newspapers. Poor old Sam, he's lost
his last red cent. The celluloid girl has left him for another
Sam, named George. The briefcase is empty, empty of dollars, leaving a poor, old man who, as he creeps into the little*

*lodging house on the Boulevard Sebastopol where he sleeps
with eight market porters in a suffocating room, carries only
one little glow of malevolent triumph [Schadenfreude] in
his heart, because he knows why this little world-beating
invention works. And he tells no one.*

At the time Tucholsky wrote this, he had become disillusioned with ineffectual German socialism and was writing pieces
for the German Communist party. His dislike and distrust of
business and businessmen were profound, rooted as they were
in his upbringing by a colorless Berlin tradesman, his experience
of the great inflation of 1922–23, and his year of working in a
bank (when he despaired of making a decent living by writing).
The picture of ruthless but none-too-intelligent businessmen was
made perhaps a little easier by setting the story in America,
for Tucholsky appreciated the figure struck by Sinclair Lewis's
George Babbitt, though in a review of the 1924 German version
of Lewis's novel, he warned his readers not to think that the
German bourgeoisie were at all above the depressing values and
problematic morality of Lewis's character. So, on one level, the
story of the zipper was a vehicle for one of Tucholsky's frequent
caricatures of the commercial classes.

On another level, however, the tale is a wonderfully revealing
picture of how the zipper was actually perceived in the 1920s. It
should be noted first that while it is clear that there are few
zippers in clothing (pouches and handbags and attaché cases are
the cited uses), everyone is supposed to have encountered it. And
most particularly, everyone is supposed to have been impressed
by it. But nobody knows how it works. The zipper instantly
becomes a symbol of a technical cleverness that surpasses not
only the ordinary but the comprehensible. While, of course,
Tucholsky profoundly understates the technical challenge that
actually confronted the zipper's inventors, as well as the marketing problems that were just then beginning to be overcome, he
senses that the most marvelous thing about this device is not
what is does but how it does it. The action of the zipper is not
only not obvious but mysterious—so much so that one could
manufacture it without understanding how it actually worked.
The sense of mystery that surrounds the zipper's action is even
today part of its image. Two separate strands enter the slider at

one end and emerge at the other tightly joined; what happens in the dark of the slider itself seems to many observers a bit of mechanical magic. Tucholsky realized this and used the mystery to reinforce his image of the dull, exploitative character of the modern businessman. In the end the only solace left to poor Sam is his sole possession of the zipper's secret: *"Und er sagts keinem."*[3]

The early date of Tucholsky's story is especially striking. Even in the United States, by 1928 the zipper's use was still largely confined to galoshes and tobacco pouches, with some headway being made in handbags, other luggage, and occasional pieces of clothing. In Germany the zipper was even more novel and less common, but it struck Tucholsky as sufficiently well known to be a convincing vehicle for a story of mechanical cleverness betrayed by commercial greed. The promise of the zipper in clothing was clear enough to be hinted at, but only as a future possibility. It was only in the late 1930s that ready-to-wear outlets in Germany, such as Alfred Zentler AG, like those elsewhere in Europe and in America, turned to zippers for garments. In one other, much less obvious way Tucholsky anticipated the zipper's progress. In ending his short tale by reference to Sam's *Schadenfreude*, Tucholsky presaged the central theme of zipper humor. The German word does not have a precise or effective English translation, but it refers to joy that one feels at the misfortune of another. As a German compiler of zipper-centered humor, Helmuth Hartmann, pointed out, "Zipper jokes are mostly about *Schadenfreude*." They tell stories of zippers that fail at particularly embarrassing moments or that catch in ways that cause discomfort. In Tucholsky's day this kind of story had not yet emerged, since the zipper had yet no important role in clothing, but his tale certainly hints at the future possibilities.[4]

Toward the end of one of the great satirical novels of the twentieth century, Aldous Huxley's 1932 work *Brave New World*, Mustapha Mond, one of the world's "Controllers," confronts the Savage John and tries to explain why Shakespeare and the Bible and other classics must be kept locked away in this world six hundred years into the future:

". . . God isn't compatible with machinery and scientific medicine and universal happiness. You must make your

*choice. Our civilization has chosen machinery and medicine
and happiness. That's why I have to keep these books locked
up in the safe. They're smut. People would be shocked
if . . . ."*

The Savage interrupted him. "But isn't it natural *to feel
there's a God?"*

*"You might as well ask if it's natural to do up one's
trousers with zippers," said the Controller sarcastically.*

In fact, to Huxley, there was nothing at all natural about zippers,
and that is just why they are such a powerful yet subtle symbol
throughout his novel. The great irony, of course, is that in the
sixty years since *Brave New World* was published, the zipper
has become such a universal part of daily life that it does seem
almost natural. The symbolism loses much of its power by the
ubiquity of the symbol. How many of today's readers really
notice Huxley's zippers?[5]

From beginning to end, however, the world of 632 A.F.
("After Ford"), a world that, in the words of American reviewer
Henry Hazlitt, has "no place in it for love, for romance, for
fidelity, for parental affection," is filled with zippers. In this
future, human beings are condemned to lives of meaningless
contentment, kept that way by artificial pleasures such as "feel-
ies" (the next logical step after "movies") and "soma," a drug
that effectively and universally banishes anxiety and concern. An
essential part of this is divorcing procreation from sex. The former is now the province of factories, in which human beings are
created in test tubes. The latter is thus converted into yet another
tool of enforced contentment, and garments are supplied with
zippers to enhance the message that sex is easy and uncompli-
cated.[6]

This is not an explicit message, but any reader in 1932 would
understand why Huxley, for example, would describe so meticu-
lously his heroine, Lenina, undressing: "Lenina pulled at her
zippers—downwards on the jacket, downwards with a double-
handed gesture at the two that held trousers, downwards again
to loosen her undergarments. Still wearing her shoes and stockings, she walked off towards the bathrooms. [p.24]"

A bit later the Savage, John, who does not know the modern
world, having been reared on an Indian reservation kept apart

from society for anthropological study, discovers Lenina's suitcase: "Then, bending over the precious box, he touched, he lifted into the light, he examined. The zippers on Lenina's spare pair of viscose velveteen shorts were at first a puzzle, then solved, then a delight. Zip, and then zip; zip, and then zip; he was enchanted. Her green slippers were the most beautiful things he had ever seen. He unfolded a pair of zippicamiknicks, blushed, put them hastily away again; but kissed a perfumed acetate handkerchief and wound a scarf around his neck. [p.96]"

Soon John has the opportunity to discover the zipper's real use: "There, on a low bed, the sheet flung back, dressed in a pair of pink one-piece zippyjamas, lay Lenina, fast asleep . . . Then suddenly he found himself reflecting that he had only to take hold of the zipper at her neck and give one long, strong pull . . . [pp.97–98]." With "zippicamiknicks" and "zippyjamas" and all the pointed references to zipping and unzipping, no 1932 reader could fail to get Huxley's message. That their own clothes were very unlikely to have zippers (though they might) made the reference to easy and mechanized sexuality all the more unmistakable.

Huxley caught the twin symbolic messages of the zipper for the twentieth century: mechanism and sexuality. The zipper as machine is perhaps less striking than the sexual symbolism, but it is no less integral to its meaning. There is something particularly fitting in *Brave New World* that sexuality is liberated and enhanced by the mechanization of clothing, for this is a world in which the mechanical gospel of "Our Ford" is pervasive. Undressing—whether of one's self or of another—is an effortless act in Huxley's society, made so by the ubiquitous zipper. In becoming effortless, the act is robbed of its allure, like so much else in this chilling, efficient world. The intrusion of machines into realms normally thought completely and safely organic, like procreation itself, is one of the central themes in this novel, and the zipper reinforces it subtly but unmistakably.

More shocking, especially to contemporary readers, was Huxley's treatment of sexuality. *Brave New World* was even banned in Australia for several years as obscene, and indeed, the pointed incorporation of "unlimited copulation" into the social order of his utopia was one of Huxley's most effective touches in stripping this world of its normal humanity. The zippers that make all this sex so easy were, it must be remembered, novel to Huxley and his readers, and this enhanced their effectiveness in reinforcing the image of promiscuous sexuality. So accustomed is the late-twentieth-century reader to zippers as symbols of sex, or at least of the easing of sexual contact, that the power of Huxley's point in this connection is hard to appreciate.[7]

The literary uses of the zipper in this direction did not, of course, cease with Huxley. Particularly striking was the persistence of the combination of sexuality with machinery that was so central to the zipper's place in *Brave New World*. The best modern example of this is probably the following scene in Tom Robbins's 1984 satire *Jitterbug Perfume*, in which the somewhat randy and loony Wiggs Dannyboy is seducing the (relatively) innocent Priscilla:

> *"Ahh, I do love zippers. Zippers remind me o' crocodiles, lobsters, and Aztec serpents. I wish me tweeds had more than the single fly.... Zippers are primal and modern at the very same time. On the one hand, your zipper is primitive and reptilian, on the other, mechanical and slick. A zipper is where the Industrial Revolution meets the Cobra Cult, don't you think? Ahh. Little alligators of ecstasy, that's what zippers are. Sexy, too. Now your button, a button is prim and persnickety. There's somethin' Victorian about a row o' buttons. But a zipper, why a zipper is the very snake at the gate of Eden, waitin' to escort a true believer into the Garden.*

At the same time that Dannyboy is waxing so poetic, he is struggling with Priscilla's dress, "to part the teeth of the Talon that ran down the length of her green knit back." It doesn't budge, however, until Priscilla finally loosens it herself: "And with one smooth stroke, she separated the interlocking tracks, the 'gator yawned, and, lo, there she sat in her underwear." Even in such a scene of seduction, the zipper's mechanical nature—here represented by its resistance to working—is never far away.[8]

The zipper has remained a tool and symbol of seduction not only in literature but in other cultural expressions, such as cartoons, motion pictures, and song. One early and notable example of the latter appeared in the Richard Rodgers and Lorenz

Hart musical *Pal Joey* in 1940. Here, seasoned newspaper reporter Melba Snyder interviews the scrapping and somewhat
phony crooner Joey Evans, and she describes with gusto one of
her more successful past interviews, with the great stripper
Gypsy Rose Lee, while pantomiming a striptease herself, singing
a song punctuated with the word "zip." With remarkable speed,
the zipper established itself as the instrument for allure and seduction, whether private or public.[9]

As with so much else in American culture, perhaps the most
powerful and evocative venue for the use of the zipper as sexual
symbol was in motion pictures. By the 1940s Hollywood had
recognized the dramatic uses of the novel fastener, which was
particularly important in an age when the explicit depiction of
the bare body or of sexual contact was censored. In a recent
essay novelist Leonard Michaels suggests that zippers were "a
major erotic trope of forties movies." He points to *Gilda*, the
1946 film starring George Macready, Glenn Ford, and Rita
Hayworth, as a prime example. In one scene of this somewhat
convoluted movie set in Argentina, Hayworth repeats her complaint to her new husband, Macready (who is a Nazi agent), that
zippers are always giving her trouble, and she asks for help
getting undressed. In this simple act the movie exploits both the
mechanical nature of the zipper (with its occasional difficulties,
especially for the nonmechanical female) and the potential that
even a balky zipper always presents of a quick and complete
disrobing. Later in *Gilda*, Hayworth begins the motions of a
striptease in Macready's club, to the dismay of Ford, who is now
her protector. The last straw in her performance, before Ford
intervenes, is the moment she again asks for help with her zipper.
The zipper is an instrument of both seduction and subjugation.
With its ease of opening and its relatively public accessibility, it
offers opportunities for attracting sexual advances, but at the
same time its mechanical nature makes the zipper a masculine
intrusion—even weapon—in the intimate environment of a
woman's clothing. The women who wrote and produced *Gilda*,
like the woman who starred in it, probably had some sense of
how their use of the zipper, still novel enough to titillate their
audience, conveyed these mixed messages.[10]

So tightly bound did its sexual image become to the zipper
that it became one of the most readily understood and powerful

metaphors for sexuality, especially for an uninhibited and promiscuous sexuality. Perhaps the ultimate expression of that
power, and one of the most memorable evocations of zippers in
modern fiction, was in Erica Jong's 1974 novel *Fear of Flying*.
Unquestionably the image that stuck in reader's minds, even
many years after encountering the book, was that of the "zipless
fuck." In a book that claimed to break new ground in giving
free expression to women's feelings about sex, this fantasy of
"ziplessness" was the one that seemed to speak to universal
desires. Jong's heroine, Isadora, explains, "It was a platonic
ideal. Zipless because when you came together zippers fell away
like rose petals, underwear blew off in one breath like dandelion
fluff." This was sex without guilt, without consequences, without games of power or love: "The zipless fuck is the purest thing
there is. And it is rarer than the unicorn." "Ziplessness" had
nothing to do with actual zippers; it was rather a symbol of
dispensing with the barriers and complications that men and
women set up between themselves. This represents the zipper
itself as a complication, rather than an invitation or simplification
of sex. This in a sense turns the zipper's usual literary role on
its head, but by doing so, Jong is able to suggest how truly
extraordinary "ziplessness" would be if it were ever achieved.
She also provided a much more enduring symbol than she could
have with "buttonless," "snapless," or any alternative.[11]

In the second half of the twentieth century, a man who might
earlier have been accused of "chasing skirts" was instead said to
have a "fast zipper." When Lyndon Johnson boasted of how
hard his staff worked, he commented, "There's not a single
playboy among them. They don't sit around, and even at eleven
o'clock at night they don't drink whiskey. Neither do they run
around with their zippers open." In Germany someone might
be said not to have a *Reissverschluss* (zipper, or "tear-open fastener"), but a *Reizverschluss* (an "allure fastener"). The zipper
became a visual metaphor as well, with cartoonists making ready
and early use of it to suggest sexual opportunity. One of the
most notorious record album covers of the 1960s was designed
by Andy Warhol for the Rolling Stones' *Sticky Fingers*, on which
a real zipper opened to reveal Mick Jagger's underwear. When
Time magazine featured in 1969 a story on the "Sexual Revolution," a zipper was the prominent symbol on its cover. The

visual message was often a direct one, when uninhibited fashion designers made zippers prominent, frontal elements of a woman's dress. Any modern reader will be familiar with any number of other means in which the zipper is used to speak about or signal sexual possibilities or activity.[12]

This association between zippers and sex—particularly open and slightly naughty sex—is worth some reflection, for its cause is certainly not inherent in the device itself. There have been, and still are, many things for opening and closing garments— snaps, buttons, laces, belts, and so forth. Each of these things might be envisioned as being used in a sexy way (and surely has been). But none of them carries the seductive message of the zipper. A number of distinctive characteristics of zippers contributes to this message. One is speed; nothing suggests so strongly a quick and effortless opening and disrobing as the zipper. This is, after all, communicated not only by the device itself but by its name. From the late nineteenth century the term "zip" had been used to imitate the sound of a speeding bullet or some other object passing rapidly through the air. The aptness of this term for the action of the zipper contributed to the speed with which that name was applied to the device, with little prompting from the manufacturers. In May 1924, a little more than a year after the introduction of Goodrich's Zipper Boots, the British manufacturer of the Lightning Fastener, Kynoch's of Birmingham, bought the front page of London's *Daily Mail* (which claimed to have the "world's largest daily net sale"). In this spectacular (and costly) advertising move, made to coincide with the company's display at the British Empire Exhibition that opened that month at the London suburb of Wembley, the term "**zip**" is used throughout, and speed is a key motif. "A pull one way '**zip**' it is open, a pull the other way '**zip**' it is closed . . . dressing becomes a matter of moments [original emphasis]." Needless to say, "undressing," too, is made a matter of moments with the Lightning, and its seductive allure is already implied.[13]

The mechanical character of the zipper is the other fundamental aspect of its image and of the uses to which it is put in literature and art. To one degree, this is even more intrinsic to the device than its sexuality, for the slide fastener was, after all, designed from the first to be a mechanical closure. Arguably, the zipper is the first machine that any of us encounters on a regular

216

ZIPPER

basis in our daily lives, and this carries with it messages both good and ill. On the positive side, it is the machinery of the zipper that is at the heart of its utility. All the promotions of the fastener, from the C-curity and Plako of the earliest days to the first forms of the Hookless and the Lightning fasteners to its modern versions, rest eventually on the convenience and ease of opening and closing with a mechanism, rather than by hand manipulation of buttons or ties. In this sense the zipper is very much part of that great trend in Western civilization in which, to use the term of the Swiss architectural critic Sigfried Giedion, "mechanization takes command." With its meshing scoops, pulled together by a (one hopes) smoothly running guide, the zipper fits comfortably into the most general image of the machine, that of meshing gears. The zipper is thus, to borrow another phrase from another notable technological critic, Lewis Mumford, a perfect representative of "paleotechnic" culture— the phase in material development characterized by metals and mechanisms.[14]

The negative messages conveyed by the zipper's mechanical nature are more complex and ambiguous. On one level, the intrusion of a machine, however small and harmless, into the intimate realms of dressing and undressing, is to some, like Aldous Huxley, an unwelcome event. It can be seen to represent the greater threat posed by the intrusion of modern technology in all realms of human life, from daily routine to lovemaking to government. More than 150 years ago Thomas Carlyle bemoaned the "Age of Machinery," in which "nothing is now done directly, or by hand; all is by rule and calculated contrivance." To Carlyle, "everything has its cunningly devised implements, its pre-established apparatus; it is not done by hand, but by machinery." The capacity of the zipper to convey this kind of image has diminished since the 1930s, for its ubiquity necessarily dulls whatever threat it may seem to imply. Yet a closer reading of later allusions to the zipper, in high literature and low, suggests another aspect of the sometimes tortured relationship between human beings and their machines. This is the ever-present threat of failure.[15]

Whereas the earlier depictions of the zipper spoke of the ease of its working, the cleverness of its mechanism, and the convenience it afforded, once the device had become commonplace, attention was more likely to be drawn to its unreliability. An important aspect of the threat that machines pose to human beings lies in their treachery. By refusing to work as they promise and are designed to do, machines become demons that betray human trust. The scene described above from *Jitterbug Perfume* is an excellent example of this demonic side of the zipper, when Dannyboy "couldn't budge the damn thing." Such scenes and characterizations of zippers can be found in a great range of postwar literary settings. The popular critic and essayist Cleveland Amory, writing in one of his last *Saturday Review* columns, provided a good example: "Toward the zipper we harbor—and harboring is one of the things we do best—nothing but ill will. The fact is that, over a lifetime of trying to make the damn things work, we have at last reached the inescapable conclusion, which should have been obvious from the first, that they don't." In a very different venue, children's literature, we find the theme again. Robin Pulver and R. W. Alley's illustrated book *Mrs. Toggle's Zipper*, for example, tells the tale of a schoolteacher stuck in her hot, winter coat. "How'd the zipper get stuck?" one of the pupils asks. "Mrs. Toggle fanned her face. 'How does any zipper get stuck? First a tiny bit of cloth gets caught in it. Then you pull and keep pulling a little too hard. And before you know it, you're trapped in your coat like a hand in a cookie jar.' " The stuck zipper, and the embarrassment or discomfort that it causes, have become one of those technological images firmly planted in our culture, born from widespread experience but nurtured by its resonance with deeper feelings about being at the mercy of fickle machines. Zippers fit easily into the class of objects known as "damn things."[16]

"Damn things" are not merely unreliable devices; they are unreliable devices that betray a seeming simplicity or ease of use. If we use a tool that obviously requires skill or hard-earned techniques to master, such as a lathe or a typesetting machine, then we are much more likely to ascribe failure at least in part to shortcomings of the user or to improper demands upon the device. But for machines that are intended to be easily used by ordinary people, whether automobiles, personal computers, or zippers, failure is often immediately ascribed to the demonic side of the machine. Typically, also, the demonic nature of the machine is linked to the fact that ordinary individuals are simply not expected to understand how they work, much less expected to be able to correct failure. In the case of such a simple machine as the zipper, this damnable nature may seem unlikely, but it is reinforced by the perception that failure in a zipper occurs at particularly unfortunate times (when one is in a hurry or in a public situation) and in places where repair is impossible (through lack of tools or the impropriety of publicly working on one's zipper). In the case of Mrs. Toggle, for example, she has to seek out the assistance of a mechanic, who has the right tools to solve her problem. Mrs. Toggle, of course, has the advantage of having a zipper stuck on her jacket; she can therefore be public about her dilemma. Much more characteristic in depictions of zippers as "damn things" is the stuck fly on a man's trouser, a source of public humiliation.

The best evidence of the zipper's place in the mechanical demonology of the twentieth century comes not from literature but from folklore. Stories about zippers have a prominent place in modern "urban legends," those tales that are a part of the oral tradition of modern urban life. These are typically stories that are repeated time and again, in many different places, frequently not as make-believe but as reports of true events. The spread and repetition of these stories are evidence not of modern experience but of modern anxieties and desires, and the ease with which the zipper stories fit into this genre tells us a great deal about how the device acquired a meaning for our culture far beyond its technological role. One of the most popular stories made its way into Ann Landers's daily newspaper column:

> *Dear Ann Landers:*
> *Your latest zipper story made me laugh out loud. It also reminded me of another zipper story that happened to a friend in Chicago.*
> *While riding the bus to work, my friend glanced at the man seated opposite her. He was reading a newspaper. Suddenly she noticed the man's zipper was open and the gap was most embarrassing. She managed to get his attention when he turned a page. Using gestures, she directed his attention to the problem. The man was horrified and set about to close the gap.*
> *The very moment he yanked up his zipper, the bus*

*lurched and another woman, seated next to him, flipped the
tail of her fox fur over her shoulder. It got stuck in the man's
zipper and they were hopelessly entangled.*

*The woman, furious, suddenly yelled, "This is my stop!"
She got up to leave and of course, the man had to get off
the bus with her. The last my friend saw of this ill-fated
couple was the two of them on the street corner, struggling
to get free from one another.[17]*

What is most striking about this story is the semblance of
truth given to it, while in fact, it is an oft-repeated tale of zipper
Schadenfreude. This is a common characteristic of urban folklore. The best-known American reporter of urban legends, Jan
Harold Brunvand, has collected several versions of this tale from
around the world. One common variation, told in venues from
Australia to Belgium to Denmark, involves a man in a theater
who attempts to pull up his zipper just as a woman squeezes past
him on the way to her seat. Her dress (sometimes described as
made of flouncy chiffon) gets caught in the zipper and resists
efforts to free it. The theater is disrupted, the man and woman
both are horribly embarrassed, and the zipper (or sloppy handling of it) is the key culprit. In another variation of this story
the long hair of a woman seated in front of a man is caught when
the man attempts to close his fly. These stories are often told
with such specific detail as to lend great verisimilitude to them;
the Muntschouwburg Theater in Brussels or the Tivoli in Melbourne is given as a definite site. A significant variation on the
"passing lady stuck in a zipper" story is the "tablecloth in the
fly" tale. In this version a man on a date (or, sometimes, visiting
his date's parents) sits down at the table, noticing as he does so
that his fly is open. He discreetly, without calling attention by
looking down, reaches to zip the fly up and does not notice that
he has caught the tablecloth in his pants. When, at the end of the
meal, the young man gets up to leave the table, he pulls the
cloth with him, and everything comes crashing to the floor.
Customarily the victim in this tale is a man a bit full of himself,
such as a college fraternity president or athlete, who thus gets his
comeuppance through this experience. In this way the demonic
zipper is used as part of a morality story.[18]

Urban legend featuring zippers is not limited to stories of

stuck zippers. In another favorite tale the zipper simply plays a facilitating role but one that makes the story much easier to relate to and thus more easily believed. Brunvand tells this as the legend of "The Unzipped Mechanic." In this tale a husband has been working on his car most of the day. "When his wife comes home from shopping and sees his legs still sticking out from underneath" the car, she decides to tease him. "She reaches down, unzips the fly of his jeans, and gives him a little tickle." The man is so surprised he starts up and hits his head so hard against the bottom of the car that he collapses unconscious. At this point the wife screams, and her husband runs out of the house to see what is the matter. The man under the car is an auto mechanic whom he called on for help. In the full version of this story paramedics are called to take the poor mechanic to the hospital, but when they ask what happened to him and hear the story, one of them laughs so hard that he drops the stretcher holding the man, whereupon he falls off and breaks his arm. This is *Schadenfreude* with a vengeance. It is also an oft-repeated tale, internationally known, sometimes given embellishments or variations, but generally with the pivotal moment being the point at which the wife reaches for the man's zipper fly. Here the ancient comic elements of mistaken identity, sex, and slapstick are all thrown together, with a readily available zipper in the middle. Urban legends tend to repeat and reformulate such classic elements but put them into modern settings, with modern people and things, and even specific details, to convey an air not of a funny story but of the truth of modern life.[19]

One reason that the zipper possesses such comic possibilities, beyond its association with clothing, undressing, and thus sex, is the widely held yet unstated perception of the zipper as unnecessary. The Spanish philosoper José Ortega y Gasset once defined all technology as the production of the superfluous, but clearly some devices would be missed more than others were they somehow whisked away from us. Zippers are undoubtedly very handy things, but as their makers discovered very quickly, they do not do something that cannot be done in some other, often simpler (if less convenient) way. Buttons really will do for the most part, or snaps, flaps, laces, or a host of simple alternatives. A nice literary depiction of this part of the zipper's image is in Jack Finney's short novel *The Woodrow Wilson Dime*. Ben

Bennell is a Manhattan advertising copy writer, deeply dissatisfied with his marriage, his job, and just about everything else in his life. Things change for him one day, when he finds a dime in his pocket with Woodrow Wilson on the face. He gradually realizes that somehow he has shifted to a parallel universe, in which most things are the same as his normal one, but some are different. He is married not to his dull spouse but to the glamorous Tessie, the Giants still play baseball in New York, the Chrysler Building is the Doc Pepper building, and trolleys still run on the streets of Manhattan. The differences in the parallel world are enough to notice, but not enough to change substantially the pattern of life. In one scene Ben discovers something else that is different. As the couple undresses for bed, Tessie complains about her buttons: "They come off all the time and spoil the line of the skirt besides." Ben mutters something about putting a zipper in instead and doesn't pay attention to Tessie's reply, until a few minutes later he bolts up in bed and shouts:

> *"When I told you to put a zipper in your skirt, what did you say?"*
> *"Why, all I said was 'What's a zipper?' Ben! What did you turn on the light for? What are you doing with the phone book!?"*
> *"What's a zipper," I quoted happily, the yellow pages a blur as I flipped through them, my creative urge ecstatic. "I am looking for the name and address of the best patent lawyer in town!"*

A few days later Ben gets $250,000 for the invention of the zipper from a safety pin manufacturer and proceeds to introduce other unknown products, such as bicycles, 7-Up, and Scotch tape. Like these other items, and like a dime with Woodrow Wilson instead of Franklin Roosevelt on it, Finney regards the zipper as a distinctive but largely dispensable detail of the modern world. It is an unintended anachronism, therefore, when, a little later in the novel, just a short time after the scene above, Ben is described as "unzipping" a costume he has rented. Finney's mistake suggests the extent to which the apparently superfluous zipper is harder to imagine out of our world than we think.[20]

From the 1930s the zipper was seen as one of the defining

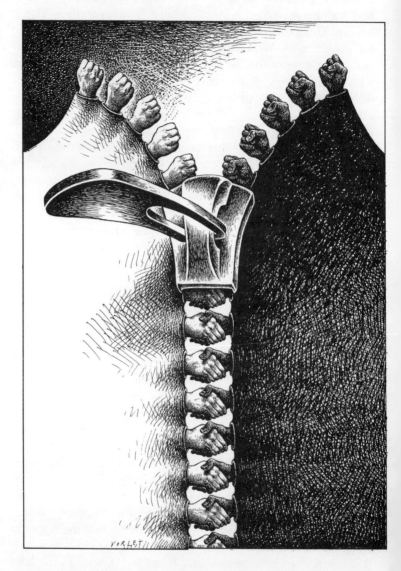

This drawing by Christophe Vorlet, accompanying a commentary about the integration of traditionally black colleges, appeared in the *Chronicle of Higher Education.* It is a powerful and imaginative evocation of the zipper's ability to show both joining and separating.   *CHRISTOPHE VORLET, BY PERMISSION*

elements of modernity. When the readers of London's *Daily*
Express late in the decade were asked to name the inventions that
seemed most distinctive of the twentieth century, the zipper was
named by more respondents than anything else. This perception
was reflected also in cartoons of the period: The appearance of
a zipper on a mummy or a churchman's gown seemed the height
of unlikely anachronism, an intrusion of the most obviously
modern into the ancient or traditional. In the years after World
War II the zipper naturally lost some of its power to convey this
idea of the up-to-date, but it acquired other meanings in specific
contexts, demonstrating powerfully the plasticity of the messages
that an artifact can be used to convey.[21]

One of the more curious yet widely recognized messages
that zippers came to be used to deliver in the postwar years was
that of generational and cultural rebellion. While the zippered
jacket had been introduced as early as the late 1920s, as a relatively expensive article of sports clothing, in the 1930s it was
wedded to an old American tradition of leather jackets. This
style was further influenced by military usage, especially for
pilots and parachutists during the war years, so that by the late
1940s the zippered leather jacket was readily available and was
associated with sporting and other outdoors activities that exposed the wearer to wind and weather. One of these activities
was motorcycling, and when Hollywood celebrated the anties-
tablishment nature of this alternative form of transportation—
noisy, powerful, exposed to the elements and thus the province
of uninhibited young men (and their "molls")—in the 1953
movie *The Wild One*, the "biker jacket" became one of the
decade's most evocative symbols of youthful rebellion. Marlon
Brando's jacket did not just use zippers to fasten, but long,
prominent zippers in the sleeves emphasized the vulgar, brash,
alienated culture that he (and his motorcycle) represented. The
prominent metallic gleam of the zippers (and the accenting metal
studs) reinforced the message of brash, unrestrained machinery
(and sexuality) in the service of rebellion.[22]

More broadly, the zipper came with increasing frequency to
be used as a general symbol of opening and closing, of joining and
separating. This was a message that could be conveyed verbally or
visually. A noisy young child told to "zip it up" understood the
demand to keep his mouth shut. A sandwich bag with a Ziploc

224

seal was one that could be opened and closed with ease. Cartoonists used zippers to play with the idea of firm closure, quick
closure, and even unlikely closure. The zipper became an icon,
in the sense of being a distinctive image that could be conjured
up in a wide variety of forms to convey its message. A classic
puzzle in which square pieces are moved around in a frame
can use the zipper as its basic image, for everyone knows and
appreciates what it should look like in its proper form. Jewelry
in the form of necklaces, earrings, and tie clasps can feature the
slide of a zipper as central pieces, for it possesses an elegant
symmetry in metal, which is appreciated only by being taken out
of its functional context. Instructions to tear an envelope open
will often be accompanied—or completely conveyed—by zipper
imagery, for it is international and wordless. By the last quarter
of the twentieth century the zipper had become as universally
understood and used a symbol as industrialized culture had yet
generated. If the meanings of this symbol seemed to shift and
turn, that was perhaps simply the ultimate sign that the device
itself had achieved some kind of symbolic transcendence over its
normally mundane utility.

C

H

A

P

T

E

R

The End of Novelty

9

The zipper's half century of novelty ended with the Second World War. So thoroughly did the war seem to mark the device's arrival into daily life that future commenters found it easy to forget that the acceptance and proliferation of the zipper were a largely accomplished fact, in both Europe and America, by 1940. The war, with its exposure of great masses of women and men to a new uniformity and to a variety of novel technologies, at the front and at home, was sometimes seen as the agent for making the zipper a ubiquitous and accepted part of normal life in the second half of the century. While this is largely a misconception, as we have seen, there is truth in the idea that the world war did take the last vestiges of oddity and curiosity off the zipper for most people. The end of novelty had many signs, some of them obvious and overt, others more subtle and, to a degree, more telling. On the obvious level, the recovery of the industry from wartime controls and restraints was swift and dramatic; by the end of the 1940s the annual sale of zippers in the United States approached one billion. The number of companies engaged in every aspect of the business exploded, as the rapidly expanding market combined with stabilization of the basic technology and the spreading familiarity with fabrication to open up the industry to all comers. The accommodation of clothing to zippers, which had commenced and accelerated in the 1930s, became the ordinary way of thinking about clothes in the postwar years. The zipper thus fitted neatly and unproblematically into the consumer culture that seemed to be the foundation for happiness and prosperity in the years meant to make up for the deprivation of depression and war.[1]

The more subtle signs of the end of novelty lay in the place given to the zipper in the scheme of everyday things and in its acquisition of a history. Novel things are characterized not by their history but by their departure from historical experience, so when something acquires a history, it sheds its novelty and enters the realm of ordinary life. Similarly, when something is new, it often possesses a mystery that is seen as the domain of a select few. While there may be some effort to explain what a new technology is and how it works, such explanations are often like introductions: limited information intended to make one feel comfortable with the unfamiliar, but not knowledge that one is meant to keep and build upon. In the decades after the war the zipper came to be seen as one of those features of life that really ought to be understood and made familiar, not as a marvel of human ingenuity or technique but as part of ordinary experience.

The emergence of a history for the zipper began relatively early, propelled not so much by the device's importance as by national pride. Although Kurt Tucholsky asked in his 1928 satire, "What did the inventor of the zipper look like?" the first serious public discussion of who had invented the zipper appeared in a Stockholm newspaper article of 1932. The Swedish public was told that although they might be led to believe that the zipper was an American invention, they should know that a Swede, Gideon Sundback, was its real creator. The roles of "Judgson" and "Colonel Walker" were described, but it was clear that until Sundback arrived on the scene in "Hobooken" their efforts were largely for naught. Swedish interest in the subject did not rest, however, with this early and somewhat inaccurate celebration of a national accomplishment. A few years later the founding director of Stockholm's Technical Museum,

Torsten Althin, took up the "problem" of the zipper's inventor
in a serious way and began gathering data on the subject. He
uncovered the work of people like Katharina Kuhn-Moos and
Peter Aronson and sent queries around Europe and America to
piece together the story. A few years later the museum's annual
journal, *Daedalus*, published an article by Sven Sköldberg, "Till
Blixtlåsets Historia" (On the zipper's history), the first documented look at the subject. Althin continued to gather material
in later years, newspapers published further popular accounts,
and the zipper came to be well known among Swedes as one of
their country's contributions to the twentieth century.[2]

At the same time that Swedish interest in the zipper story
was quickening, the American pioneers were beginning to think
of their own legacy. As early as 1925 Lewis Walker recounted
to the Meadville Literary Union the origins and progress of the
Hookless Fastener Company up to that time, but this was little
more than small-town boosterism. In the fall of 1932 Walker,
now feeling comfortable with his company's prosperity, as well
as intimations of his own mortality, approached Ida Tarbell with
the prospect of putting together the tale of the hookless fastener.
It was almost three decades after she had vaulted into the ranks
of America's most famous writers with her muckraking *History
of the Standard Oil Company*, and the choice might have seemed
an odd one for the conservative businessman. But Tarbell had
been born and reared in Meadville's corner of Pennsylvania, in
the heart of the old oil boom region around Titusville and Oil
City, and thus represented the finest local talent around. The
project apparently never yielded more than an interview with
Gideon Sundback (with the Colonel sitting at his elbow), and
even this was not to be found among Tarbell's papers when
they were gathered together for deposit in Meadville's Allegheny
College (a copy was found in the Talon files). In 1937 Talon's
patent attorney, T. L. Chisholm, put together a summary of
company history, and the next year, when Meadville observed
its sesquicentennial and when the Colonel's death was marked
with tributes local and national, the first, cursory public treatments of the zipper's history made their way into print.[3]

The Swedish connection was important even in the American
context. Beginning in 1939, an enthusiastic Swedish American,
J. A. Sundin, began writing Sundback and others to get the

zipper story straight. He located Peter Aronson's widow in Connecticut and made an effort to see that Aronson received equal billing with Sundback in the Swedish treatments of the story. Sundin also attempted to reach Harry Earle, hoping to get his impressions of Judson. It's not clear if he found Earle, but if he did, it would not have been a happy sight. The old salesman, who turned eighty in 1934, was in the Marcus L. Ward Home for Aged and Respectable Bachelors and Widowers, in Maplewood, New Jersey. He was in sad circumstances, with no savings and living off charity. In an exchange of letters with Gideon Sundback in 1939 he complained bitterly of his treatment by Lewis Walker, believing that the Colonel had squeezed him out of the fastener business and its history. For his part, Sundback treated Earle with great kindness, giving him some funds in his last years and gently seeking his recollections of the early days with Judson. Sundback, who in the early 1940s began to collect the elements of the zipper story for his own purposes, did not get much of value from Earle, whose memory was understandably shaky in his old age. When Earle died at the age of eighty-nine, in early 1944, his son wrote to inform Sundback, thanking him for "all you have done for Dad."[4]

Sundback himself did not do a great deal with the zipper story. He was careful to correct historical accounts that he thought did not allocate credit precisely, and he seemed particularly annoyed by those that appeared to give too much credit to Colonel Walker. But he was also conscientious about informing correspondents about the work of Judson and Earle. He may have been stirred somewhat by the inquiries he began getting from Swedish Americans and from Sweden itself in the late 1930s, and his prodding of Earle seems to have stemmed from some plans to put together a history himself, perhaps in response to some queries from the Franklin Institute, in Philadelphia. There's no evidence that Sundback completed such a work, but he continued to respond to inquiries and correct others' accounts.[5]

The first serious American treatment of the zipper as a historical subject was an article by P. J. Federico, of the U.S. Patent Office. Federico undertook numerous brief historical investigations of American inventions, and in the mid-1940s he latched on to the zipper. After several letters between Federico and Sundback and others at Talon, he published an article on "The Invention and

Introduction of the Zipper" in the *Journal of the Patent Office* **229**
Society in 1946. For his primary audience of patent attorneys and
examiners, Federico pieced together the technical history of the
slide fastener, with particular attention given, naturally, to the
sequence of patents taken out by Judson, Sundback, and others,
beginning in 1893. The article set out in an authoritative fashion
the basic outlines of the history of the zipper not as a novelty but
as a fundamental part of twentieth-century technology.[6]

For his part, Gideon Sundback was able to enjoy the bit of
notoriety that came his way as the zipper's inventor. In 1939 he
retired from his post as consulting engineer of Talon but kept
active by overseeing Canada's Lightning Fastener Company, visiting the plant in St. Catharines, Ontario, every couple of weeks.
He characterized his situation as "active retirement" and devoted
more and more of his energies to the pleasures of tree farming,
planting almost half a million trees on some property he held
about thirty miles outside Meadville. In 1947, at age sixty-seven,
he agreed to Talon's absorbing the Canadian and Mexican companies that he had founded, and in return, he took a place on
Talon's board of directors. He enjoyed such attentions as the
honorary doctoral degree he received from Allegheny College in
1937 and the medal he was awarded by the Swedish Royal Academy of Sciences in 1950. A popular article on the zipper by
Bertram Vogel, published in *Coronet* in 1949, spread word of his
contributions more widely, although he remained a bit sensitive
about the credit received by Colonel Walker (which had been
promoted in a much-reprinted piece by Bruce Catton a decade
before). Sundback never stopped tinkering; he described with
enthusiasm to a Canadian interviewer in 1952 his method of
applying zippers to shoes, in a sense trying to complete the task
that had moved Whitcomb Judson sixty years before. When he
died in mid-1954, he must have felt comfortable with his modest
bit of fame, as well with the acceptance of the technology he had
shaped.[7]

Another sign of the zipper's increasingly secure place in the
scheme of twentieth-century things was the spreading sense that
it needed to be "understood." Novelties are typically appreciated
for their clever departure from the normal and expected way of
doing things, and a familiar understanding of their working is

THE END OF NOVELTY

directed toward appreciating their cleverness and their departure from the ordinary. When novelty diminishes, however, then it is expected that a device will be understood simply as part of the accepted technological order: "This is how things are done." The extent to which the zipper's working was mysterious to people encountering it for the first time was illustrated well by Kurt Tucholsky's story in which no one, except the inventor, could explain it. It is not surprising, therefore, that showing how the zipper worked was an early promotional technique. The transformation of this into a part of education signaled the zipper's shift from novelty to normality.

On April 23, 1924, there opened in a field in a bit of a backwater of North London, known as Wembley, the British Empire Exhibition. The great structure of the fair was the large concrete Empire Stadium, which had been completed the year before in time for the final match of Britain's Football Association Cup competition. Next to the stadium there arose a large collection of somewhat ornate buildings, whose styling seemed to have been influenced by the recent uncovering of King Tut's tomb in Egypt. Inside the large palaces of Engineering and of Industry, as well as around the lake that had been sculpted into the landscape for the event, were scattered more than thirty kiosks erected by a variety of companies to promote their products. These provided welcome diversions, it was reported, from the primary exhibition spaces, so earnestly dedicated to showing the glories of Britain and its worldwide dominions. Among the kiosks erected by such well-known firms as Mackintoshs' toffees, Wilkinson sword (who added to the expected array of knives and blades "the Chinese Game Mah-Jongg"), and Lipton's teas was space taken by Kynoch's of Birmingham. There, in the bay of the Palace of Industry taken by the parent Nobel company, the makers of the Lightning Fastener attempted to introduce the British public to their novel product. One of the tools fashioned for this purpose was a giant mechanized fastener, whose slide moved up and down hundreds (if not thousands) of times a day, not only to show what made the thing work but also to demonstrate its reliability. One of Kynoch's managers reported to Lewis Walker that it was "making quite a splash" with the display, although it was not so striking to have caught the attention of reporters of the exhibition. Here, then, was a novelty, competing with dozens of sights for public attention.[8]

Almost thirty years later another model of a zipper was put on display, but in very different circumstances. On an island in the river Isar, in the center of the city of Munich, the Deutsches Museum von Meisterwerken der Naturwissenschaft und Technik (German Museum of Masterworks of Natural Science and Technology) has presented to its public since 1925 examples of important inventions and crafts, demonstrations of basic scientific principles, and celebrations of the best products of German technology. During the Second World War the extensive buildings suffered great damage from Allied bombing, and many years were thereafter devoted to reconstruction and replacement. In the course of this, in early 1952, the president of the German Federal Republic, Theodor Heuss, came to view the museum's progress. According to museum lore, the highly regarded Heuss, at the completion of his tour, turned to his hosts and asked, "But where is your zipper display?" While the documents don't tell us the president's arguments, the alacrity with which museum officials then proceeded to seek out a zipper model suggests that the case was made that an institution devoted to communicating the best of science and technology simply could not leave out such a basic part of modern life. Quickly museum staffers wrote to the zipper makers in Nuremberg to solicit a "10–20 times enlarged demonstration model of a zipper." After the better part of a year the giant zipper was placed on display in the museum's gallery of mechanisms, as part of the basic educational displays. Within six years it had been removed, to the dismay of the Nuremberg makers. According to the curator of physics, it just did not belong in the long-term scheme of things. The zipper was now, by the mid-1950s, neither novel nor interesting enough to make it into a museum devoted to "masterworks" and basic principles.[9]

Whatever the interpreters of a "higher" concept of technology might think, it is clear that by the early 1950s most people in both Western Europe and America would have agreed with President Heuss that the zipper was an integral part of daily life. The great commercial success of the industry in the decade after the war was the most powerful testimony of this. Sales in 1946 picked up right where they left off in 1941—up almost 25 percent from the last full year of production before wartime controls. They continued to climb during the 1940s, peaking in 1950 at 1.37 billion zippers sold in the United States alone. Recovery was similarly swift in Europe, where even production in the wrecked Nuremberg factory of ZIPP-Werk was back to its prewar level by 1950, despite the enormous dislocations of the German economy through the late 1940s. Renewed controls of strategic metals during the Korean emergency, plus an economic downturn, put a damper on American sales in the early fifties, although the industry successfully fought off major restrictions on its supplies, and it substituted aluminum for copper-based alloys on a massive scale.[10]

Even before the war was over, clothing manufacturers and others anticipated a pent-up demand for zippers. In a survey taken in mid-1945 more than 90 percent of American apparel makers stated their intention to increase their use of zippers. It was expected that more than 85 percent of trousers would use zippers, and more than four-fifths of all (nonpullover) sweaters. The extent to which clothing manufacturers and designers assumed that the zipper had a permanent place in their products is remarkable. It is only necessary to recall that before 1937 the zipper was still largely neglected by most of them, and during the years from 1942 to 1945 the item was not available to most clothing makers. There had been, therefore, only a few years in which zippers could secure their place in ordinary clothing, but the belief that it had done so was almost universal by the late 1940s.[11]

The zipper makers, for their part, expected demand to outstrip their ability to supply for several years after the war. These expectations help explain a dramatic change in the complexion of the zipper industry in the first postwar years. While there were no more than about a dozen makers of zippers in the United States before the war, by 1950 there were about 170 companies engaged in slide fastener manufacture. In the prewar industry almost all engaged in the business were "integrated" manufacturers, who fabricated every part of their product, but in the postwar years there arose a large number of firms that produced fastener parts or chain and others that assembled these parts and chain into finished zippers. The largest category of companies were the "assemblers," which tended to be very small firms, largely serving the garment industry. The small size of the assemblers, which were concentrated in the New York City area, enabled them to be very flexible in filling orders for the makers of men's and women's clothing, able to shift quickly to different demands for colors, fabrics, and zipper lengths. The equipment needed to take chain and other zipper parts and make complete fasteners was inexpensive, labor was largely unskilled, and selling could be very focused, in terms of both location and type of customer. Even the sector of the industry made up of new integrated manufacturers and chain makers was relatively easy to enter during these years. Chain machines could be purchased used or made by skilled mechanics, and the technology was now well and widely known. The war produced a sizable number of skilled tool- and diemakers looking for outlets in the civilian market, and the production of zipper machinery, to supply overseas customers as well as new domestic ones, was an attractive direction for some of these. New types of chain machines, using flat wire rather than the formed wire of Sundback's basic design, were easier to construct and maintain and could turn out zipper chain at a faster rate (although there was debate about how the quality compared). Several of these machine producers became chain manufacturers, supplying the bulk of components for the assemblers. The transformation from a small, oligopolistic industry into one diffused and highly competitive was sudden and shocking.[12]

The assemblers that transformed the industry were products of the war. The restrictions on new production created a novel demand for used zippers taken from discarded clothing, and small companies, with little capital, arose to meet this. These firms thrived on the services they could provide to apparel manufacturers and thus developed close ties with consumers in the garment industry. At the war's end it became evident that the garment makers found the flexibility and responsiveness of these small suppliers an attractive alternative to the large zipper companies, and the business of assembling parts emerged. The number of assemblers grew from less than half a dozen in 1945 to as many as 120 five years later. Because of the close relationship with the garment industry, the zipper assembly business was particularly attractive to many of the immigrants, especially Jewish ones, fleeing the social and economic chaos of Europe.[13]

The shift to the small assemblers was particularly encouraged by the spreading use of zippers in women's clothing. Whereas the variations in color and length of zipper used in trouser flies was modest, for women's skirts and dresses the range demanded by the many small firms that supplied these garments was enormous. The small assembly shops were better equipped to respond to these needs than firms like Talon or Conmar. Since almost 43 percent of all zippers sold in 1950 went into women's clothes, this steered a great deal of the increasing demand to the small companies. The increasing importance of the women's market also favored the shift to the lighter, smaller aluminum fasteners from the traditional copper alloy variety. These were cheaper (largely because of the low material cost), and their quality was less consistent, additional factors that favored the small assemblers, which had less at stake in quality control and could rapidly respond if a customer detected problems. An assembler could fill a garment maker's order in a matter of days, while the larger producers persisted in maintaining a six-week order cycle. The assemblers thus could compete fiercely in pricing: An aluminum fastener that cost an average of 8.4 cents if bought from an integrated producer in 1950 could be bought for 5.8 cents from the typical assembler, a 30 percent savings. The larger firms steadily lost ground in the late 1940s and 1950s: whereas Talon's share of the market in 1941 was estimated at 70 percent, by 1950 it was less than half that proportion, and the assemblers were estimated to have as much as 30 percent of the zipper market by the mid-1950s.[14]

The changes in the industry meant that the boom in zipper sales and usage did not translate into prosperity, either for the larger producers or even for the assemblers, taken as a whole. The profit rate for Talon plunged in the postwar years, from a 1946 ratio of profits to assets of more than 19 to less than 4 percent in 1952. The assemblers, for their part, had a high failure rate: Between 1951 and 1956 fifty-eight companies either folded or got out of the zipper business, and all but nineteen of these were assemblers. The problems plaguing the producers, both large and small, were not ignored. In the fall of 1952 several zipper makers, primarily smaller ones, met together in New

York City to organize a Zipper Industries Association. Unlike the well-established Slide Fastener Association (organized as suc- cessor to the Slide Fastener Manufacturers Association in 1950), the proposed ZIA was to be more than a friendly trade organiza- tion, but a means for bringing order to the market. One of the promoters analyzed the situation succinctly: "One of the reasons that conditions are so bad in this industry is that it is awfully easy to get into and to make a start in this industry—what we call 'the ease of entry into this industry' and it is one of the important things in determining anti-trust violations. One of the things that struck us is the small amount of capital needed to get into the industry. This is particularly true of the chain producers and assemblers where a small amount is required to get into the industry, resulting in a great many people going into the industry and causing over-production." In addition, it was pointed out, all basic patents had expired and thus posed no restraint to entry, and "there is no complicated know-how" required to get into the business. The result was not only overproduction but "a great deal of unfair, illogical, and self-destructive competition."[15]

How "unfair" or "illogical" the competition was probably depended on one's point of view, but there is no question it was self-destructive. The records of the Slide Fastener Association show that membership reached a peak in mid-1951, at sixty-five, and declined swiftly thereafter, falling to thirteen by the end of 1955. This was not an accurate reflection of true numbers in the industry, those companies joining the association probably representing the more stable ones in the business. If this was the case, the weeding out of companies was probably even swifter than these numbers suggested. Nonetheless, when A. B. Carlip wrote his Columbia University Ph.D. dissertation in economics on the zipper industry in 1960, he concluded that the division of the industry between integrated manufacturers and smaller assemblers and components suppliers seemed permanent and that the large companies would never regain their prominence. He also noted that since the end of World War II imports had not been important in the American market.[16]

It was true that whatever problems the larger zipper produc- ers had in the 1950s, imports were not among them. Indeed, this was the decade in which American producers like Talon finally reached overseas as well as spread out at home. The joining of Talon with the Sundback interests in 1947 reversed the inward-looking marketing approach that the Colonel had set for the company three decades before. The moves abroad continued to be conservative, however, as Talon continued to stay out of Europe during this period. Joint ventures with local companies produced factories in Argentina, Jamaica, and Hong Kong. Even more important for the future, Talon joined the stream of American manufacturers that were pulling out of the old industrial heartland of the Northeast and heading south. Lured by the inducements that drew other northern firms, such as nonunion labor, cheaper land and energy, and a steadily improving transportation system, Talon first moved in 1949 into the old pine-logging town of Morton, Mississippi. A few years later Cleveland, Georgia, was enjoying the benefits of another Talon plant, and early in 1954 yet a third southern factory opened in Woodland, North Carolina, where production centered on a cheaper fastener for the womenswear market, called the Falcon. The largest of the southern operations followed shortly, in the middle of the textile-producing region of Gaston County, North Carolina. Here, at Stanley, the company focused its sizable tape weaving operations and later its primary nylon zipper facility. The company's answer to its new, fiercely competitive environment was a combination of cost-cutting measures and technical innovations, which worked for several years to reverse its decline in market share and profitability.[17]

The zipper makers never stopped experimenting and innovating. Even in the years after World War II, when energies were focused on keeping up with burgeoning demand and then dealing with cutthroat competition, research and development did not cease, although it did fall off considerably from the prewar years. Economist Carlip counted a total of 526 slide fastener patents issued between 1935 and 1954, although only half as many were issued in the second ten years as in the first. As might be expected, Talon received the largest number of patents in this period, 189 (36 percent), with the rest being distributed among the smaller companies and individual inventors. But Carlip also estimated that Talon used only about 13 percent of the patents it was issued and that even many of the patented product innovations that made it to market had only limited impact (the machine

and process patents may have been more useful). The most important results of research efforts continued to be the development of new applications, which typically required little or no
modification of the zippers themselves. This was yet another
reason that the large companies were so ineffective in blocking
the smaller competitors: Anyone could exploit an application
once it was known and the market was developed.[18]
Just as Carlip was counting patents and drawing his conclu-
sions, however, there emerged the most important modification
in zipper design and fabrication since Gideon Sundback's original
Hookless #2, and its appearance was eventually to transform
the industry in ways the economist clearly did not imagine.
Experiments with plastic zippers had yielded fruit as early as the
1930s, when the bright colors and quiet action of the first celluloid zippers caught the eyes and ears of Elsa Schiaparelli and
other couturiers. Celluloid, and even the somewhat sturdier acetate that followed, were not durable materials, and fashioning
them into the basic Sundback design was not easy or cheap, so
in spite of the real desire for color and lighter-weight fasteners,
the first plastic zippers did not make much of an impact outside
high fashion (and even there the influence was apparently ephem-
eral). A bit later a more satisfactory plastic zipper was molded
from polystyrene. It was sturdy and dependable but still too
expensive to compete with traditional alloys. Another, much
cheaper plastic fastener that did away with the zipper scoops
altogether was introduced in the early 1950s. Superficially resem-
bling a zipper and utilizing a similar form of slide, this device
consisted of two grooved bands of extruded plastic. When the
slide brought the bands together, they were forced into each
other, thus providing a closure. Talon's version was called the
Plasti-Zip, and it was adapted to cheap applications that bore
little stress, such as garment bags and portfolios. The principle
is still to be found, without the slide, in varieties of plastic
sandwich bags (Ziploc). It was readily apparent, however, that
this design provided no substitute for the metal zipper in most
uses.[19]
The fundamental problem was that while plastic was an attractive material for a slide fastener, it did not function well with
the design of the metal zipper. A new design was to change
things. Actually the design that Nicholas Wahl came up with in

1939 was not really that new. The concept of a fastener made of interlocking spirals could be traced back at least as far as the German patent taken out by Max Wolff in 1890. But the steel springs that Wolff suggested simply did not have the proper combination of elasticity and security to make a useful fastener, not even when shaped from wavy steel wire, as put forward in a later patent. George Prentice had tried out a similar design, attempting to supply competitors of Goodrich's Zipper galoshes in the 1920s, only to change quickly to a Sundback-like fastener. Metal wire, however configured, simply did not supply what this design needed. What was needed was a material whose elasticity could be controlled with great precision, whose shape could be formed to close tolerances, and that was not expensive. Before the 1930s such a material simply did not exist.[20]

By the time the decade was over, however, the perfect material had emerged, although realizing its promise would take almost another twenty years. Working in the laboratories of E. I. du Pont de Nemours in Wilmington, Delaware, a brilliant Iowa-born chemist, Wallace Hume Carothers, was trying to mimic nature in a way no one had done before, to produce an artificial silk. There were numerous silk substitutes, primarily cellulose nitrate and cellulose acetate, but Carothers wanted better, so he went back to nature itself and attempted in a sense to mimic the silkworm by putting together the basic building blocks of a protein. The result was a remarkable superpolymer, a polyamide that was like silk in many ways, fell short in some directions (it could never be made as resilient as natural proteins like silk or wool), but far surpassed its model in many others. While the first hint of the new material could be seen in experiments as early as 1930, it was not until 1934 that the Du Pont chemists had a recognizably promising substance and only in 1937 that they filed for the basic patent. Three weeks after that filing, on April 29, the moody Carothers, who had just turned forty-one, ended his life with a dose of cyanide taken in a Philadelphia hotel room. The material he had ushered into being was one of the most versatile products ever to come from a chemistry laboratory. Nylon could be made in a wide variety of forms and consistencies. As the public was to soon find out, to its astonishment, the same material could make its way into stockings, parachutes, fishing lines, brush bristles, window screens, and ropes. It took a bit longer, but it also turned out to be the answer for the spiral zipper.[21]

This was not, of course, readily apparent in 1939. Nicholas Wahl and his three brothers immigrated to the United States, where, while operating a costume jewelry business, they attempted to interest potential developers in their spiral zipper design. They did not get very far, and soon the demands of preparedness and war diverted the capital and enterprise that might have been available to the effort. The Wahls were not able to take quick advantage of the zipper boom of the late forties, but by the early fifties they had found backing and a Connecticut company, Cue Fastener, Inc., to take up the required development work seriously. Progress was not rapid, however, and experimenters in Europe began to overtake the American efforts. W. Erich Heilmann began his Opti-Werk company in a small factory in Germany's Harz Mountains soon after the end of World War II and in less than a decade had built it up to a major zipper producer. When Nicholas Wahl traveled to Opti's offices in Essen in 1955 to promote his spiral design, he found a genuine enthusiast in Heilmann. In a matter of months, nylon spiral zippers were on sale in Germany and France, and their advantages of light weight and true and fast colors were making them conspicuous alternatives to metal fasteners.[22]

Even if problems of quality and price still plagued the nylon zipper, it was evident at this point that they posed a potential threat to the traditional device. In the mid-1950s Talon began reaching out beyond its traditional base, promoting a spring-operated shoe fastener (Shu-Lok), acquiring a button and snap manufacturer, and eventually approaching the Cue Fastener company for a piece of the nylon zipper action. Talon was in no way satisfied with Cue's product, but it needed the Wahl patents and the plastics-forming expertise of the Connecticut company. Considerable additional research and development were required to come up with a satisfactory product, forcing the Talon engineers into very new realms of chemistry and extrusion machinery and necessitating close cooperation with Du Pont's nylon experts to devise precisely the right formulation of the material. Finally, in March 1960, Talon introduced its Zephyr fastener, touting not only its color and small size but also its "self-healing" properties. A nylon coil fastener, unlike a metal one, can be pulled open manually, to release a snagged thread, for example, and then reclosed with little difficulty. In addition, the rounded edges of the flexible nylon are far less threatening to fraying cloth (or exposed skin) than a zipper's metal scoops. Little wonder, then, that the Zephyr appeared to be the salvation of the large zipper maker's fortunes.[23]

By some measures, the Zephyr and similar products of other companies were successes. Only three years after its introduction, half of those polled in a consumer survey (all women) were aware that there was a new zipper on the market, although only a fraction knew the name Zephyr or even knew that it was made of nylon. Most respondents said they preferred the new zipper over the old metal ones. On the other hand, about one-fifth of those who had used it reported problems, most commonly through ironing. There are many who can still remember, no doubt, the dismay with which they lifted a new skirt or pair of trousers from the ironing board, only to discover that the iron's heat had melted the nylon zipper, thus destroying it. The fact is that despite their intensive research efforts and much-trumpeted quality controls, the American zipper makers had introduced their product too soon. While nylon indeed could be (and quickly was) formulated to withstand a hot iron (at least for a short time), too many zippers hit the market before the problem became apparent. Other quality problems plagued Talon's production. The buyers for Levi Strauss of San Francisco, the world's premier maker of blue jeans and a huge zipper consumer, complained bitterly of the massive failure of the Zephyr, especially on its Panatela line. Levi Strauss debated moving its account to a rival zipper manufacturer, like Scovill. There was even a hesitant mention of the possibility of purchasing from a promising new Japanese supplier, YKK.[24]

These difficulties were not insurmountable, and after a rocky start the 1960s turned out to be glorious years for the American zipper makers. The total number of zippers sold climbed steadily for much of the decade, going from 1.2 billion units in 1960 (which was less than the 1950 total) to almost 2.3 billion in 1968 and peaking at 2.33 billion in 1972. By 1974, when statistics began to be gathered on the question, more than 43 percent of the total zipper sales were nonmetallic zippers, which by this time included not only nylon spirals but also advanced versions

of heavier-duty continuously cast plastic fasteners, often using
other polymers, such as polyester or polystyrene. The shift to
plastic was accompanied by a return to the dominance of large,
integrated producers over smaller assemblers and component
makers. The capital needs for plastic zippers, patent protection
for new designs and machinery, and new levels of expertise required in everything from molding equipment to dying combined
to force the assemblers to scramble ever harder for a shrinking
share of the market, with the result that most of them disappeared. By the early 1970s it was estimated that Talon accounted
for as much as 70 percent of U.S. zippers, a proportion the
company had not seen since Gideon Sundback's basic patents
had expired almost four decades before.[25]

A decade later, however, Talon's share was half that, and
falling. The fate of the pioneering zipper maker was tied to a
combination of choices and circumstances that made its story
something of a parable of the troubles of American manufacturing in the 1970s and 1980s. The inflexibility in response to changing competition that had plagued the company in the 1950s was
joined by the kind of managerial and fiscal mishaps that tortured
many American businesses in the period, making the once-proud
and dominant industrial sector of the economy seem incapable
of either maintaining the values that had given it prosperity and
power or changing with sufficient know-how and swiftness to
confront foreign competitors finally enjoying the fruits of two
generations of peace.

Some of the problems that plagued Talon were the results
simply of bad business decisions. For example, in the late 1960s
the zipper assemblers, which had been largely shut out of the
nylon coil business that had taken such a huge portion of precisely the clothing market that had been their sustenance and
thus had appeared at times on the brink of extinction, found new
life as a result of a Talon miscalculation. An independent chain
producer persuaded the Meadville company to license its production of coil, then proceeded to supply to those assemblers willing
to convert their manufacturing to the new material and machinery. Enough of them did so to revive the assembly business,
and the old zipper giant once again found itself competing at a
disadvantage.[26]

But already the giant was not what it used to be. Not many

The world's largest zipper company is the creation of **Tadao Yoshida** (1908–1993), whose "cycle of goodness" included the construction of integrated manufacturing facilities throughout the world.   *YKK (U.S.A.)*

years after Talon introduced the Zephyr fastener in 1960, its
stock was purchased by the large and growing conglomerate
Textron, Inc., and in 1968 Textron absorbed the Meadville company
entirely. The conglomerate was a benevolent parent and
clearly believed at first that it had made a fine acquisition. Beneath
the surface, however, there was trouble brewing even at
this point. By the early 1970s an increasing proportion of Talon's
profit was coming from the home sewing market—the old notions
counter sales (since the reemerging assemblers cut down
profits of sales to garment producers and other bulk consumers).
These had for many years been handled by a separate firm, the
Donahue Sales Company, of New York City, which naturally
took its own share of the profits. The managers at Textron,
driven by more of an accounting mentality than the Meadville
people had been, did not see the point of this arrangement and
proceeded to purchase Donahue in the mid-1970s. This was
apparently just before it became evident that the home sewing
market was shrinking dramatically and permanently, with the
shifting demographics of the American household and especially
the wholesale movement of women (erstwhile home seam-
stresses) into the work force. The remaining profit center of
Talon's business shrank beyond recognition, and the conglomerate did not feel so paternalistic any longer. In 1981 Textron sold
Talon to a Boston-based holding company, which a couple of
years later sold it to its Meadville managers, who continued to
struggle to turn things around, but with an ever-shrinking capital
base. Finally, in 1991, Talon was purchased by the British textile
firm Coats Viyella PLC, which was also the owner of Birmingham's
Lightning Fastener Company and the German firm
Opti-Werk. Yet this remarkable consolidation of zipper pioneers
did not strike most observers as the end of international competition
but, rather, perhaps as a leveling of the field.[27]

The primary reason for this strange conclusion was the dramatic
rise of the Japanese zipper company YKK, which constituted
the competition everyone had to look out for, worldwide.
YKK's recovery from the ashes of World War II and its subsequent
ascendancy to international zipper preeminence were as
remarkable a success story as twentieth-century business has
witnessed. In the first years of the war Tadao Yoshida had been
lucky. Government orders and supplies of metal had kept his

business going better than, say, the hobbled zipper makers in Meadville and Birmingham; in fact, 1944 sales were four and a half times his best prewar year. In the last months of the war, however, his luck ran out. In an air raid on Tokyo in March 1945, his Komatsugawa factory in Tokyo was completely destroyed, and his business wiped out. The ink was hardly dry on Japan's surrender in August, however, before Yoshida had begun reconstruction, this time in his native Toyama Prefecture, about 150 miles northwest of Tokyo, on the Sea of Japan. Three months later he was turning out zippers again, although the export market that had been the source of his prewar success was closed to him. In 1947 he was allowed to resume shipments abroad, and they began to grow steadily. On perseverance alone, Tadao Yoshida could have survived and flourished in postwar Japan.[28]

Yoshida brought more to his enterprise, however, than simply pluck. His ambitions were driven by a philosophy that he called the "cycle of goodness." Tracing its origins to boyhood exposure to Andrew Carnegie's "Gospel of Wealth," Yoshida summed up the idea as "goodness will cycle back to us if we sow seeds of goodness and render goodness to others." In the dozens of talks on his philosophy that he had translated into English and published, Yoshida made it clear that this idea was intended to be not simply ethical preaching but a practical approach to success in business, one that stressed quality and effort and sharing of benefits. Without our trying to judge the extent to which Yoshida's life or business actually lived up these fine-sounding precepts, it is possible to appreciate the immensity of his success and some of the key steps that led to it. Perhaps the key moment was the day in 1947, at just the time that Yoshida was resuming his export business, that a visitor from the United States brought him samples of American zippers. A close inspection of the entirely machine-made product, whose price was not out of line with his own, opened Yoshida's eyes, as he told the story, to the quality production possible from correctly designed and maintained machinery. The scarcity of capital in postwar Japan made it impossible for him to abandon right away the hand production that had always sustained the Japanese zipper makers, but in 1950 Yoshida purchased four chain machines from the United States—those same relatively inexpensive machines that had made independent component production so important in the

U.S. zipper industry. Mechanization increased markedly the productivity of the company that Yoshida had dubbed YKK in 1948. But it also apparently began a remarkable transformation of his entire approach to zipper making.[29]

The key, Yoshida began to see, was integration, not just the core integration of zipper-making processes that firms like Talon had long represented, but total integration—from ingot and yarn to finished fastener. While some steps toward vertical integration were taken as far back as 1948, the serious demonstration of what such an approach could mean began in 1954, with the construction of a large integrated production factory in Kurobe, not far from Yoshida's boyhood home. The drive toward integration was partly fueled by his calculation always to put one-half of his profits back into the firm. The result was an intensification of capital—the constant expansion of plant and machinery as well as the rapid replacement of older machines. Compared with the conservative investment philosophy of older Western companies, this practice, augmented by a passionate concern for maintaining quality, could, in retrospect, have hardly led anywhere but to an almost dominant commercial position. It should be noted that Yoshida was never part of the old Japanese industrial establishment and did not seek special assistance from the traditional business or government structures. His zipper enterprise, after all, could never command the attention or power that accrued to the makers of steel, automobiles, or electronics. His success instead was owed to an almost passionate devotion to one product—to making it right and making it competitively. The passion for competition would, not surprisingly, bring to Yoshida his share of detractors especially when, in 1959, he began erecting plants overseas.[30]

YKK's expansion abroad was an integral part of Yoshida's strategy. Very unlike Lewis Walker, whose policies had locked Talon out of foreign markets for thirty years, Tadao Yoshida saw the movement of production around the world as a natural part of his "cycle of goodness." The making of zippers in the places where they were consumed brought all the benefits of his enterprise to the customers, including the jobs that zipper manufacture supported. It also meant that his company could effectively respond to local shifts in consumer demand, to customer problems and special needs, and to opportunities pre-

246 sented by the local market. The sweep of YKK's ensuing spread was breathtaking. From those 1959 plants in India, Indonesia, and New Zealand, YKK and affiliates spread in following years to Malaysia, Thailand, Costa Rica, the Netherlands, Puerto Rico, Taiwan, England, and Italy, and by 1991 there were 171 plants and offices in forty-two countries. While the factories in Japan were enormous, they produced in that year only about 30 percent of the more than 1.25 million *miles* of zippers made by the company. The first factory in the United States was opened in New York City in 1964, under the aegis of YKK (U.S.A.), which had been set up in 1960. The entry into the huge U.S. market was a bit tentative, but the effort gathered momentum as the decade progressed. It was in the 1970s that YKK made its real American push. In 1972 it had less than 10 percent of the market, but two years later it opened a very large manufacturing facility in Macon, Georgia (which has since grown to occupy more than two and a half million square feet). By 1978 YKK was challenging Talon for primacy in the American market, and sometime in the 1980s it clearly surpassed the pioneer. The Macon factories now produce several *million* zippers every day. And the American YKK story has been repeated in country after country around the world. No wonder that other zipper makers sometimes sound besieged.[31]

A visitor to Meadville today is not likely to come into town as he would have in Colonel Walker's day, by way of the Erie Railroad or, perhaps, via the road running between Pittsburgh and Erie, which now carries the label of U.S. Route 19. No, he can't take a train and is much more likely to head up from Pittsburgh by means of the interstate highway, I-79. The expressway does not actually go to the town but skirts it, in the manner of such expressways and small towns, by a few miles. So the traveler will exit the highway and proceed eastward by way of a road that is labeled with the combined numbers of U.S. Routes 322, 19, and 6. But even that road, just as it approaches the town, passing by a couple of shopping centers on the way, veers off to the north, constituting itself as the "Meadville Arterial Highway." The alert driver will perhaps notice at this point the shallow waters of French Creek and the more prominent sprawl of railroad tracks that gives a hint of the town's industrial character.

But our visitor may have gotten the message that the late twentieth century is avoiding Meadville.

If he makes the required right turn toward the middle of the
town, he will find more pointed reminders that this is not a
country village, serving only to provide Crawford County's
farmers with supplies and its lawyers with courthouse employment and young men and women with the education offered
for nearly two centuries at Allegheny College. Smokestacks rise
above the rolling landscape, to suggest a town in which things
are made. Or, rather, were made, for the smokestacks are mostly
without purpose these days. Oh, yes, there are still some things
made in Meadville in these days, but zippers are not among them.
Indeed, only by straining a little bit can one make out a faded
"Talon" on one or two of the outlying brick buildings. A more
obvious, though less direct and pertinent, reminder of this part
of the town's past would be the local radio station, WZPR,
whose call letters suggest a day, only a generation or two gone,
when the making of zippers was the economic heart and soul of
Meadville.

When, about a decade ago, Talon gave its last Meadville
zipper factory to the public agency in charge of "redevelopment," the town had already received a series of economic blows.
The railroad car maintenance and repair shops that Conrail had
taken over from the Erie were closed between 1976 and 1982,
throwing almost 1,000 people out of work. With the reduction
of Talon's workers in the town to 250, the total unemployment
rate climbed to just under 20 percent. The scars of economic
decline are still visible; the vacant buildings on Chestnut Street
and Market Street testify to Meadville's share of the troubles
faced by so many of America's middle-size towns, especially in
the Rust Belt that stretches across the Northeast from New
England to southern Wisconsin. The "Downtown Mall" just a
few blocks from the former commercial heart is now less a promise of the future than a reminder of the kind of "redevelopment"
schemes that pockmark places in cities and towns all across
America, products of a philosophy of urban renewal now out of
fashion.[32]

The impression that Meadville makes on the visitor is not
necessarily negative, however. Just off Chestnut Street, at the
corner of Park Avenue, one encounters the Diamond, a town

green very much in the tradition of Meadville's New England founders. Here can be found the courthouse, a couple of churches, a small bandstand, the obligatory war memorials and statues, and the public library and historical society. The effect, graced with tall and stately trees, is as charming a small-town vignette as could be wished for. Up the hill several blocks from the Diamond sits the David Mead Inn, where the town's more important folk still meet for lunch (if they don't go out to the Country Club) and where our visitor will want to stay if he chooses to avoid the motels nearer the interstate. It's not a very historic place, despite being named for the town's founder, but the inn carries on some of the traditions of small-town life, hosting the local associations that, even in the 1990s, keep the fabric of civic life from completely fraying away. The Colonel would have been at home here.

But there is much else in Meadville that Lewis Walker would not be so happy about. The still factories and the shuttered shops would disturb him, for he was a very loyal town booster. The turnover in Talon's ownership over the past two decades would have displeased him, for he was clearly a man who believed in a certain steadiness of course and institutional dedication. And, while the Colonel was never a seeker after the limelight, he could not help being bothered by the obliteration of his name and memory in the adopted home to which he had brought a bit of notoriety and prosperity a bit more than a half century ago. When, in late 1991, the *Meadville Tribune*, which in an earlier guise had faithfully chronicled the coming of Hookless to town, ran an almost full-page feature marking the hundredth anniversary of Whitcomb Judson's first fasteners, not a word was printed about the Colonel's role in the story. A complaint from an old Talon man brought only the disingenuous reply that the piece had been a syndicated feature, conveniently neglecting the fact that there had in fact been appended a local note about Talon, but without any mention of the central role that the company (and its founder) once played in the city's life. Almost as if to complete the circle, the *Tribune* carried an announcement in early 1993 that by the end of that year—one hundred years after Whitcomb Judson had received the patents for his "clasp lockers or unlockers"—Talon would leave Meadville for good.[33]

Near the beginning of his famous 1948 study of technology and modern culture *Mechanization Takes Command*, the Swiss critic and historian Sigfried Giedion made these remarks about what he called "anonymous history": "For the historian there are no banal things. Like the scientist, the historian does not take anything for granted. He has to see objects not as they appear to the daily user, but as the inventor saw them when they first took shape. He needs the unworn eyes of contemporaries, to whom they appeared marvelous or frightening. At the same time, he has to establish their constellations before and after, and thus establish their meaning."[34]

We are accustomed to asking questions about the great technological achievements that so obviously shape our world. The creation of new powers and new things is an exciting and often portentous expression of the human capacity for altering the world, so we inquire where these things came from, who made them, and how they affected us. In answering such questions, we devise and reinforce our images of technology and of the shape and meaning of our material world. And yet there may linger the suspicion that in probing only technologies of power and magnitude, we somehow miss something of what makes our creations truly expressions of humanity.

Just *because* the zipper was so apparently "banal"—even silly—the history of its origins and spread illuminates corners of the technological order that are otherwise hard to see, blinded as we are by the brighter lights of grander machines and inventions. Look at the world around us, and notice that most human artifice is "common," "trivial," "unimportant." Yet it is just this universe of things that truly gives our world its shape, feel, and meaning. How are we to pretend to understand how our world comes to be what it is, and how human beings function within it, if we do not probe these corners that become visible only in the dimmer light of the ordinary?

There are three very simple questions at the heart of this exploration: Why was the zipper invented? How did the zipper become a part of everyday life? And what difference did it make? As everyone knows, simple questions often do not have simple answers. In this particular case, the complications of the answers are particularly revealing because the zipper turns out to be an invention for which neither need nor function—the two things that we typically think of as central to engendering a technology—explain its origins or success. A moment's reflection will suggest why this should not surprise us too much. What, indeed, does a zipper do that cannot be done by simpler, older means? Do not buttons function well for skirt plackets or trouser flies? Are not snaps often quite satisfactory for jackets or purses? Does not a simple tie or drawstring secure a flap or a pocket if we wish? This is not to say that we do not now perceive the zipper as often superior to these or other alternatives, but merely that such superiority is not compelling.

The familiar story is that the zipper was invented because fastening the high-top shoes popular at the end of the last century was a chore, particularly for the overweight man who had the inspiration. To be sure, Whitcomb Judson's first fastener patents refer to shoe fastening, and there is no reason to doubt that this was the application that he had in mind. But this tells us nothing about *causes*. There are indeed occasions when a specific problem seems to lead to a specific invention. A good example of such a "solution-invention" is the air brake that George Westinghouse invented to improve railroad safety—a narrowly defined answer to a specific, widely recognized difficulty. Inventions of this kind are important—they are arguably the goal of much of engineering research—but they are not the key sources of novelty.

A large number of inventions (it is beside the point whether or not they are in the majority) simply do not fit into the category of solutions, and the attempt that many observers make to force them is a source of great misunderstanding about technological change. The fastening of shoes may be a chore, but it is one that no one could argue justifies the complexity of a zipper, certainly not at the outset of its difficult and time-consuming invention. There are many, much more straightforward means to diminish the chore, not the least of which is our modern one of reducing the number of fastenings on a shoe, often to zero. These solutions were readily apparent to late-nineteenth-century shoe wearers if they cared about the problem. Even more important, there is no evidence that they did, in fact, see fastening as a "problem."

The origins of the zipper cannot be explained as problem solving, but rather as problem *seeking*. As an opportunity-invention, the slide fastener was the creation of a kind of thinking that is less concerned with solving particular problems and more with devising clever alternatives to the world as known. In such a case, far more common than is often suspected, invention is the product of the perception of opportunities for novelty. The ingenious mind devises—sometimes in great quantity—means for accomplishing tasks that are sufficiently distinct from the ordinary to pose the possibility of profit and utility. Where such ideas actually come from is a great and interesting question that is beyond our scope here. What is clear without delving to psychology and cognitive processes is that the human mind is indeed capable of formulating novel ways of doing or making things and does so often, stimulated not by specific hurdles to be overcome but rather by possibilities that present themselves through new knowledge, new resources, or new combinations of the familiar. Examples of this kind of invention are extremely common, ranging from the mechanical pencil to the microwave oven, although their significance in shaping the technological order is vastly underappreciated.[35]

By the end of the nineteenth century, in America at least, the pursuit of novelty was an activity that was broadly valued by the larger culture. This marks an astonishing change from the historical norm, in which novelty was generally neither sought nor welcomed. The situation in which the zipper's inventors and promoters worked and eventually flourished was perhaps unique, at least up to that time. Here was a society in which men and women who wanted to get ahead in life were urged to explore the possibilities of making the world anew. This has been referred to as an age of technological enthusiasm, but it was more fundamental than that. In many ways it was not technology itself that was celebrated but novelty. After all, the users of zippers might be aware that they were using a machine and that the device depended on other machines for its existence, but they were more keenly attracted to the newness of the zipper, just as they became more receptive to new music, new dances, new styles, new literary forms, as well as other new technologies.

The full importance of this kind of opportunity-invention can be appreciated by recognizing that making the zipper that we know and admire today required twenty years of dogged effort, as design after design was tried and discarded. The initial versions of the device consisted of traditional forms of fasteners, such as clasps or hooks and eyes, brought together by a slider. None of these functioned well, although some were marketed by hustling salesmen, who were careful to avoid their "marks" after the sell. For two decades entrepreneurial energy and money were plowed into this problematic invention. Why? Largely, it would seem, because the ingenuity embodied by the invention's basic idea—automatic and mechanical closure—was too attractive to abandon. It appeared to be a novelty with promise; it was certainly not because there was a clear-cut demand for the invention.

Just as the invention of the zipper is not to be accounted for by need, so, too, its success in the market cannot be attributed to "demand." There simply was no demand for zippers, either in its primitive first form or in its final, "perfected" design twenty years later. As might be expected for such opportunity-inventions, the creation of demand for the device was as much a challenge to entrepreneurs as the technical challenge of making it function. The two challenges, of course, were not independent of each other. Without a problem to solve, the opportunity-invention must have its function defined for it, usually in terms of perceived demand possibilities. For the zipper, this had its complications. The perceived market for shoes, for example, was quickly abandoned, and along with it certain functional requirements. Defined then as a "universal fastener," the device ran into another common problem for such inventions: Being touted as good for everything, it is not clear that it is actually useful for anything. This strategy, too, was abandoned, to be replaced by a narrow focus on clothing, particularly women's skirts and, secondarily, men's trousers. This strategy, too, proved a failure, even after the functional deficiencies highlighted by these uses had led to the truly original and clever design of the modern zipper. More than two additional decades, in fact— a total of more than forty years after its initial invention—passed before the zipper was widely accepted in these applications.

The zipper's experience during those two decades of intense marketing efforts provides an extraordinary glimpse at the role novelty plays in making an invention part of ordinary life. These decades, during which the zipper never ceased to be seen and promoted as a novelty, witnessed a variety of attacks on the problem of making the zipper wanted. Confronting at last the essential problem that their product was more complicated, more expensive, and less reliable than traditional alternatives for most uses, the zipper makers parlayed their product's most distinctive attributes—its cleverness and novelty—into marketable assets. In some realms this could succeed quickly, if not spectacularly, so products such as money belts, tobacco pouches, and galoshes emerged with zippers to set them apart from otherwise identical competitors. Gradually the list of such uses lengthened, serving to enlarge the numbers of those who had seen the gadget in operation, until finally, in the 1930s, the zipper's technical refinement and proved reliability combined with the quirks of fashion and the lure of modernity to enlarge its domain to include a wide variety of the articles of everyday life, including the intimate realm of clothing.

During this period, too, the zipper began to acquire something more than markets. It began to take on meanings. In this way it was like all the things that provide us with the material vocabulary of daily life and discourse, but the zipper was exceptional in the explicitness of the messages that men and women attached to it. For this reason the means by which the zipper assumed meaning and began to convey them are particularly instructive to study. Anyone reading this is aware that these devices have associations, although articulating them may require an extra effort. The central meanings attached to zippers should come as no surprise: sexuality, mechanism, cleverness, opening and closing, attaching and releasing, revealing and hiding. The image of the zipper is one of the cardinal material images of the twentieth century, finding expression in literature, art, humor, folklore, science, music, technology, and language. Whether it be the German motorist, who enters the rapid stream of traffic on the autobahn by means of the *Reissverschluss-Verfahren* (the "zipper procedure," in which alternate cars slip in between those already on the road), the molecular biologist who describes a "zipper protein," or the plastics manufacturer who promotes the Ziploc bag for sandwiches, the visual and mechanical images of the zipper convey actions and performance with little chance for ambiguity. Beyond this mundane level, of course, is a host of deeper relationships, manipulable by the jokester who tells of a man with "the fastest zipper in town," the gossip who passes on the story of "the unzipped mechanic," or the feminist author whose most vivid fantasy is that of a "zipless" roll in the hay. We would be hard pressed to find anything that we use or make that has such a host of signifying functions.

There is one additional significance that the zipper should have. It is a remarkable reminder of the capacity of individuals to see the world differently from the way it is and to remake it into a new form. This may seem an absurdly inflated characterization of the meaning of something so trivial as a zipper, but as this story has attempted to show, the full glory of this novelty lay in eventual reduction to ordinariness. What an extraordinary sequence of actions and intentions led to this result! The place of the zipper in modern life is ultimately the result of the inspired notions of a dreamy-headed inventor, the dogged persistence of a small-town entrepreneur, the analytical and imaginative calculations of a skilled engineer, and the enormously varied reactions of men and women willing to experiment and gamble in everything from galoshes to evening gowns. It is also the product of the values of a culture that, by the first decades of our century, readily made room for novelty yet often knew not what to do with it.

In our own time we continue to struggle with the new, imbuing it with both hope and dread. Novelty is, after all, the fundamental source of our future. Each of us enters the world as a novelty and spends our life trying to understand that balance between the new and the familiar that will give our own existence meaning. Our technologies and artifacts are, in the last analysis, extensions of our selves and our capacities. Therefore, the pursuit of novelty and its successful integration into life are the central means by which we cope with being human.

Notes

1. "Witty Inventions and Thinking Men"

1. The application file for U.S. Patent 504,037 can be found in the Records of the U.S. Patent Office, RG 241, Washington National Records Center, National Archives and Records Administration, Suitland, Maryland. The application file for U.S.P. 504,038 (the 1891 application) is missing; it is reasonable to assume that the same examiner was responsible for both applications. Anderson was also the examiner of record for Judson's 1896 patents.

2. The fullest account of Whitcomb Judson's life comes from his obituary, published in the *Muskegon News Chronicle*, Wednesday, December 8, 1909, (in Talon files, Crawford County Historical Society* [hereafter Talon files]; letter from Mac Leigh, Muskegon, Michigan [n.d.])

---

*Most early extant corporate records of Talon, Inc. and its predecessor companies are to be found in the collections of the Crawford County Historical Society, Meadville, Pennsylvania. At the time of research for this work, many of these records were not yet in the society's collections. They have subsequently been added. Where no other reference is given in these notes, correspondence to, from, and between individuals associated with Talon and predecessors is to be found in the Talon files of the Crawford County Historical Society.

3. A discussion of the comparative merits of power transmission systems at this period can be found in Louis C. Hunter and Lynwood Bryant, *A History of Industrial Power in the United States. 1780–1930*. vol. 3, *The Transmission of Power* (Cambridge, Mass.: MIT Press, 1991), pp. 180–84.

4. Details of the Judson system are described in "The Judson Pneumatic Railway System," *Engineering News* (July 13, 1889), pp. 28–30. See also *Street Railway Journal*, vol. 5 (1889), pp. 175–78. The essential features are described in the first patents, all issued May 7, 1889: 402,674; 402,839; 402,933; and 402,934.

5. "Notes on the Washington, DC Street Railways," *Street Railway Journal*, vol. 6 (July 1890), pp. 324–27; LeRoy O. King, *100 Years of Capital Traction: The Story of Streetcars in the Nation's Capital* (Dallas: LeRoy O. King, 1976), p. 19; John H. White, Jr., "Public Transport in Washington before the Great Consolidation of 1902," *Records of the Columbia Historical Society* (1969), pp. 227–28. Since the experimental Judson line was outside the controlled area of the capital, overhead trolleys were allowed in the electification; inside the controlled area (south of Florida Avenue), underground electrical conduits were used.

6. Lewis Walker, "Origin and Progress of Big Meadville Industry; the Story as Told by Colonel Walker to Literary Union in September, 1925," typescript of article in the *Meadville Tribune Republican*, January 22, 1927, in Talon files.

7. P. J. Federico, "The Invention and Introduction of the Zipper," *Journal of the Patent Office Society*, vol. 28 (December 1946), p. 862.

8. Ibid., p. 857.

9. Some details of the formation of the Universal Fastener Company are to be found in James Gray, *Talon, Inc.: A Romance of Achievement*, p. 14. This work was commissioned by Talon (the eventual successor to Universal Fastener) for the fiftieth anniversary of the company's founding in 1913. Gray's study was eventually published by the company, but in a heavily edited and much condensed version, in 1963, with the notation on the title page that the work is "an abridgment of the original manuscript by James Gray." This published work is probably most accurately cited as: Talon, Inc., *Talon, Inc.: A Romance of Achievement* (Meadville, Pa.: Talon, 1963). Gray's work, however, was circulated in at least two more complete forms to company insiders. Citations to Gray (given simply by the author's name) in this current work will be to an offset printed version, circulated in softcover form, in 1963, unless otherwise specified. No version found of Gray's manuscript includes specific citations to his sources. The only biographical source on Harry Earle, found in Gray's files at Talon, is a copy of the application that Earle made for admission to the Marcus L. Ward Home for Aged and Respectable Bachelors and Widowers, Maplewood, New Jersey, August 9, 1937.

10. Article of Incorporation, Earle Manufacturing Company, filed October 31, 1887, in Secretary of State, Incorporations, vol. S, p. 532. (Minnesota State Archives, Minnesota Historical Society, St. Paul).

11. Earle application to Ward Home, 1937.

12. Minutes, Universal Fastener Company, December 3, 1895, excerpts in Talon files. These excerpts were prepared in 1934 and included in a package of historical material delivered to Lewis Walker 3d for his use in a paper he was writing as a student at Lehigh University. According to the cover letter on this material, it was reviewed by his uncle Wallace Walker and his grandfather Colonel Lewis Walker. Where the original source of this information is clear, it is cited as here (and as above in reference to Colonel Walker's talk before the Literary Union in 1925 [n.6 above]). Where the source of the information is unclear, it is cited as "Talon history notes, 1934."

13. Arthur J. Cox and Thomas Malim, *Ferracute: The History of an American Enterprise* (Bridgeton, N.J.: Cowan Printing, 1985), p. 53.

14. Gray, pp. 14–15; the order from the Post Office was reported in the excerpts from minutes of the Universal Fastener Company, in Talon files.

15. Minutes, Universal Fastener Company meetings of June 1 and September 4, 1896, excerpts in Talon files; letter from Harry L. Earle to G. Sundback, February 12, 194[2], in Talon files.

16. Minutes, Universal Fastener Company, excerpts in Talon files; Gray, pp. 15–16.

17. U.S. Department of the Interior, U.S. Patent Office, *Report of the Commissioner of Patents for the Year Ending Dec. 31, 1900* (Washington, D.C. Government Printing Office, 1901), pp.viii–ix. The commissioner was Charles H. Duell.

18. Fred G. Dieterich, *The Inventor's Universal Educator: an Educational Cyclopaedia and Guide for Inventors, Patentees, Manufacturers, Mechanics, and All Others Connected Directly or Indirectly with Patents* (Washington, D.C.: publ. by the author, [1899]), p. 18.

19. Edison quoted in Matthew Josephson, *Edison* (New York: McGraw-Hill, 1959), p. 355; the commissioner's reference to Edison is in the *Report of the Commissioner . . . 1900*, p. xi.

2. Hustle and Bustle

1. "Lengthened Shadow of a Man," *American Newcomer Society, n.d.*, passim; Gray, pp. 4–8.

2. Gray, pp. 8–9; Lewis Walker letter book (1880s–1900s) in possession of David Conner, Meadville, Pennsylvania, includes copies of letters related to Pneumatic Railway affairs in 1891; the mistaken reminiscence is in Walker, "Origin and Progress . . . 1925."

3. Walker, "Origin and Progress . . . 1925."

4. Excerpts from Universal Fastener Company minutes, Talon files.

5. Gray, pp. 18–19.

6. "Fastener Manufacturing and Machine Company," booklet in Talon files.

7. Unidentified clipping under the head of "[M]ercantile and Financial Times," dated August 16, 1902, from clipping in scrapbook of Mrs. Ruth Klingener, Meadville, Pennsylvania.

8. Excerpts from Universal Fastener Company minutes, Talon files.

9. Lewis Walker makes reference to Ross Judson's success in "Origin and Progress . . . 1925."

10. Gideon Sundback, in testimony in Hookless Fastener Co. v. Lion Fastener Co., Records of Appeal no. 5282 and 5304, U.S. Cir. Court of Appeals, Third Cir., Philadelphia, pp. 40–41, in Record Group 276, Federal Records Center, National Archives and Records Administration, Philadelphia. The original case was heard in 1932 (Hookless Fastener Co. v. Lion Fastener Co., U.S. Dist. Court, Western Dist. of Penn., Equity #2617). Sundback's description of fabrication was also copied into Talon history notes, 1934.

11. This advertisement is reproduced in *Talon: A Romance* . . . , p. 24.

12. Excerpts from *Vogue* (December 27, 1906), *The Delineator* (April 1907), and the *Woman's Magazine* (March 1907) taken from copy of C-curity promotions; *Woman's Home Companion* and *Ladies' World* excerpts in the form of clippings—all found in scrapbook of Mrs. Ruth Klingener.

13. E.g.: *Lewiston* (Maine) *Evening Journal* (June 11); *Portland Evening News*; *Rutland* (Vermont) *Daily Herald* (June 7); *Burlington Daily News* (June 7)—clippings in Klingener scrapbook.

14. Items from Klingener scrapbook; *Collier's* piece ran on October 5, 1907.

15. "The Opportunity" brochure (August–September 1907), file copy in Klingener scrapbook.

16. "The C-Curity Placket Fastener," booklet in Talon files. The final note is reproduced in an edition of the booklet pictured in *Talon: A Romance* . . . , p. 26.

17. G. Sundback in Hookless v. Lion, p. 35.

18. "Contract" form and "Special Agents Contract" form from Automatic Hook and Eye Company (no date, but with specific reference to C-curity), "The Opportunity," from Klingener scrapbook.

19. Unidentified clipping, from scrapbook of Ruth Klingener, Meadville, Pennsylvania. Since the date for this item is unknown, it is not clear if the "Genius from Hoboken" referred to was Judson or one of the company's later mechanics.

20. Excerpts from minutes, Talon files; Peter Aronson's background in part described by Ruth Klingener, his granddaughter, Meadville, Pennsylvania (personal communication).

21. Personal information on Gideon Sundback is from several sources. The most valuable are the personal recollections of his daughter, Ruth Klingener, as communicated in conversations with the author and supported by materials from the scrapbooks that Gideon Sundback kept, and the typescript of an interview that Gideon Sundback gave to Ida Tarbell in October 1932 (in Talon files). Additional information is from Gray, pp. 23–24, and Sundback's testimony in Hookless v. Lion.

22. Gray, p. 24; recorded interview with G. Sundback by Cecil Linder, December 30, 1952, St. Catharines, Ontario, in possession of Ruth Klingener, Meadville, Pennsylvania; personal communication with Eric Sundback, December 12, 1991.

23. Tarbell interview, 1932; excerpts from minutes of Automatic Hook and Eye Company, Talon files.

24. Sundback in Hookless v. Lion, pp. 38–40.

25. Tarbell interview, 1932–original wording. The typescript of this interview was reviewed, edited, and corrected by Sundback himself. Quotations generally incorporate these alterations, except where noted.

26. Sundback in Hookless v. Lion, p. 40.

27. Tarbell interview, 1932; Sundback in Hookless v. Lion, p. 41.

28. Excerpts from minutes of Automatic Hook and Eye Company, miscellaneous papers in Talon files, undated general letter from Clarke Sales Company.

29. Gerald Carson, The Old Country Store (1954; New York: E. P. Dutton, 1965), pp. 165–68; Christopher Morley, Parnassus on Wheels (New York: Grosset & Dunlap, [1917]).

30. Miscellaneous papers in Talon files: Clarke Sales Company letter to Joyce, dated October 14, 1908; undated general letters and notices from Thomas J. Cooper; general letter to agents, dated December 31, 1908.

31. Reminiscences of Wilson Wear are from two sources: an untitled, undated report, written by Sam Kinney, the Talon sales manager in the 1930s, in the Sundback papers of Ruth Klingener, and the Tarbell interview with Sundback, 1932. Personal recollections of Wear have also been reported by Ruth Klingener.

32. Correspondence file, "Wilson Wear," in Talon files; Kinney report; Tarbell interview with Sundback, 1932; advertisements and clippings from Klingener scrapbook.

33. Gray, pp. 25–26; advertisement for le Ferme-tout Américain in possession of Ruth Klingener; account book of Automatic Hook and Eye Company (June 1911–July 1913), Talon files.

● **1.** *Die Entstehung des Dieselmotors* (Berlin: 1913), translated and excerpted in Friedrich Klemm, *A History of Western Technology* (Cambridge: MIT
Z Press, 1964), p. 346. A good recent discussion of the stages of technological change is Joel Mokyr, *The Lever of Riches* (New York: Oxford University
I Press, 1990), pp. 9–11 and 155.

2. On Diesel, see Donald E. Thomas, Jr., *Diesel: Technology and Society*
P *in Industrial Germany* (Tuscaloosa,: University of Alabama Press, 1987),
esp. chs. 4 and 5.
P
3. "Safety Pins," *Safety Pins and Other Essays* (London: Jonathan Cape,
E 1925), p. 81.

4. On the history of clothing fasteners there is little written. The one book
R devoted to the subject is a small work, published by a major snaps and zipper manufacturer: Herbert Manchester, *The Evolution of Fastening Devices: From the Bone Pin to the Koh-i-noor* (Long Island City: Waldes Koh-i-noor, 1922); in addition, some information can be found in Sara Frances Robinson, "Fastening Devices of Historic Costume," M.A. thesis in home economics, Texas State College for Women, 1940.

5. Manchester, pp. 16–20.

6. Information on buttons can be gleaned from many clothing histories, such as Diana De Marly, *Fashion for Men: An Illustrated History* (London: B. T. Batsford, 1985). Books for button collectors are another source; examples include Grace Horney Ford, *The Button Collector's History* (Springfield, Mass.: Pond-Ekberg, 1943) and Primrose Peacock, *Buttons for the Collector* (Newton Abbott, England: David & Charles, 1972).

7. Nancy Bradfield, *Costume in Detail: Women's Dress, 1730–1930* (Boston: Plays, Inc., 1968).

8. Examples include Roswell Judson and William Lynch, "Improvement in Fastening Wearing Apparel, Shoes, &c.," U.S.P. 75,924 (1868); Thomas H. Smith, "Mail-bag Fastening," U.S.P. 285,518 (1883); M. V. B. Ethridge, "Mail Bag Fastening," U.S.P. 297,245 (1884); and Luther Russell, "Fastening Device for Mail-bags, Trunks, &c." U.S.P. 375,684 (1887). Variations on the Howe type of device appeared also in European patents, such as the German patent (23,668) issued to Gottfried Klotz in 1883; discussed in Karl F. Nägele, *100 Jahre Reissverschluss* (Stuttgart: published by the author, 1958), pp. 112–13; an English translation of much of this work is in the Talon files.

9. Application files for U.S.P. 1,060,378 (Sundback) and U.S.P. 1.060,412 (Aronson), in Records of the U.S. Patent Office, RG 241, Washington National Records Center, National Archives and Records Administration, Suitland, Maryland.

10. U.S. Department of the Interior, U.S. Patent Office, *Report of the Commissioner of Patents for the Year Ending Dec. 31, 1900* (Washington, D.C.: Government Printing Office, 1901), p. xi.

11. A good review of European patents is in Nägele, pp. 114–26; another helpful list of relevant patents is in the Exhibits, Hookless Fastener Co. v. Greenberg and Josefsberg, U.S. Dist. Court, Southern Dist. of Calif., in Records of the District Court of the U.S. for the Southern Dist. of Calif., Equity Case no. 883-Y, in Record Group 21, National Archives, Pacific Southwest Region, Laguna Niguel, California.

12. The Patent Office's response to Sundback's claims as well as many notices of subsequent infringement cases can be found in the application file for U.S.P. 1,219,881, in Records of the U.S. Patent Office, RG 241, Washington National Records Center, National Archives and Records Administration, Suitland, Maryland.

13. The quotation is from a letter to Elvira Aronson, August 4, 1908; this and other letters from 1907 and 1908 are in the possession of Ruth Klingener, Meadville, Pennsylvania.

14. Gray, p. 26; account book of Automatic Hook and Eye Company (June 1911–July 1913), a complete profit and loss statement for 1904–1912 is on p. 59 (entry of April 23, 1913).

15. Account book, Automatic Hook and Eye Company (June 1911–July 1913); Gray, pp. 26–27; Tarbell interview, 1932.

16. Account book, Automatic Hook and Eye Company (June 1911–July 1913).

17. Ibid.,; letter, A. F. Russell to Wilson Wear, February 8, 1912, in Talon files.

18. Account book, Automatic Hook and Eye Company (June 1911–July 1913); letters from Elvira to Gideon Sundback in Sweden, in possession of Ruth Klingener.

19. Interview with Ruth Sundback Klingener, Meadville, Pennsylvania.

20. The quotation is from the Tarbell interview, 1932; the expenses are recorded in account book, Automatic Hook and Eye Company (June 1911–July 1913).

21. Sundback testimony in Hookless v. Lion, p. 44.

22. Letters quoted in Gray, p. 29.

23. Sundback testimony in Hookless v. Lion, p. 44.

24. Walker's reactions to the Hookless fastener are recounted in Sundback's Tarbell interview of 1932, at which Walker was apparently present (at least part of the time).

25. Gray, p. 30; Tarbell interview, 1932.

26. Account book, Automatic Hook and Eye Company (June 1911–July 1913); Gray, pp. 30–32; letter from Josephine Baldwin, Elyria, Ohio, to Lewis Walker, February 11, 1914.

27. This story is told in a letter from T. L. Chisholm to James Gray, December 13, 1960, Talon files.

• N O T E S

28. James O'Neill to Lewis Walker, May 16, 1915; Walker to O'Neill, May 19, 1915, in Talon files; quotation from Arthur and Barbara Gelb, *O'Neill* (New York: Harper & Row, [1962]), p. 43; the light bulb episode is at the beginning of Act 4, *Long Day's Journey into Night* (New Haven: Yale University Press, 1956).

29. *Meadville Evening Republican*, August 8, 1913 and September 16, 1913; Sundback's second hookless patent was U.S.P. 1,236,783 (issued August 14, 1917).

30. L. Walker to Frank Russell, November 15, 1913, Talon files.

31. L. Walker to F. Russell, November 25, 1913; L. Walker to W. Wear, December 2, 1913, Talon files.

32. L. Walker to F. Russell, May 4, 1914; W. Wear to L. Walker, February 9, 1914.

33. W. Wear to L. Walker, April 23, 1914, and May 18, 1914.

4. Novelty in a New World

1. Frank B. Jewett, "The Promise of Technology," *Science* (January 7, 1944): 6, quoted in P. J. Federico, "The Invention and Introduction of the Zipper," p. 855.

2. Tarbell interview, 1932.

3. T. L. Chisholm, typescript history (untitled), dated May 3, 1937, in Talon files.

4. Ibid. In his court testimony Sundback referred to making fasteners with "spherical projections," Sundback testimony in Hookless v. Lion, p. 48 of record; Edwards, Sager & Wooster, attorneys, to Commissioner of Patents, October 1, 1915, in Application file, U.S. Patent 1,219,881, in Records of the U.S. Patent Office, RG 241; opinion of Judge Woolley, in Lion v. Hookless Fastener Co. and Hookless Fastener Co. v. Lion Fastener Co., Appeals no. 5282 and 5304, U.S. Cir. Court of Appeals, 3d Cir., (72 F.2d 985), issued September 20, 1934.

5. Sundback testimony in Hookless v. Lion, pp. 45–49 of record.

6. L. Walker to F. Russell, May 4, 1914, Talon files.

7. Tarbell interview, 1932.

8. Sundback testimony in Hookless v. Lion, pp. 49–50 of record; L. Walker to T. A. Lamb, December 7, 1914; L. Walker to Lewis Walker, Jr., December 9, 1914.

9. Sundback testimony in Hookless v. Lion, p. 53 of record; Tarbell interview, 1932; L. Walker to T. A. Lamb, September 24, 1914.

10. Tarbell interview, 1932; L. Walker to W. Wear, October 26, 1914; W. Wear to L. Walker, October 27, 1914.

11. L. Walker to W. Wear, August 17, 1915; W. Wear to L. Walker, August 18, 1915; L. Walker to W. Wear, September 17, 1915; W. Wear to L. Walker, September 21, 1915.

12. E. S. Templeton to L. Walker, December 18, 1914; L. Walker to E. S. Templeton, December 21, 1914; L. Walker to T. A. Lamb, December 7, 1914; L. Walker to L. Walker, Jr., December 9, 1914.

13. Gray, pp. 37–38; Wallace Walker is included in *The National Cyclopedia of American Biography*, vol. 28 (1940), p. 7; the correspondence between Lewis Walker and his sons that has been found in the Talon files and elsewhere constitutes the largest original record remaining documenting the Walkers' involvement in the fastener's history—about three cubic feet of letters, mainly from the years 1915 to 1918.

14. Irving Howe, *World of Our Fathers* (New York: Harcourt Brace Jovanovich, 1976), pp. 304–05.

15. Ibid., pp. 154–62, provides a brief overview of the garment trade in the East Side; John Higham, "Introduction" to Abraham Cahan, *The Rise of David Levinsky* 1917; (New York: Harper & Row, 1966), pp. v–viii.

16. L. Walker to Lewis Walker, Jr., December 31, 1915.

17. Ibid., January 6, 1915.

18. Ibid., December 30, 1914; December 31, 1914; January 2, 1915.

19. Lewis Walker, Jr., to L. Walker, December 29, 1914.

20. Ibid., December 30, 1914; January 5, 1915; December 28, 1914.

21. Ibid., January 21, 1915; February 5, 1915.

22. Ibid., February 11, 1915.

23. L. Walker to Lewis Walker, Jr., and Wallace Walker, February 10, 1915.

24. Cahan, pp. 372–74.

25. Ibid., p. 443.

26. Lewis Walker, Jr., to L. Walker, January 5, 1915.

27. Ibid., January 22, 1915; December 31, 1914; January 29, 1915; March 6, 1915; March 4, 1915.

28. "Supplement to Index of Jan. 30, 1915," for February and March, in Talon files.

29. Lewis Walker, Jr., to L. Walker, January 30, 1915.

30. L. Walker to Lewis Walker, Jr., February 2, 1915; February 5, 1915.

31. Lewis Walker, Jr., to L. Walker, July 28, 1915.

32. Ibid., July 29, 1915.

33. L. Walker to Lewis Walker, Jr., August 3, 1915; C. M. Goldberg to L. Walker, August 11, 1915; Lewis Walker, Jr., to L. Walker, August 14, 1915; August 19, 1915.

264   **34.** Lewis Walker, Jr., to L. Walker, August 28, 1915. Direct correspondence between Meadville and Goldberg shows that he continued work for Hookless for at least a year.

z

5. Zip

1. L. Walker to G. W. Loomis, May 17, 1915.

2. Gray, pp. 30–31; Lewis Walker correspondence files, "T. A. Lamb" (1913–1915); G. Sundback correspondence files, in Talon files. The earliest stockholders' list found, from 1922, lists 1,149 shares in Lamb's name, 38 percent of the total and nearly twice that held by the senior Walker; the total Walker family holdings amounted to about 21 percent.

3. Gray, pp. 41–42; Lewis Walker correspondence files, "T. F. Soles," especially letters from L. Walker to T. F. Soles, January 14, 1915, and February 18, 1915; Hookless Fastener Company stockholders' list, June 1922, Talon files.

4. L. Walker to George Schlecht, January 26, 1915.

5. Frank W. Lawrence to L. Walker, July 9, 1915; L. Walker to F. W. Lawrence, July 12, 1915.

6. References to the No. 3 are in Lewis Walker, Jr., to L. Walker, July 28, 1915; to experiments with tape, Lewis Walker, Jr., to L. Walker, July 19, 1915. David Conner (personal communication) has speculated that the No. 3 was the fastener design featured in the patent Sundback applied for in April 1915 (issued October 1917 as U.S.P. 1,243,458), in which the design of the scoop was modified, and the cloth tape was specified as having "oppositely-twisted cords," which aided the finished fastener in lying flat rather than curling to one side. If this is the No. 3 that the records of that summer refer to, then this was probably the basic form of fastener produced for several years, even if it was never referred to as "Hookless #3" in later usage.

7. Report on "Manufacturers Using the Fastener," February 22, 1916; Hookless Fastener Company account book (July 1913–May 1919), Talon files.

8. Report on "Manufacturers Using the Fastener," February 22, 1916; letter to "Hookless Fastener Co." from "Your New York representatives," undated, in Talon files.

9. Hookless Fastener Company account book (July 1913–May 1919); L. Walker to Lewis Walker, Jr., and Wallace Walker, September 23, 1915, and November 1, 1915; L. Walker to Lewis Walker, Jr., March 26, 1917.

10. Hookless Fastener Company account book (July 1913–May 1919); Lewis Walker, Jr., to Hookless Fastener Company, July 19, 1917; U.S. Tariff Commission, "Cost of Production of Slide Fasteners and Parts Thereof," Rep. No. 113, 2d ser., 1936.

11. E. W. Taylor to Lewis Walker, Jr., April 21, 1916, and May 4, 1916; Jack Nadel to W. D. Walker, January 26, 1938; Jack Nadel letters in Hookless correspondence files, 1916 (e.g., to Lewis Walker, Jr., May 5, 1916).

12. Gray, p. 45; Report on "Manufacturers Using the Fastener," February 22, 1916; "Estimated cost. . . ," March 18, 1916.

13. Lewis Walker, Jr., to J. W. Apple, June 22, 1917; L. Walker to Lewis Walker, Jr., October 9, 1917.

14. Preston William Slossen, *The Great Crusade and after: 1914–1928* (New York: Macmillan, 1930), pp. 54–56; Ralph M. Hower, *History of Macy's of New York, 1858–1919* (Cambridge: Harvard University Press, 1943), pp. 380–81.

15. L. Walker to Lewis Walker, Jr., and Wallace Walker, July 25, 1917, and July 26, 1917; Wallace Walker to Hookless Fastener Company, July 26, 1917.

16. Lewis Walker, Jr., to L. Walker, October 8, 1917, and January 23, 1915; L. Walker to Lewis Walker, Jr., January 25, 1915.

17. Gray, pp. 46–49; Lewis Walker, Jr., to L. Walker, December 15, 1917; Hookless Fastener Company account book (July 1913–May 1919), Talon files.

18. L. Walker to Lewis Walker, Jr., October 9, 1917; Lewis Walker, Jr., to J. W. Apple, June 22, 1917; Tarbell interview, 1932.

19. Gray, p. 47.

20. Gray, pp. 47–49; Hookless Fastener Company, account book (July 1913–May 1919), Talon files; summary of customers, dated June 11, 1920.

21. Hookless Fastener Company account book (July 1913–May 1919); summary of customers, dated June 11, 1920; advertisements in Talon files.

22. *New York: A Guide to the Empire State* (New York: Oxford University Press, 1940), p. 490; C. Cody Collins, *Love of a Glove* (New York: Fairchild Publishing Co., 1947), pp. 59–64. According to this last source, as late as 1947, Gloversville and Fulton County produced about 80 percent of the more than twenty-five million pairs of gloves made in the United States.

23. Collins, pp. 115, 123; Helen Mary Lehmann, *Leather Goods and Gloves* (New York: Ronald Press, 1922), pp. 188–89, 196–97; Fred B. Carl, "The City of Gloversville," in *History of the Mohawk Valley*, ed. Nelson Greene (Chicago: S. J. Clarke Publishing Co., 1925), pp. 1656–59.

24. L. Walker to Lewis Walker, Jr., January 23, 1917; Lewis Walker to Lewis Walker Jr. and Wallace Walker, February 8, 1917, February 9, 1917, and February 13, 1917; Hookless Fastener Company account book (July 1913–May 1919); summary of customers, dated June 11, 1920.

25. Summary of customers, dated June 11, 1920; letter from F. S. Mills to Lewis Walker, Jr., May 26, 1927; Gray, pp. 53–54.

26. Valerie Cumming, *Gloves* (New York: Drama Book Publishers, 1982), pp. 76–78; Collins, pp. 75–77.

27. Sundback's continued devotion to the flat metal machine can be inferred from his application for a second patent on the device, filed October 19, 1918. It was issued as U.S.P. 1,434,857, November 7, 1922.

28. Lewis Weiner, "The Slide Fastener," *Scientific American* (June 1983), pp. 134–36; thanks to David Conner for his efforts to explain zipper fabrication.

29. Weiner; Nägele, pp. 40, 44, 74–75.

30. "President's Report for the Directors to the Stockholders' Meeting Held July 1, 1919," Talon files.

31. "President's Report . . . July 1, 1920"; Tarbell interview, 1932.

32. "President's Report . . . July 1, 1920"; "Application" correspondence files for 1927–28 (the only such years that have survived) include numerous rejections to prospective customers on the grounds that "allotments" for certain uses were already sold; R. J. Ewig to Hookless Fastener Company, December 24, 1921; Lewis Walker, Jr., to R. W. Ewig, December 28, 1921.

33. "President's Report . . . July 1, 1921"; Memo "To the President and Board of Directors . . ." from Lewis Walker, Jr., February 20, 1922; "President's Report . . . July 1, 1922"; *Meadville Tribune Republican*, August 31, 1921, and February 12, 1922.

34. "Talon Production, 1913–1943" "To the President . . ." from Lewis Walker, Jr., February 20, 1922.

35. Account books, Hookless Fastener Company (1913–1923), Talon files; Gray, p. 58 (Gray mistakenly puts the initial Goodrich order in July 1921).

36. Gray, pp. 59–63; W. D. Walker to Lewis Walker, Jr., February 7, 1923, Talon files.

37. The 70 percent figure is from U.S. Tariff Commission, *Cost of Production of Slide Fasteners*, p. 14; telegrams, Wallace Walker to Hookless Fastener Company, October 22 and November 26, 1924. On general adoption of the term "zipper," see the *Supplement* to the *Oxford English Dictionary*, which provides the following from an advertisement in *Scribner's Magazine*, October 22, 1925: "No fastening is so quick, secure, or popular as the 'zipper';" for the term "zip fastener," the following usage is from the *Daily Express* for September 6, 1927: "The airwoman's costume of tango suede, complete from the zip fastening to the little hat . . . is attracting many admirers." The term "zip" is used to described the action of the fastener in an advertisement in the *London Daily Mail*, May 22, 1924.

6. "Growin' like the Deuce"

1. Data for sales and earnings in this chapter are taken from a summary of Hookless Fastener Company/Talon, Inc., production, 1913–1943, found in the Talon files, Crawford County Historical Society. The purposes or source of the summary are not indicated. The data therein are reported by calendar year; the data in annual reports to stockholders, beginning in 1919, are reported by fiscal year (originally beginning June 1) and thus differ from the summary data but are consistent with them. The following table summarizes data from the company's first twenty years.

Year	Fasteners Sold	Sales $	Net Profit	Change (#-%)	Change (Sales-%)	Change (Net-%)
1913	180,000	$19,730.26	$2,739.57			
1914	193,611	$21,808.70	$291.05	7.56%	10.53%	−89.38%
1915	196,664	$23,971.77	$8,299.87	1.58%	9.92%	2751.70%
1916	131,327	24,761.08	$5,402.91	−33.22%	3.29%	−34.90%
1917	24,072	$9,319.08	$11,417.69	−81.67%	−62.36%	111.32%
1918	90,056	$28,469.27	$2,537.51	274.11%	205.49%	−77.78%
1919	66,769	$22,311.91	$4,889.22	−25.86%	−21.63%	92.68%
1920	110,500	$26,469.95	$7,714.44	65.50%	18.64%	57.78%
1921	342,152	$81,244.10	$11,178.76	209.64%	206.93%	44.91%
1922	759,187	$137,389.00	$19,776.22	121.89%	69.11%	76.91%
1923	2,026,572	$401,549.04	$107,823.34	166.94%	192.27%	445.22%
1924	4,081,282	$813,582.21	$276,038.07	101.39%	102.61%	156.01%
1925	5,189,837	$1,158,667.53	$443,709.47	27.16%	42.42%	60.74%
1926	8,517,167	$1,855,751.64	$704,037.15	64.11%	60.16%	58.67%
1927	11,944,899	$2,517,085.46	$931,121.21	40.24%	35.64%	32.25%
1928	8,240,906	$1,561,369.20	$357,978.07	−31.01%	−37.97%	−61.55%
1929	17,004,306	$2,945,257.85	$986,692.25	106.34%	88.63%	175.63%
1930	20,041,122	$3,408,039.30	$1,193,167.04	17.86%	15.71%	20.93%
1931	23,994,985	$4,153,555.63	$1,614,084.95	19.73%	21.88%	35.28%
1932	18,286,271	$3,492,125.84	$1,027,507.98	−23.79%	−15.92%	−36.34%
Average yearly change 1920–29				87.22%	77.84%	104.66%

2. "President's Report to the Stockholders, March 18, 1929," in Talon files.

3. "President's Report for the Directors at the Annual Meeting, July 1, 1924," in Talon files.

4. The best source on European developments is Nägele. The author was an engineer who successfully manufactured zipper machinery for many years; his historical survey is not very reliable but appears to be the only substantial effort made to document non-American developments in the industry.

5. Sundback's foreign rights were confirmed by contracts beginning July 1908 and confirmed in later ones in 1913, 1918, and 1921, according to Gray, pp. 50–51; Wallace Walker to G. Sundback, May 31, 1917; Lewis Walker to L. Walker, Jr., and Wallace Walker, June 4, 1917. Bruhn's role is described in letter from Hugo Bruhn, of Sweden, to K. A. Harrington, August 19, 1954, in records of ICI Metals Division, Lightning Fastener

268 Company papers, Archives Division, Birmingham Central Library (hereafter Lightning Fastener Records).

6. Gray, pp. 50–51, 83–84; account books, Hookless Fastener Company (1913–1923) R. Finch to L. Walker, May 3, 1924.

7. Gray, pp. 83–88.

8. Untitled and undated summary of SAFE history in Lightning Fastener Records; statement of sales, Lightning Fasteners Ltd., 1919–1953, in Lightning Fastener Records; SAFE files, in Lightning Fastener Records.

9. "History of the Slide Fastener—ZIPP Make—in Germany," translated document from the German, in Lightning Fastener Records.

10. Ibid.; statement of sales, Lightning Fasteners Ltd., 1919–1953, in Lightning Fastener Records; William L. Shirer, *The Rise and Fall of the Third Reich* (New York: Fawcett Crest, 1962), pp. 357, 1411. Reference to the Soviet capture of a German zipper factory is in Leslie Lieber, "Who Put the Zip in Zippers?," *This Week* (June 4, 1961).

11. Nägele, p. 39; "Die abenteuerliche Flucht des schweizerischen 'Reissverschluss-Königs,'" *Schweizer Illustrierte Zeitung*, October 12, 1949, pp. 5–7; "75 Years of Koh-i-Noor," booklet from Koh-i-Noor National Enterprise (Prague: 1982); Manchester, op. cit.; conversation with Otto Smrček, Prague, September 1991; conversation with Milo Waldes, September 1992.

12. U.S. Tariff Commission, "Cost of Production of Slide Fasteners; "Zippered Import," *Business Week* (July 18, 1936), p. 30; letter from Alex Gregory, YKK (U.S.A.), Marietta, Georgia, October 26, 1992.

13. "Post-War Prospects of the Metal Group, Section XXIII-Lightning Fasteners," report prepared by ICI Metals, Ltd., Witton, Birmingham, September 1943, in Lightning Fastener Records; "Bickford & Co., Wiener Neustadt, 75th Anniversary," in Lightning Fastener Records.

14. "Meadville," prepared by the Meadville Chamber of Commerce, June 1941; *Historical and Industrial Review of Meadville, Pa.* (Meadville: Tribune Publishing Co., [1912]).

15. *Meadville Tribune Republican*, August 21, 1921; December 4, 1922; April 7, 1924; January 7, 1925; February 27, 1926; April 9, 1926; June 5, 1926; December 24, 1926; December 27, 1926.

16. *Meadville Tribune Republican*, January 26, 1927.

17. The *Hookless Scoop* (December 1926); Hookless Fastener Company payroll ledger, 1922–24, Crawford County Historical Society; tours of zipper factories in Prague (Koh-i-Noor), 1991, and Rhauderfehn, Germany (Opti), 1992.

18. Application correspondence files, 1927–28, in Talon files.

19. "100,000,000 Units," *Fortune* (September 1932), pp. 58–61.

20. Ibid.; Alfred B. Carlip, "The Slide Fastener Industry: A Study of

Market Structure and Innovation," Ph.D. dissertation, Columbia University, 1960, pp. 96–98, 101–02.

21. Ibid., pp. 102–05.

22. Report by W. L. Gilmore, general manager, to the president, board of directors, and stockholders, July 1, 1927; Gray, pp. 71, 75; examples of advertisements can be found in the *Saturday Evening Post* (September 4, 1926), p. 64; (September 18, 1926), p. 117; (October 2, 1926), p. 97; (October 16, 1926), p. 84; (April 14, 1928), p. 219; (May 12, 1928), p. 199; and (June 9, 1928), p. 175; David Conner provided the explanation about the advantages of the shorter name.

23. The key Prentice case is Hookless Fastener Co. v. G. E. Prentice Mfg. Co., filed January 1932, decision of appeal handed down February 4, 1935 (75 F. 2d 264); others included HFC v. G. E. Prentice Mfg. Co. (18F. (2d) 1016, Cir. Court of Appeals, 2d Dist.); HFC v. G. E. Prentice Mfg. Co. (68F. (2d 940, Cir. Court of Appeals, 2d Dist.).

24. Gray, pp. 87–88.

25. Gray, p. 99; Hookless Fastener Co. v. Lion Fastener, Inc. (72 F. (2d) 985, Cir. Court of Appeals, 3d Cir.); Hookless Fastener Co. v. Lion Fastener, Inc. (84 F. (2d) 579, Cir. Court of Appeals, 3d Cir.).

7. Bye-bye Buttons

1. Untitled report by Sam Kinney (ca. 1937), from files of Ruth Klingener (hereafter referred to as Kinney report).

2. Report on applications, June 11, 1920; Kinney report; "100,000,000 Units," p. 60; U.S. Tariff Commission, "Cost of Production of Slide Fasteners," pp. 14, 17.

3. Kinney report; Gray, pp. 78–80.

4. "Merchandise Equipped with TALON, the Original Slide Fastener," Hookless Fastener Company catalog, [1929]; "100,000,000 Units," p. 60; "Designing to Sell," *Sales Management* (February 20, 1932), p. 254.

5. "The Merchant to the Child," *Fortune* (November 1931), pp. 71–78, 100–06; information on O'Brien and the Bureau of Home Economics from Carolyn Goldstein, University of Delaware/Smithsonian Institution.

6. "The Merchant to the Child," p. 100; Ruth O'Brien, "Child Study and Clothes," *Earnshaw's Infants' and Children's Department*, vol. 14 (April 1930), p. 564; Ellen Miller, "Clothing Your Child," *Catholic Woman Magazine* (April 1927), from unpaginated offprint in Records of the Bureau of Human Nutrition and Home Economics, U.S. Department of Agriculture, Record Group 176, Series 14, U.S. National Archives and Records Administration, Suitland, Maryland (thanks to Carolyn Goldstein for assistance in using this collection.); Jessica G. Cosgrave, "Behaviorism in Bringing Up Children," *Delineator* (May 1929), pp. 36, 93–94. See also Hillel Schwartz,

270 "The Zipper and the Child," *Notebooks in Cultural Analysis* (Durham, N.C.: Duke University Press, 1985), vol. 2, pp. 18–19.

7. "Earnshaw, George Frederick," *National Cyclopedia of American Biography* (New York: John T. White Co., [1943]), vol. 30, pp. 408–09; "Vanta originated it . . . the nation carries on," Earnshaw Knitting Company advertisement, *Earnshaw's*, vol. 18 (March 1934), inside front cover; "Vanta" advertisement, *Earnshaw's*, vol. 14 (April 1930), pp. 498–99; Iva Irene Sell, "Clothes for the Pre-School Child," *Journal of Home Economics* (July 1928), from unpaginated galley sheets in records of the Bureau of Human Nutrition and Home Economics.

8. Ruth O'Brien to R. H. Macy [Company], February 8, 1928, in records of the Bureau of Human Nutrition and Home Economics; J. C. Flugel, *The Psychology of Clothes* (London: L. & V. Woolf/Hogarth Press, 1930), p. 231; historical summary prepared for Lewis Walker II, 1934, in Talon files; "Manufacturer's Price List, Talon Slide Fastener," July 1, 1929, in Talon files; "General Manager's Report," January 18, 1932, in Talon files; "History of the Application of the Slide Fastener," typescript memoir by W. D. Craig, 1943–44, in collection of Ruth Klingener; "Hookless Fastener Gets Store Buyers Active Support with Industrial Film," *Sales Management*, vol. 35 (October 10, 1934), pp. 364, 366.

9. "Hookless Fastener Gets Store Buyers . . ."; "Slide Fasteners Battle Buttons to Hold Up Tots' Togs," *Sales Management*, vol. 36 (March 1, 1935), p. 274; Herbert L. Stephen, "Tough Market Capitulates," *Printers' Ink* (November 14, 1935), pp. 34–40.

10. Advertisements in *Earnshaw's Infants' and Children's Department* and *Parents Magazine*, various issues, 1933 and 1934 (all ellipses are in the originals); Winifred Davenport, "Self-Help Clothes," *Parents Magazine*, vol. 8 (November 1933), pp. 29, 74; Esther Mason and Elinor M. Brown, "Learning to Dress," *Parents Magazine*, vol. 9 (October 1934), pp. 22–24, 85.

11. "Tough Market Capitulates," p. 40; "100,000,000 Units," pp. 60–61; "Slide Fasteners Battle Buttons . . . ," p. 274; Carlip, p. 82; Craig memoir; advertisement in *Earnshaw's Infants' and Children's Department*, vol. 18 (March 1934), inside cover.

12. Carlip, p. 82; Paul H. Nystrom, *Economics of Fashion* (New York: Ronald Press, 1928), pp. 376–77.

13. O. E. Schoeffler and William Gale, *Esquire's Encyclopedia of 20th Century Men's Fashions* (New York: McGraw-Hill, 1973), pp. 124–28.

14. Report of General Manager for Stockholders' Meeting, July 1, 1927, Talon files; Craig, "History of the Application. . . ."

15. Craig memoir; Manchester, pp. 36–38.

16. Eugene Du Bois, "Who Said Depression?," *Brooklyn Daily Eagle* (May 7, 1935), sec. 2, pp. 1, 21; "Slide Fasteners: Roosevelt Safeguards Domestic Industry," *Newsweek* (July 21, 1934), pp. 29–30; "Zippered Imports," *Business Week* (July 18, 1936), pp. 30–31; Craig memoir; "100,000,000 Units."

17. Kinney report.

18. Ibid.

19. Ibid.; Gray, pp. 90–91.

20. Kinney report.

21. Ibid.; "Who Said Depression?"

22. Gray, pp. 92–93, 97; "Meadville *v.* the U.S.," *Time* (September 15, 1941), pp. 67–68; "Men's Wear Sixth Annual Summer Clothing Survey," *Men's Wear* (September 22, 1937), p. 38, and Talon advertisement, pp. 78–79.

23. Various articles on the Paris showings in *Women's Wear Daily*, August 13–August 17, 1937; "Now Everything's Zippers," *Life* (November 8, 1937). Thanks to Robert Kaufmann of the Metropolitan Museum's Costume Institute for locating this last item, from which the quotation is taken.

24. Gray, p. 94; Elizabeth Ann Coleman, *The Genius of Charles James* (Brooklyn: Brooklyn Museum, 1982), p. 12; Billy Bay, "Elsa Schiaparelli," in *Hommage à Elsa Schiaparelli*, ed. Guillaume Garnier (Paris: Musée de la Mode et du Costume, 1984), pp. 36–37; Elsa Schiaparelli, *Shocking Life* (New York: E. P. Dutton, 1954), pp. 87–88; for plastic zippers, basic patents are U.S.P. 2,068,354 (1933), 2,166,905 & 2,273,773 (1935). My thanks to Elizabeth Ann Coleman of the Museum of Fine Arts, Houston, and Claudia Kidwell, of the Smithsonian Institution, for special assistance with this subject.

25. Cecil Beaton, *The Glass of Fashion* (New York: Doubleday & Co., 1954), pp. 221–22; Prudence Glynn, *In Fashion: Dress in the Twentieth Century* (New York: Oxford University Press, 1978), pp. 26, 39; Valerie Steele, *Paris Fashion: A Cultural History* (New York: Oxford University Press, 1988), pp. 248–50.

26. "On and Off the Avenue," *The New Yorker* (September 25, 1937); Talon advertisements in *Vogue* (February 1, 1935), p. 88; (February 15, 1935), p. 18; (September 15, 1935), p. 32; (September 1, 1937), p. 37; (September 15, 1937), p. 51; (November 1, 1937), p. 28; Gray, pp. 93–94.

27. Gray, p. 95.

28. Ibid., pp. 97–98, 103–04.

29. Carlip, p. 50, with data from Slide Fastener Association, Inc., "Historical Sales Data, the Zipper Industry."

30. Talon, Inc., "Talon, Inc. and Subsidiary Companies, Sales by Application, 1937, 1938, and 1939," in Talon files; "The Annual Slide Fastener Survey," *Apparel Manufacturer* (August 1952), p. 61; "College Boys Are Zippered Up," *Sales Management* (October 20, 1940), p. 33.

31. "Vanishing Zipper," *Business Week* (September 27, 1941), pp. 44–45; "Meadville v. the U.S.," *Time* (September 15, 1941), pp. 67–69.

32. "Vanishing Zipper"; "Meadville v. the U.S."

33. "Product Line Refined, Expanded," *Meadville Tribune*, Talon anniversary supplement (May 14, 1963), p. 8; Gray, pp. 112–13.

34. Nägele, p. 81; Dun and Bradstreet, *The Slide Fastener Industry in 1950* (New York: Dun & Bradstreet, 1951), p. 46; Donald Kirk, "Zipper King," *New York Times Magazine* (June 9, 1974), p. 20; letter from Alex Gregory, YKK (U.S.A.), Inc., October 26, 1992; Carlip, p. 129.

35. "Product Line Refined, Expanded;" untitled clipping from *Meadville Tribune Republican*, February 17, 1943; photographs of "Fabric Conservation Exhibit" for the War Production Board, May 9–16, 1944, in files of Slide Fastener Association.

8. "Alligators of Ecstasy"

1. There are many studies of the literary and intellectual responses to technology. Among the best known (all focusing on the United States) are Leo Marx, *The Machine in the Garden* (New York: Oxford University Press, 1964); John F. Kasson, *Civilizing the Machine* (New York: Grossman, 1976); Cecelia Tichi, *Shifting Gears* (Chapel Hill: University of North Carolina Press, 1987).

2. Bryan P. Grenville, *Kurt Tucholsky, the Ironic Sentimentalist* (Atlantic Highlands, N.J.: Humanities Press, 1981), passim; Kurt Tucholsky, *Castle Gripsholm*, trans. Michael Hofmann (London: Chatto & Windus, 1985), introduction by M. Hofmann, pp. 7–13; Kurt Tucholsky, *Tucholsky, ein Lesebuch für unsere Zeit*, ed. Roland Links (Berlin: Aufbau-Verlag, 1990); Tucholsky's story is translated in Helmuth Hartmann, *Open-Shut: A Book around and about Zip-fasteners*, trans. Alan Braley (n.p.: published by the author, 1980), the excerpts that follow are from Braley's translation, pp. 13–17.

3. The Germans seemed to have been particularly ready to express this sense of wonder and mystery of the zipper's working. A history of Germany's ZIPP-Werk, found in the Lightning archives in Birmingham, makes specific reference to this reaction from the German public.

4. Hartmann, pp. 25, 65.

5. Aldous Huxley, *Brave New World* (1932; New York: Bantam Books, 1968), p. 159. All subsequent quotations are taken from this edition.

6. Henry Hazlitt, "What's Wrong with Utopia," *Nation* (February 17, 1932), pp. 204, 206, reprinted in Donald Watt, ed., *Aldous Huxley, the Critical Heritage* (London: Routledge & Kegan Paul, 1975), pp. 215–16.

7. Watt, p. 3.

8. Tom Robbins, *Jitterbug Perfume* (1984; New York: Bantam Books, 1985), pp. 272–73.

9. Thanks to Ellen Miles for finding this and bringing it to my attention.

10. Leonard Michaels, "The Zipper," in *The Best American Essays, 1992*, ed. Susan Sontag (New York: Ticknor & Fields, 1992), pp. 244–52 (originally in *The Threepenny Review*, 1991).

11. Erica Jong, *Fear of Flying* (New York: New American Library, 1974), pp. 11, 14.

12. *Reizverschluss* is mentioned in Hartmann, p. 30, who also quotes Johnson, p. 34; *Time* (July 11, 1969).

13. The *Oxford English Dictionary* gives this as the original usage of the word, dating from the 1870s; the final volume of the original *OED* was published in April 1928, apparently too early to incorporate "zipper," which appeared in the first *Supplement* to the Dictionary; *London Daily Mail*, May 22, 1924, p. 1. Thanks to Paul Willer for supplying this.

14. References are to Sigfried Giedion, *Mechanization Takes Command:* A Contribution to Anonymous History (New York: Oxford University Press, 1958) and Lewis Mumford, *Technics and Civilization* (New York: Harcourt Brace, 1934), perhaps the two most influential critiques of modern technology published in this century.

15. Thomas Carlyle, *Signs of the Times*, quoted in Albert Borgmann, *Technology and the Character of Contemporary Life* (Chicago: University of Chicago Press, 1984), p. 59.

16. Cleveland Amory, "Curmudgeon-at-Large," *SR/World* (October 23, 1973), p. 53; Robin Pulver, *Mrs. Toggle's Zipper* (New York: Four Winds Press, 1990), not paginated.

17. *Washington Post*, October 5, 1991. Thanks to Susan Oetken for spotting this.

18. Jan Harold Brunvand was kind enough to supply several versions of these stories, which appeared both in his newspaper columns ("Urban Legends," United Feature Syndicate, e.g.: November 21, 1988, March 12, 1990, and March 30, 1992) and in his books—e.g.: *The Vanishing Hitchhiker* (New York: W. W. Norton, 1981), pp. 138–39. A published version of the "tablecloth in the fly" story appears in Maynard Good Studdard, "The Trouble with Zippers," *Saturday Evening Post* (November 1981), p. 67.

19. Brunvand, "Urban Legends" column for weeks of June 15, 1987, and July 17, 1989.

20. Jack Finney, *The Woodrow Wilson Dime* in *Three by Finney*, (1968; New York: Simon & Schuster, 1987), p. 58.

21. References to the *Daily Express* survey of 1938 are in file, "Blixløs" (no. 2281), in the Archives of the Tekniska Museet, Stockholm, citing the London journal *Pinpoints* (May–June 1939).

22. O. G. Schoeffler and William Gale, *Esquire's Encyclopedia of 20th Century Men's Fashions*, (New York: McGraw-Hill, 1973), pp. 128–32; John Bentley Mays, "Deciphering the Zip Code," *Toronto Globe and Mail*, February 27, 1991.

• **1.** In a peculiar mistake, the distinguished English historian A. J. P. Taylor claimed that World War I [*sic!*] had broken the blockade that button manu-

z facturers had enforced against the zipper and that the war had exposed thousands of men to the device. Could Taylor have been thinking of the

I Second World War, when such a claim, while still erroneous, at least had some logical foundation? A. J. P. Taylor, *English History, 1914–1945* (New

P York: Oxford University Press, 1965), p. 52. Thanks to Alex Magoun for bringing this to my attention.

P **2.** The Swedish interest in the zipper's history is documented in a file (no. 2281) in the Archives, Tekniska Museet, Stockholm. Among specific items

E are: "Blixtlåsets historia aer en spaennande . . ." *Stockholms Tidningen* (1932—clipping not further identified); "Museum på jakt efter blixtlåsets

R uppfinnare," *Svenska Dagbladet* (July 11, 1938); "Hur, Blixtlåset Kom Till," *Nya Norrland* (July 22, 1938);" Vem uppfann blixtlåset?," *Jamtlands Tidning* (July 5, 1954). Thanks to Inger Björkland of the Tekniska Museet for making this material available and to Alice Klingener of the University of Illinois for providing translations. "Till Blixtlåsets Historia," *Daedalus-Tekniska Museets Årsbok* (1940), pp. 84–96.

3. The Literary Union address, the Tarbell interview with Sundback, the Chisholm history, and a large collection of obituaries and tributes to Colo-nel Walker are in the Talon papers, Crawford County Historical Society. See also "History of Talon, Inc.," *Meadville Tribune Republican* (sesqui-centennial Special), May 12, 1938. References to Walker's approach to Tarbell are in an editorial, *Meadville Tribune*, November 9, 1963.

4. Correspondence between J. A. Sundin and G. Sundback, in Talon files; between J. A. Sundin and Torsten Althin, in archives of the Tekniska Museet, Stockholm; and between G. Sundback and Harry Earle, Sr. and Harry Earle, Jr., in Talon files. A copy of Earle's application for admission to the Marcus L. Ward Home for Aged and Respectable Bachelors and Widowers is in the Talon files, as the result of inquiries made by James Gray. The dates for Harry Earle, Sr., were November 5, 1854, to January 28, 1944. The colonel had not, in fact, completely turned his back on Earle. The salesman apparently kept in touch over the years, and letters between the two men in 1927 refer to loans that Walker assisted Earle in getting as well as Earle's embarrassment at leaving an unpaid bill at Meadville's Lafa-yette Hotel. H. Earle to L. Walker, February 8, 1927; L. Walker to H. Earle, July 23, 1927, Talon files.

5. Sundback correspondence, in Talon files; the reference to the Franklin Institute is from a letter, G. Sundback to Harry Earle, Sr., January 13, 1942; see also "Extract from letter to Victor Freeburg from Gideon Sund-back dated December 7, 1939," in Archives, Tekniska Museet, Stockholm.

6. Federico correspondence with Sundback and with T. L. Chisholm, 1945–1946, in Talon files. The Federico article appeared in *Journal of the Patent Office Society*, vol. 28 (December 1946), pp. 855–76.

7. Gray describes the integration of Sundback's interests into Talon, pp. 128–29; the self-characterization is in a letter to J. A. Sundin, May 19, 1939, in the Talon files; the interview was recorded in Canada, December 30, 1952, in the holdings of Ruth Klingener. The article by Vogel was "The Zipper: A Story of Success," *Coronet* (May 1949). Sundback's sensitivity about Walker's credit was mentioned in a letter from T. L. Chisholm to James Gray, December 13, 1960, in Talon files. The merger between Lightning, Canada and Talon was reported in the *Meadville Tribune Republican*, August 28, 1947.

8. For descriptions of the Wembley exhibition, see John E. Fielding, ed., *Historical Dictionary of World's Fairs and Expositions, 1851–1988* (New York: Greenwood Press, 1990), pp. 235–38; John Allwood, *The Great Exhibitions* (London: Studio Vista, 1977), pp. 127–29; [Marjorie G. Cook], *The British Empire Exhibition, 1924, Official Guide* (London: Fleetway Press, 1924); and [Donald Maxwell], *Wembley in Colour* (London: Longmans, Green and Co., 1924). The exhibit was advertised in the *London Daily Mail*, May 22, 1924, p. 1. The remark to Walker was in a letter, R. Finch to Lewis Walker, May 3, 1924, in Talon files.

9. Some of the story of Heuss's visit to the museum and the request for a zipper was told me by Hans-Liudger Dienel of the museum staff, who, along with curator Hartmut Petzold, assisted me in finding the correspondence between the museum and ZIPP-Werk, GmbH, Nuremberg in the Deutsches Museum records.

10. "Historical Sales Data," reported to the Committee on Statistics, Slide Fastener Association, June 28, 1954, in SFA files; Lightning Fasteners Ltd., "Statement of Sales, 1919–1953," in Lightning Fastener Company papers, Archives Division, Birmingham Central Library. The shift to aluminum is documented in Dun and Bradstreet, p. 8 and passim.

11. Perkins Bailey, "The Slide Fastener Picture," *Apparel Manufacturer* (February 1944), p. 33; "A Guide to Slide Fasteners," *Apparel Manufacturer* (August 1944), pp. 45–55; "What Garment Makers Want from Slide Fastener Industry," *Apparel Manufacturer* (August 1945), pp. 54–58.

12. Dun and Bradstreet, pp. 13–14; interview with Jerry Gould (YKK [U.S.A.]), February 1, 1993; Nägele, pp. 74–79.

13. Interview with Jerry Gould; Dun and Bradstreet, pp. 7–8.

14. Carlip, pp. 144–156; Dun and Bradstreet, pp. 7–8, 15, 45.

15. Carlip, pp. 156–57; "Firms Who Have Discontinued Zipper Business since January 1, 1951," memo issued by Slide Fastener Association, November 6, 1956, in SFA files; remarks of Samuel I. Rosenman at organizational meeting of the Zipper Industries Association, October 16, 1952, in SFA files.

16. "Comparative Analysis of Membership, S.F.A., Inc.," 1956, in SFA files; Carlip, pp. 144, 156–57.

276 17. Gray, pp. 131–32, 138–43, 152; "Product Line Refined, Expanded," *Meadville Tribune* (Talon fiftieth anniversary supplement), May 14, 1963, p. 8.

18. Carlip, pp. 157–66.

19. Nägele, pp. 49–50; "Product Line Refined, Expanded," p. 8.

20. Nägele, pp. 22, 27

21. Morris D. Schoengold, *Encyclopedia of Substitutes and Synthetics* (New York: Philosophical Library, 1943), pp. 227–28; David Hounshell and John K. Smith, Jr., *Science and Corporate Strategy: Du Pont R&D, 1902–1980* (New York: Cambridge University Press, 1988), pp. 229, 239, 257–62.

22. Gray, pp. 153–54; Nägele, p. 50; Hartmann, p. 66; "Sonderausgabe," *Opti News* (house organ of Opti-Werke, Essen, Germany), May 14, 1987; Lewis Weiner, "The Slide Fastener," *Scientific American* (June 1983), pp. 136–38.

23. "Product Line Refined, Expanded," p. 8; Gray, pp. 154–56.

24. "Zephyr Consumer Survey" by Gallup & Robinson organization, dated January–March 1963, in Talon Company files; Levi Strauss memorandums (undated) in Talon Company files.

25. Sales statistics from files of the Committee on Statistics, Slide Fastener Association records; "Change of Strategy for Talon Zippers," *New York Times*, December 7, 1981, p. D4.

26. Interview with Jerry Gould, February 1, 1993.

27. Memorandum from David Conner, March 1992; details of the mergers and purchases were reported in the *Meadville Tribune* April 3, 1968, and October 18, 1983.

28. "History of YKK," chronology, and other information, communicated in correspondence from Alex Gregory, YKK, October 26, 1992; Donald Kirk, "Zipper King," *New York Times Magazine* (June 9, 1974), pp. 18–20, 30.

29. Kirk, pp. 30, 35–40; Tadao Yoshida, *How YKK Sees and Thinks: Yoshida's Philosophy*, 4 vols. (Tokyo: Senko Kikaku, 1980–83), vol. 1, pp. 7–8.

30. Kirk, pp. 35–40; Yoshida, vol. 1, pp. 14–20, 73–76.

31. "This is YKK," YKK annual report (1991); "YKK Close-Up" (report of YKK [U.S.A.], 1990); additional information supplied by Alex Gregory, YKK; Kirk, p. 40; "Will Success Spoil YKK," *Fortune* (October 16, 1978), p. 109.

32. "Gift of Plant by Talon Zips Up Meadville Era," *Pittsburgh Press*, April 3, 1983 (unpaginated clipping in files of Crawford County Historical Society).

33. *Meadville Tribune*, December 2, 1991, and December 15, 1991.

34. Giedion, p. 3.

35. Of course, many—perhaps most—inventions are not pure examples of either breed but hybrids. There may be needs or specific desires that spur inventive activity, but these needs often provide no direction to the would-be inventor. The direction is provided by the perception of opportunity, an insight into possibilities for combining elements of the natural or artificial world in novel ways. The perceived opportunities may, in turn, guide the entrepreneur or inventor toward novel possibilities far removed from the original perceived demand.

Index

Page numbers in *italics* refer to illustrations.

Abercrombie & Fitch, 135
Adams, Henry, 204
Age of Machinery, 217
Agriculture Department, U.S., 177
air forces, 60
airplanes, 22, 60, 63, 136, 151, 204–5
Akron, Ohio, 147–48, 164, 166
Alfred Zentler AG, 209
Allegheny College, 26, 227, 229, 247
Alley, R. W., 217–18
Althin, Torsten, 227
aluminum, 58, 201, 232, 234
American Bell Company, 2
Amory, Cleveland, 217
Anderson, Thomas Hart, 2–3, 12
anti-Semitism, 110, 111–13, 118
anti-trust violations, 235
Apparel Manufacturer, 197
Arnold-Constable Company, 111
Aronson, Peter, *31*, 81, 227, 228
    daughter of, *see* Sundback, Naomi
        Elvira Aronson
    fastener invention and patent of, 32,
        60, 70, 72

French and English sales promotions
    of, 58–60, *59*, 70, 72, 75, 97,
    154, 157, 158
Sundback and, 32, 48, 58–60, *58*,
    75, 77, 97
Swedish birth and emigration of, *31*,
    32, 45, 46
Arthur, William C., 199–200
Atlas Underwear Company, 166
Australia, 130, 136, 160
Auto-Glove Company, 139, 140
Automatic Hook and Eye Company,
    48–60, 68–70, 74–83, 127
establishment of, 36–45
financial difficulties and closing of,
    57–60, 75, 78, 80–84, 99
products of, *see* C-curity fastener;
    Plako Garment Fastener
sales campaigns of, *37*, 38–44, 49,
    50–60, *54*, *59*, 65, 74–75, 76,
    116
stockholders in, 29, 83–84, 99, 105
Sundback's management of, 74–
    81

automobiles, 36, 80, 88, 89, 138, 150–51, 175, 204–5
  electric, 63
  mass production of, 63, 150
aviators' suits, 133, 136, 155

Babbitt (Lewis), 85, 208
Barrett Machine Tool Company, 162
behaviorism, 177
Bell, Alexander Graham, 2
Bell Laboratories, 91
Berlin, 158, 206–8
B. F. Goodrich Rubber Company, 147–49, 152–54
  Zipper Boots of, 148–49, 150, 152–53, *152*, 157, 158, 164, 166–68, 184, 216, 238
Bickford & Company, 160
biotechnology, 22
B. Kuppenheimer, 188
Blake & Johnson, 22–23
Bloomingdale's, 181
book salesmen, 53, 54–55, 56
boots, 34, 35, 43, 74, 131
  rubber, *see* B. F. Goodrich Rubber Company
Boston, Mass., 117, 127, 136, 181
Brando, Marlon, 224
Brash, Dr., 110–11
Brave New World (Huxley), 209–12
British Empire Exhibition, 216, 230–31
Brooklyn Daily Eagle, 186
Bruhn, J. T., 155
Brunvand, Jan Harold, 219–21
Bryden Horse Shoe Company, 20–22
Bullock's, 181
Bureau of Home Economics, 182
  Division of Textiles and Clothing, 177–80
Burr, Aaron, 45
buttons, viii, 43, 44, 66–67, 131, 188, 198, 200, 215, 221, 250
Bye-Bye Buttons, 181

cable cars, 6, 10
Cahan, Abraham, 113–14
Calhoun, Ida Josephine, 71
Canada, 156–57, 170–71
Canfield, Frank, 70–71
Carlip, A. B., 235, 236–37
Carlyle, Thomas, 217
Carnegie, Andrew, 134, 244
Carothers, Wallace Hume, 238
Carroll, Miss (buyer), 118
Castle Garden, 38
Cataract Construction Company, 7
Catasauqua, Pa., 20–23
Catton, Bruce, 229
C. Campart, 155

C-curity fastener, 37, 45–53, *52*, 68, 70, 98, 105, 127, 157, 216
  manufacturing of, 37–38, 42–45, 49–51, 74, 100, 165
  mechanical problems with, 41, 42, 45, 49, 50–51, *52*
  promotion and sales of, *37*, 38–44, 49, 50, 53, 56, *59*, 74
celluloid, 237
census:
  of 1870, 53–54
  of 1900, 45
Champion DeArment Company, 162
Chicago, Ill., 1–2, 11–12, 28–29, 117, 133, 188
children's clothing, 176–83, *179*
child study, 177–80
Chisholm, T. L., 94–95, 227
Chronicle of Higher Education, 223
Citroën, 157
City Ale Brewing Company, 163
Civil War, U.S., 4
Clarke, Howard, 53
Clarke Sales Company, 53, 55–56, 74
clasps, viii, 131, 252
cloak and suit makers, 113–15, 116
Closgard Wardrobe Company, 137
Coats Viyella PLC, 243
Collier's Weekly, 40
Colonial Fastener Company, 170–71
Colton, Charles S., 155
Columbian Exposition (Chicago), 1, 63
Columbia University, 235
commercial travelers ("drummers"), 40–41, 42–43, 53–58, 60, 65, 74, 76, 77, 86–90
communism, 208
compressed air engine, 6–10, *8*
Congress, U.S., 9–10
Conmar, 234
Converse, 167
Cooper, Thomas J., 53, 55–56
Coronet, 229
corsets, 34, 35, 43, 176
Craig, W. D., 180
Cue Fastener, Inc., 239
Czechoslovakia, 160–61, 186

Daedalus, 227
Daily Express (London), 222
Daily Mail (London), 216
Dali, Salvador, 194
Delamater, Victor, 36, 45, 75, 76, 82
Delamater family, 26, 29, 81, 125
Delaware, Lackawanna & Western Railroad, 45
department stores, 107, 109, 111, 112, 115, 122, 129, 130, 181
Depression, Great, 20, 175, 186, 199

Deutsche Amac-Vergaser-und-
  Apparatebau, 158
Deutsches Museum von Meisterwerken
  der Naturwissenschaft und
  Technik, 231
Diesel, Rudolf, 62–63, 64, 98
Dieterich, Fred G., 24
Donahue Sales Company, 243
Dr. Denton, 180
Dress Creators' League, 195
dressmakers, 40, 41, 42, 44, 109, 111,
  114
Dressmakers' Protective Association,
  44
Drury Lane Theater, 38
DuBois Overall Company, 166

Earle, Harry L., 16–23, *19*, 45
  companies formed by, 5, 9, 11–12,
    16–23, 26, 29–36
  death of, 228
  early business career of, 19
  entrepreneurial skills of, 4, 9, 19–20,
    19, 29, 32, 34–36, 43, 49–50,
    154
  impoverishment of, 20, 49, 228
  investors found by, 20–23, 29, 32
  Judson's relationship with, 4–5, 9,
    12, 16, 18–20, 22–23, 30–35,
    153
  patents of, 20
  slide fastener investment of, 17,
    19–23, *19*, 49
  Sundback and, 49–50, 228
Earle Automatic Bagger & Tallyer, 20
Earle Automatic Band-cutter & Self-
  feeder, 20
Earle Manufacturing Company, 5, 20
Earnshaw, George F., 178–79, 183
Edison, Thomas Alva, 3, 4, 19, 25, 32,
  60
E. I. du Pont de Nemours, 194, 238,
  239
electricity:
  generation of, 7, 46
  lighting systems using, 3, 60
  rapid development of, 60, 63, 150
  transport systems using, 6–7, 9, 10
electromagnetic radiation, 63
Ely, George H., 23, 30
Elyria Fastener Company, 23
enamels, 186
engines:
  compressed air, 6–10, *8*
  internal combustion, 2, 6, 55, 63, 64
  steam, 7, 32
Erie, Pa., 82, 83, 89, 125, 133
Erie Canal, 138
Erie Railroad, 162, 246, 247

Esquire, 184, 190
European Universal Fastener
  Company, 23
Everfloat Life Preserver Company, 137
Ewig, Robert J., 134–35, 136–37, 145,
  149
E-Z Lok fastener, 167, 169–70

Falcon fastener, 236
fashion, viii
  dressmakers and, 109
  French, 115, 132, 191–95
  men's, 187–91, *198*
  women's, 109, 115, 132, 191–95,
    193, 215, 237
Fashion Originators Guild of America,
  195
Fastener Manufacturing and Machine
  Company, 32–36
Fear of Flying (Jong), 214–15
Federico, P. J., 228–29
Ferme-tout Américain, *59*, 60, 154,
  157
Ferracute Company, 21
Filene's, 181
Finney, Jack, 221–22
Firestone, 167
Fitzgerald, F. Scott, 150
flaps, viii, 221, 250
Flugel, John Carl, 180
Ford, Glenn, 213–14
Ford, Henry, 63, 150
Forster, Henri, 72–73, 95–97, *96*, 155
Fortune, 182
Forty-second Illinois Cavalry, 4
France, 58–60, *59*, 66, 72, 75, 97, 138,
  154, 162
  fashion of, 115, 132, 191–95
  Nazi occupation of, 157–58, 199
Franklin Institute, 228
Freidenrich, Van Cott Company, 129,
  137
Freidenrich & Company, 129
Friend & Shrier, 129
F. S. Mills Company, 139–40

gadgets, 55, 125, 133
garment industry, 44, *103*, 107–22,
  127, 128–32, 153, 200
  factories and showrooms of, 107–15,
    118, 233–34
  Jewish immigrants in, 107–22, 234
  labor conditions in, 107
  labor unions and, 112, 117, 120
  personal business contacts in,
    110–22, 115, 120–21
  ready-to-wear trade in, 108, 109,
    114
  specialty clothing in, 109, 111, 116

General Electric Company, 2
General Motors, 150–51
German silver (nickel-copper-zinc alloy), 58, 101, 143, 159, 185, 199, 200, 201, 232
Germany, Federal Republic of, 231, 232, 239
Germany, Imperial, 45, 46
Germany, Nazi, 115, 157–60, 162, 199, 202
Germany, Weimar, 158–60, 206–9
Giedion, Sigfried, viii, 216, 249
Gilda, 213–14
Gilmore, W. L., 180, 182–83
Globe-Superior Company, 166
Glovers Review, 138
Gloversville, N.Y., 138–40, 166, 174
gloves, 16, 34, 43, 66, 74, 138–40, 147, 174
Goldberg, Charles M., 119–22, 131
Goodyear, Charles, 3, 99
"Gospel of Wealth" (Carnegie), 244
Great Britain, 60, 71–73, 97, 155–56, 162, 202, 243, 246
Guiterman Brothers, 137, 146, 176

Hallett and Hackmeyer, 176
Hamburg American steamship line, 45
Hamilton, Alexander, 45
handbags, 139, 150, 174–75, 184, 207
Hart, Lorenz, 212–13
Hart, Schaffner and Marx, 188
Hartmann, Helmuth, 209
harvesting machine, 4
H. A. Seinsheimer, 188
Hayworth, Rita, 213–14
Hazlitt, Henry, 210
H. D. Lee Mercantile Company, 168, 176
Heilmann, W. Erich, 239
Heuss, Theodor, 231
Higham, John, 108
Hippodrome theater, 111
History of the Standard Oil Company (Tarbell), 227
Hitler, Adolf, 199
Hoboken, N.J., *31*, 32–50, 82, 113, 165
Hood, 167
Hookless Fastener Company, 92–97
advertising by, 169
board of directors of, 126, 153–54, 197
competitors of, 154–55, 158–62, 167–71
Development Department of, 184
economic downturns and sales declines at, 145–46, 152–53, 159, 167–68, 175

employees of, 164–66, *165*, 168, 171
establishment of, 82–90, 92, 99, 227
financial condition of, 105, 125–27, 151–54
patent suits involving, 95–96, 97, 168, 169–71
production increases and expansion of, 145–49, 151–52, 154, 163–64, *165*–67, 168
sales campaigns of, 86–90, 99, 106–24, 125–37, 138, 144–48, 173–77, *179*, 180–96, *193*, *196*
stockholders of, 125–27, 154, 168
Sundback at, 85–86, 88, 90, 99–102, 118, 145, 146, 157
see also Automatic Hook and Eye Company; Talon, Inc.
Hookless Fastener #1, 100, 101, 216
invention and development of, 77–82, *79*, 85, 88, 91–94
mechanical problems with, *79*, 80–81, 85, 92–94
Hookless Fastener #2, *93*, 94–106, *94*, 237
clothing manufacturers' experimentation with, 114–18
design and performance of, *93*, 94–99, *94*, 100, 106, 112, 128
foreign sales of, 130, 136
installation and use of, 112–13, 117, 119–20, 127–28
manufacturing of, 98, 99–102, 106, 118, 120, 128, 132, 141–44, *142*
military uses of, 130, 133–37, 155, 156
non-garment applications of, 132–33, 134–35, 137–38, *139*, 140–41, 144
pricing of, 112, 113, 117–22, 129, 130, 141
promotion and sales of, 102–24, 125–37
Hookless Fastener #3, 128, 180
Hookless Fastener #4, 135, 137–38, 146
Hookless Fastener #5, 144, 146, 166, 180
Hookless Fastener #6, 144, 146
Hookless Scoop, *103*, 164–65, *165*
hooks and eyes, 39, 43, 44, 66, 71, 77–78, 113, 118, 120, 122, 252
horse cars, 7, 10
Howe, Elias, 3, 67–68, *69*
Hudson River, 46, 81
Huxley, Aldous, 206, 209–12, 217
Hyatt, John Wesley, 32

ICIANZ, 160
Imperial Chemical Industries (ICI), 156, 160, 170, 194

internal combustion engine, 2, 6, 55, 63, 64
"Invention and Introduction of the Zipper, The" (Federico), 228–29

Jagger, Mick, 215
James, Charles, 192
Japan, 130, 161–62, 186, 201, 202, 240, 243–46
Jewett, Frank, 91, 99
Jews:
  Eastern European, 107, 108, 113–14
  in garment industry, 107–22, 234
  German, 108, 114
  stereotyping of, *see* anti-Semitism
Jiffy Lock Company, 137
Jitterbug Perfume (Robbins), 212, 217
J. L. Hudson Company, 181
Johnson, Lyndon B., 215
Johnson, William, 138
Jong, Erica, 214–15
Jordan Marsh, 181
Journal of the Patent Office Society, 229
Joyce, James M., 55
Judson, Ross, 36
Judson, Whitcomb L., 2–25, 5, 228–29
  agricultural machinery sold by, 4–5, 5, 11–12, 19
  background and education of, 4
  character and personality of, 10, 50, 98
  Civil War service of, 4
  death of, 10, 18, 75
  Earle's relationship with, 4–5, 9, 12, 16, 18–20, 22–23, 30–35, 153
  non-fastener patents of, 3, 5–6, 5, 8, 11, 18, 36
  pneumatic street railway invention of, 5–11, 8, 19, 20, 28–29
  slide fastener designs of, vii, 2–4, 5, 11–18, 13, 15, 22–24, 36–38, 37, 39, 41, 42, 45, 60, 64, 70, 78, 81, 91, 141, 153, 197
  slide fastener manufacturing and, 16, 20–23, 21, 26, 29–38, 31, 45, 64
  slide fastener patents of, ix, 2–3, 11–18, 13, 15, 21, 25, 32, 34, 36, 50, 63, 68, 70, 71–72, 82, 106, 248, 250
  technical ingenuity of, 4, 9, 10–11, 18, 64, 68
  Walker's relationship with, 10, 11, 28–32, 153
Judson Pneumatic Street Railway Company, 9–10, 11, 19, 20, 28–29

Kartel der deutschen Reissverschluss-Industrie, 159
Keilly, Jack, 176–77, 180–81
Keilly, Joan, 180, 181
Kettering, Charles, 63
Keystone View Company, 163
Kinney, Sam, 175–77, 187–90, 195
Kitty Hawk, N.C., 63
knitwear, 185, 232
Knox College, 4
Kodak cameras, 2
Korean conflict, 232
Kover-Zip, 161, 186
Kuhn-Moos, Katharina, 72–74, 95–97, 96, 155, 170, 227
Kynoch's Limited, 155–56
  see also Lightning Fastener Company (England)

labor movement, 107, 112
laces, 39, 131, 215
La Crosse Rubber Mills, 167
Ladies' Home Journal, 175, 195
Ladies' World, 39–40
Lake Shore & Michigan Southern Railway, 19
Lamb, Theodore, 83, 94, 102, 125–26
Landers, Ann, 219
Lanvin, 192
Lawrence, Frank, 127
Lee, Gypsy Rose, 213
Lepper, John G., 32
Levi Strauss, 240
Lewis, Sinclair, 85, 208
Life, 192, 195
Liggett's drugstores, 135
Lightning Fastener Company (Canada), 156–57, 158, 229
Lightning Fastener Company (England), 60, 156, 157, 160, 194, 216, 230, 243
Lind, Jennie, 38
Lion Fastener Company, 168, 171
Locktite tobacco pouch, 139–40, 139, 141, 144, 166
London, 154, 170, 230
Long Day's Journey Into Night (O'Neill), 84
L. Shidlowsky & Company, 116–17
luggage, 137–38

McCall's, 195
McCreery's, 109, 112
McCroskey Reamer Company, 85, 162
McGunnegle, W. S., 83
Macready, George, 213–14
mailbags, 16, 22, 85
Manville Brothers, 23, 31, 32

Marcus L. Ward Home for Aged and Respectable Bachelors and Widowers, 20, 228
Marines, U.S., 89
Marschalk, Henry E., 88–89
Marshall Field's, 112
Martin, Burt A., 40
Martin, Frederick H., 147
Meadville, Pa., 26, 45, 75, 77, 81–90, 108, 246–48
industry and commerce in, 162–63, 186–87, 190, 247–48
zipper production in, *see* Hookless Fastener Company; Talon, Inc.
Meadville Evening Republican, 84–86, 88
Meadville Literary Union, 227
Meadville Theological Seminary, 163
Meadville Tribune, 248
Meadville *Tribune Republican*, 163–64
Mechanization Takes Command (Giedion), 249
Men's Wear, 190
Merrill-Palmer School, 177
Mexico, 89, 229
Michaels, Leonard, 213
Miller, Ellen, 177–78
Minneapolis, Minn., 4–5, 19–20
Model T, 63
Mohawk Indians, 138
Molyneux, Edward, 192, 195
money belts, 134–35, 136, 137, 145
Morley, Christopher, 54–55, 66
motion pictures, 60
Mrs. Toggle's Zipper (Pulver and Alley), 217–18
Mumford, Lewis, 216
Munn & Company, 71
Muskegon *News Chronicle*, 10
Mystik Boot, 148, *152*

Nadel, Jack, 131
Nannette Manufacturing Company, 183
National Bearing Metals, 163
Navy Department, U.S., 136
New Jersey:
manufacturing and commerce in, 21–22, 32, 45
Swedish immigrants in, 45–46, 48
New York, N.Y., 11, 20, 22, 32, 35, 44, 53, 97, 138
garment industry of, 44, *103*, 107–22, 127–32, 153, 200, 233–34
Lower East Side of, 108, 110–11, 113–14
New Yorker, 190, 195
New York World, 131

New Zealand, 130, 160, 246
Niagara Falls, N.Y., 7, 46, 157
Nicoll, Leonard, 111
Nissei Trading Company, 130
Nobel Industries Ltd., 156, 160, 230
North German Lloyd steamship line, 45
NuBone Corset Company, 133, 137
NuGild, 185
Nuremberg, 158–60, 206, 231, 232
nylon, 80, 200, 236, 238–40, 241

O'Brien, Ruth, 177–80
Office of Production Management, 199
O'Neill, Eugene, 84
O'Neill, James, 84
Opti-Werk, 239, 243
Ortega y Gasset, José, 221
Osborne Machinery Company, 4
O'Shaughnessy, J. F., 32

Paige, Doris, 164–65
Pal Joey (Rogers and Hart), 213
Paquin, Mme., 192
Parents Magazine, *179*, 182
Paris, 115, 132, 154, 191–95
Paris International Exhibition (1900), 204
Parnassus on Wheels (Morley), 54–55
Patent Act of 1836, 3
Patent Office, U.S., ix, 2–3, 11, 24–25, 35, 70–71, 95, 96, 228–29
Pennsylvania, 29, 74, 227
Pennsylvania, University of, 106
Pennsylvania National Guard, 28
Pennsylvania Railroad, 45
Pennsylvania Station, 45
Philadelphia, Pa., 117, 132, 181, 228
phonograph, 64
Piguet, Robert, 192
Pitts Agricultural Works, 5
Pittsburgh, Pa., 46, 49, 106, 107, 109, 112, 246
Plako Garment Fastener, 51–61, 98, 101, 157, 216
French and English promotion of, 58–60, *59*, 72, 75, 97, 154, 157, 158
installation and use of, 51, *54*, 55–56, *59*, 65, 136
laundering and rusting of, 51, *53*, 77, 101
manufacturing of, 51, *52*, 57–58, 74–77, 80, 82, 84, 85, 86, 100, 151, 165
mechanical problems with, 51, *52*, 56–57, 60, 65, 77–78, 95
patents on, 58, 70

promotion and sales of, 51–60, *54, 59*, 75–76, 77, 86–90, 102, 105, 116–17, 127, 128, 154, 155
Plako Hose and Sleeve Supporter, 57–58
plastic, 32, 60, 159, 191, 192–94, *193*, 200, 202, 237, 241
Plasti-Zip, 237
Popular Mechanics, 131
Post Office Department, U.S., 22
Poux, Noel J., 168, 171
Prentice, George E., 167, 169–70, 238
Princeton University, 189, 198
Psychological Care of Infant and Child (Watson), 177
Pulver, Robin, 217–18

radio, 60, 63, 80, 151, 181, 204–5, 247
railroads, 45, 55, 56
Ready Fastener Manufacturing Company, 155, 157
Regan, Miss (buyer), 111
Reissverschluss, 158, 159–60, 215
Reissverschluss-Verfahren, 253
Renaissance, 204
Rinne-Rippe fastener, 160
Rise of David Levinsky, The (Cahan), 113–14
R. J. Ewig & Company, 145
Robbins, Tom, 212
Rockefeller family, 29, 134
Rodgers, Richard, 212–13
Roebling and Sons, 57
roller bearings, 32
Rolling Stones, 215
Roosevelt, Franklin D., 199, 222
Rouen, 157–59
Rouff, Maggie, 192
rubber, 127–28
manufacturers of, 167; *see also* B. F. Goodrich Rubber Company
vulcanization of, 3, 99
Russ Automatic Labeling Company, 125
Russell, Alger, 75–77, 87
Russell, Frank, 45, 48, 75–76, 82, 86–89, 99, 100, 133
Russell, Lillian, 39, 140
Rust Belt, 247

S. A. Azamon, 160
safety pins, 66
Sales Management, 198, *198*
San-S Shokai, 161–62
Saturday Evening Post, 169, 190
Saturday Review, 217
Schadenfreude, 209, 219, 220
Schiaparelli, Elsa, 192–95, *193,* 237
Schuss, Nathan, 112–13

Scientific American, 1–2, 71
Scovill, 240
Sears, Roebuck & Company, 43
Self-Help program, 180–83
sewing machine, 3, 24, 68
Shakespeare, William, 54, 55, 209
Sheldon, Mr. (buyer), 117
Shocking Life (Schiaparelli), 194
Shoe Hardware Company, 167
shoes, 2, 3, 5, 12, 34, 85, 127–28, 250, 252
Siddons, Sarah Kemble, 38
Simplex Electric Heating Company, 136
skirt plackets, 34, 38–40, 50, 55, 65, 70, 195, 234
Sköldberg, Sven, 227
slide fastener, *see* zipper
Slide Fastener Association, 235
Slide Fastener Manufacturers Association, 202, 235
Sloan, Alfred P., 150
S-L "scrapless" machine, *142,* 143
snaps, viii, 39, 66, 113, 120, 122, 138, 215, 221, 250
Snuggle Rug Company, 176
socialism, 208
Société Anonyme Fermeture Éclair (SAFE), 157, 159
Soles, Alice Walker, 126
Soles, Louis, 126
Soles, Thomas Franklin, 126–27
Soviet Union, 160, 162
Spirella Company, 163
sportswear, 109, 129, 183–86
Sprague, Frank, 7, 9
Stall & Dean, 137
steam engine, 7, 32
steel, 58, 80–81, 101, 106, 200–201, 238
Stevens, John, 32
Sticky Fingers, 215
Stiles, Mr. (buyer), 111
Strawbridge & Clothier, 181
Sunday, Billy, 150
Sundback, Naomi Elvira Aronson, *31*
courtship, marriage and motherhood of, *31, 48, 49, 58,* 60, 74, 77
death of, 77
factory work of, *31,* 74
Sundback, Otto Frederick Gideon, 46–53, *47, 103*
Aronson and, 32, 48, 58–60, *58,* 75, 77, 97
background and education of, 46, *47,* 49
character and personality of, 49, 77, 92
daughter of, 77

Sundback, Otto Frederick Gideon
(*continued*)
death of, 229
Earle and, 49–50, 228
Elvira Sundback and, *31, 48,* 49, *58,*
60, 74, 77
engineering skills of, 46, *47,* 49, 51,
57–58, 75, 77, 81, 87, 90, 98,
100–101, 141–44, *142*
fastener patents of, 50, 58, 70,
73–74, 78, *79,* 85, *93,* 95–97,
111, 130, 155, 160, 161, 168,
169–71, 237, 241
foreign ventures of, 155–58, 229
hookless invention of, 77–82, *79,* 85,
88, 91–106, *93, 94;* see also
Hookless Fastener #1
invention of the modern zipper by,
47, 93, 94, 226–29
plant management and production
of, 74–81, 85–86, 88, 90,
99–102, 118, 145, 146, 157
production machinery designed by,
100–101, 106, 128, 132, 141–44,
142, 158, 170–71, 233
recognition and honors accorded to,
229
slide fastener improvements of,
50–51, *52, 57,* 73–74, 76
Swedish birth and immigration of,
46, *47,* 226–28
technical challenges of, 48–49,
57–58, 65, 77
tree farming of, 229
Walker and, *79,* 80–86, 89–90,
92–94, 100–102, 106, 109, 116,
133, 226, 228, 229
Sundback, Ruth Margit, 77
Sundin, J. A., 227–28
sweatshops, 107, 114
Sweden, 32, 45, 46, 77, 226–27, 228
Swedish Royal Academy of Sciences,
229
Swiss Federal Patent Office, 72
Switzerland, 72–73, 92, *96,* 160

tailors, 40, 41, 42, 109, 111, 112–13,
114
Talon, Inc., *169,* 190
advertising campaigns of, 169, 175,
179, 181–82, 190, 195–96, *196*
board of directors of, 197, 229
British acquisition of, 243
companies absorbed by, 229, 236
competitors of, 234, 236, 238–40,
241–46
expansion and moves of, 236
foreign ventures of, 236

"gap-osis" campaign of, 195–96,
196, 200
Meadville closing of, 248
postwar market share of, 234, 241,
243
prosperity of, 190–91, 197–98, 200
stockholders of, 197, 243
Sundback's position at, 229
Textron acquisition and sale of, 243,
248
war matériel made by, 201–2
wartime downsizing of, 199, 201
Zephyr fastener of, 239–40, 243
see also Talon Fastener
Talon Fastener:
fashion industry and, 187–95
innovations of, 184–86
pricing of, 175, 181, *185*
promotion and sales of, 169,
173–77, *179,* 180–96, *193, 196*
separable version of, 184–86, 188
Tarbell, Ida, 227
Taylor, Effie Wright, 131
Teapot Dome scandal, 150
Technical Museum (Stockholm), 226
Teflon, 64
telegraphy, 4, 19, 60
telephone, 3, 60
Textron, Inc., 243, 248
*Theory and Construction of a Rational
Heat Engine* (Diesel), 63
thermodynamics, 64
Thurber, James, 196, *196*
"Till Blixåsets Historia" (Sköldberg),
227
Time, 215
Titanic, 63
tobacco pouches, 123, 139–40, *139,*
141, 144, 157, 158, 166, *185,*
207, 209
Triangle Shirtwaist Company tragedy,
107
trousers, 43, 65, 137, 187–91, 197–98,
202, 232, 234
Tucholsky, Kurt, 206–9, 226, 230

underwear, 166
Universal Fastener Company, 12,
16–23, 26, 29–30, 68, 82, 153,
154
Universal-Verschluss, 155, 158
"Unzipped Mechanic, The"
(Brunvand), 220–21
U.S. Rubber, 167

vacuum cleaners, 43
Van Dreissche Company, 139
Vanity Fair Silk Mills, 166

Vogel, Bertram, 229
Vogue, 39, 195
Vorlet, Christophe, *223*
Vorwerk and Son, 155
vulcanization, of rubber, 3, 99

Wagman Manufacturing Company, 139
Wahl, Nicholas, 237–38, 239
Waite, Charles M., 137
Waldes, Jindrich (Henry), 160–61
Waldes Koh-i-Noor, 160–61, 186
Walker, Lewis, Jr., *103*, 106–22, 166
    death of, 197
    education of, 106
    sales campaigns of, 106–22, 123,
        125–34, 137, 145–48, 174, 175
Walker, Lewis "the Colonel," *19*,
    26–32, *27*, 51, 57, 58, *103*, 227,
    230
    background and education of, 26, 29
    character and personality of, 28, 30,
        81, 83, 84, 125
    correspondence of, 30, 77, 80, 81,
        83–84, 86–89, 99, 102, 105,
        108–9, 118, 125, 127–28, 134
    death of, *103*, 197, 227
    hookless fastener as life's work and
        legacy of, 29, 106, 125, 153–54,
        248
    Hookless Fastener Company
        established by, 82–90, 92, 99
    investment in pneumatic railway
        system by, 10, 28–29
    investment in slide fastener by, 10,
        16, *27*, 28–32, 35–36, 39,
        43–45, 77, 79–90
    Judson's relationship with, 10, 11,
        28–32, 153
    legal and business career of, 26–28,
        27, 29–30, 81–82, 83, 84, 125
    management style of, 165
    sales strategy of, 86–90, 102–5,
        108–9, 116, 118–19, 121, 129,
        130, 133, 137, 144–45, 236, 245
    social and civic life of, 28, 30
    sons of, *see* Walker, Lewis, Jr.;
        Walker, Wallace
    Sundback and, *79*, 80–86, 89–90,
        92–94, 100–102, 106, 109, 116,
        133, 226, 228, 229
    travel expenses of, 83
    vigor of, 125, 197
    Wear and, 86–90, 99, 102–5, 116
Walker, Martha, 125
Walker, Susan Adelaide Delamater, 26
Walker, Wallace D., *104*, 197
    bachelor life of, 115
    death of, 199

sales campaigns of, 106–22, 123,   **287**
    125–31, 147, 148, 174
war service of, 132
Walls, Miss (buyer), 115, 118, 122
Wanamaker, John, 115
Wanamaker's, 115, 122, 130
W. & J. Sloane, 186
War Department, U.S., 136
Warhol, Andy, 215
War Industries Board, 133
War Production Board, 202
Washington, D.C., 2–3, 9–10, 29,
    129, 137
Watson, John B., 177
W. B. Bradbury Company, 198
Wear, Wilson "Willie," 56–68, 74, 76,
    77, 127, 130
    Colonel Walker and, 86–90, 99,
        102–5, 116
Weber and Field's Music Hall, 39
Weehawken, N.J., 45–46
Wells-Lamont, 139
Western Union, 19
Westinghouse, George, 46, 63, 250
Westinghouse Electric and
    Manufacturing Company, 46–48
Wharton School, 106
White, H. V., 130, 136
Whitney, Eli, 22
Wildman, F. A., 50
Wild One, The, 224
William J. Ganz, 181
Williamson, James, 11, 28–29
Wilson, Woodrow, 221–22
Windsor, Duke of, 190, 191
Wolff, Max, 238
Woman's Home Companion, 39–40,
    179
Woman's Magazine, 39
Woodrow Wilson Dime, The (Finney),
    221–22
Work, Benjamin G., 149
World War I, 63, 132–37, 141, 144,
    150, 151, 156, 158, 177, 183
World War II, 133, 159–60, 198–201,
    222, 225, 231, 232, 239, 243–44
Wright Brothers, 22, 60, 63, 75
WZPR radio, 247

Yale University, 189
YKK, 240, *242*, 243–46
YKK (U.S.A.), 246
Yoshida, Tadao, 161–62, 201, 202,
    242, 243–45
Yost company, 162

Zephyr fastener, 239–40, 243
"zip," 215–16

"Zip," (Rodgers and Hart), 213
Ziploc bags, 224, 237, 253
Zip-On Manufacturing Company, 176, 180
zipper:
  alternatives compared with, viii, 35, 43, 113, 202, 221, 250
  art and language of, 214–16, *223*, 224, 253–54
  assemblers of, 233–34, 241, 243
  common uses for, vii–viii, 16, 22, 23, *33*, 34, 39, 65, 85, 124
  cultural implications of, 205–24, 253–54
  foreign patents and production of, 72–74, 95–97, 155–62, 171–72, 239, *242*, 243–46
  home sewing market for, 243
  humor and, 209, 219–21
  importing of, 161–62, 186, 235
  installation and operation of, vii–viii, 12–18, *13*, *15*, 21, 41–42, 71
  laundering and rusting of, 51, *53*, 77, 101
  literary depictions of, 206–15, 217–18, 221–22
  as machine, vii–viii
  mechanical problems with, 41, 42, 45, 49, 50–51, *52*
  metals and materials used for, 58, 80–81, 101, 106, 143, 159, 185, 186, 191–94, *193*, 200–202, 232, 236–41
  military uses of, 130, 133–37, 155, 156, 200, 224
  originality and novelty of, ix, 2, 12, 39, 106, 141, 225–26, 229–31
  patent history of, ix, 2–3, 11–18, *13*, *15*, *21*, 25, 32, 34, 36, 50, 58, 67–74, *69*, 78, *79*, 82, 93, 95–97, *96*, 106, 111, 130, 154, 155, 168, 169–71, 228–29, 236–37, 241, 248, 250
  postwar manufacturing boom in, 225–26, 232–35, 243–46
  press exposure of, 131, 186, 192, 195, 229
  sales statistics on, 197, 225, 232, 234, 240–41
  separable, 184–86, 188
  sexuality and, 211–16, 253, 254
  spiral, 238, 239–40
  as a term, 20, 34, 134, 148–49, *152*, 158
  triviality of, 61, 205, 249
  urban legends on, 218–21
  widespread acceptance of, 190–91, 196–97
  see also specific zipper models
"Zipper Boot, The," 164, 166
Zipper Industries Association (ZIA), 235
ZIPP-Werk, 158–59, 232